INSIDE
FOREIGN
POLICY

**The Department of State Political System
and Its Subsystems**

by JOHN H. ESTERLINE
and ROBERT B. BLACK

Mayfield Publishing Company

For
Mae and Bruce and Marie

Manufactured in the United States of America
Mayfield Publishing Company,
285 Hamilton Avenue, Palo Alto, California 94301

This book was set in Century Medium by Libra Cold Type
and was printed and bound by the George Banta Company.
Sponsoring editor was C. Lansing Hays, Carole Norton
supervised editing, and Janet Wilson was manuscript editor.
Michelle Hogan supervised production. The book was designed by Nancy Sears and the cover by Ireta Cooper.

Contents

iii

List of Charts

Preface

Upon returning to academe after two decades in the United States Foreign Service, I was impressed by the methodological progress which characterizes contemporary textbooks on the subject of foreign affairs. Conceptualization, simulation, and model building have developed into important classroom tools. However, I was also struck by what I perceive to be a gap between concept and hypothesis on the one hand, and reality on the other. The specifics of how the major foreign affairs agencies operate and interact with one another are conspicuously missing in most textbooks.

The gap has been somewhat narrowed by several recent studies. John Francis Campbell's *Foreign Affairs Fudge Factory* (New York: Basic Books, 1971) is one step along the road which, I believe, students of the foreign policy process should take. The Campbell work underscores the large size of the "fudge factory" and the difficulty of coordinating roles within the expanded foreign affairs bureaucracy. Campbell resents the Department of State's bureaucratic competitors. In stressing their impact upon the foreign policy system he tends to obscure the fact that the coordinating role in foreign policy is *assigned* to the Department of State and that the department *is* at the vortex of the foreign affairs bureaucracy. Morton H. Halperin

VI   INSIDE FOREIGN POLICY

takes us another step along the road in his *Bureaucratic Politics and Foreign Policy* (Washington, D.C.: Brookings, 1974), which affords a series of useful generalizations arising from Halperin's analysis of memoirs, autobiographies, and private conversations of actors at the highest levels of government. In addition, William I. Bacchus has made an important contribution in his *Foreign Policy and the Bureaucratic Process* (Princeton: Princeton University Press, 1974), which is a definitive study of the country director system in the Department of State.

Much more needs to be done, however, to link the real world of foreign affairs management to academic investigation and to the teaching of foreign affairs-related courses. It is for this reason—to provide a bridge between bureaucratic practice and classroom theory—that I undertook the writing of this volume with my co-author, Robert B. Black. *Inside Foreign Policy* concentrates on interactions within and among State, USIA, and AID, "the three foreign affairs agencies" as they are known in the federal bureaucracy. Employing a modified systems approach, it provides data, observation, and analysis by two actors who have participated in the foreign policy system abroad and in Washington for a combined period of more than forty years. The authors' hope is that students can use the materials contained in this volume to build upon, and perhaps to modify, the various theoretical bases emphasized in other textbooks.

The volume also explores interactions within United States diplomatic missions abroad and between those missions and the Washington bureaucracies, an aspect of the foreign policy process not heretofore addressed in textbooks, yet highly significant in the formulation and implementation of policy. The case of the Dominican Republic in 1965 as discussed herein is an example of how such interactions can influence outcomes. Emphasis on the role of United States diplomatic missions seems particularly appropriate at this time: in 1974 the United States Foreign Service marked its fiftieth year of operation in its present form.

The superb and affectionate assistance of my wife—her logic, her editing, and her typing—made this volume possible. I wish also to acknowledge the patience and cooperation of my co-author, Robert B. Black, during the long process of writing and rewriting. He and I, of course, are accountable for any errors.

J. H. E.

Claremont, California
January 1975

Prologue

The summer of 1971 was a period of surprises for the student of foreign affairs: presidential adviser Henry Kissinger's secret flight to Peking, announcement of a Nixon dual-representation game plan to accommodate two Chinas in the United Nations—which proved unsuccessful—and inauguration of new foreign economic policies, including the first devaluation of the U.S. dollar in almost forty years. These were only preludes to further significant foreign policy change. Within the following year the United States withdrew its armed forces from Vietnam, an American president visited the capital of China for the first time in history, a critically important strategic arms limitation agreement with the Soviet Union was signed, and President Nixon met with Soviet leaders in Moscow. Before Nixon's resignation in August 1974, he and Soviet leader Brezhnev would meet at the summit twice more, U.S. influence in the Middle East would rise dramatically, and the European Economic Community would significantly reduce its tariff barriers against American agricultural exports.

Each of these policy outcomes was a consequence of initiatives undertaken by Richard Nixon and Henry Kissinger. The dramas and successes of the 1971-74 period highlighted the concept of personal diplomacy, leading many observers to the conclusion that the Department of State and its sub-systems—for that matter, all foreign policy subsystems including Congress—had fallen into functional and role-playing disarray. Observers seized upon the Nixon-Kissinger manifestations of personal diplomacy as final proof of the eclipse of the bureaucracy in foreign policy formulation.

Some observers have suggested that, unlike previous fairly regular swings of ascendancy and descendancy, the current "decline" of the Department of State is not a consequence of the character and style of its leaders, of reduced appropriations, or of wartime displacement by the military of the Department of State's role. Rather, they conclude, since World War II the prolif-eration of bureaucratic subsystems that play foreign policy roles and maintain personnel at U.S. missions abroad has produced an inevitable division of responsibility, and the resulting fragmentation has destroyed the pre-eminence of the Department of State within the foreign policy system. An even worse development, it is contended, is that the department maintains its position of primus inter pares among competing interests only with dif-ficulty; consequently, no single bureaucracy is "in charge" of the conduct of foreign policy. In the view of one observer, "The Department of State, once the proud and undisputed steward of foreign policy, has finally acknowledged what others have long been saying: that it is no longer in charge of the United States' foreign affairs and that it cannot reasonably be expected to be so again."[1]

One can conclude from such observations and the trend of recent develop-ments that, in the midst of competing interests and confused role-playing, a presidential foreign policy take-over was not only inevitable but necessary. It might appear that the advent of Nixon, a president with a strong personal interest in foreign affairs—a president who promised on the eve of his election in 1968 that "I am going to call the turn," and then proceeded to do so with the brilliant assistance of Kissinger—simply hastened the demise of the Department of State as a principal role player.

But is that what really happened? Is the Department of State really a withering arm of the executive?

Scholars are nearly unanimous in viewing the institution of the presidency as the unique contribution of the United States to the process of government. In developing the concept of a president with specific responsibilities, Ameri-

---

1 Terence Smith, "Foreign Policy, Ebbing of Power at the State Department," *New York Times*, January 17, 1971. For other views see Graham Stuart, *The Department of State* (New York: Macmillan, 1949); Dean Acheson, "The Eclipse of the State Department," *Foreign Affairs*, July 1971; Dean Acheson, *Present at the Creation: My Years in the State Department* (New York: Norton, 1969); John P. Leacacos, *Fires in the Basket* (Cleveland: World Publishing Company, 1968).

cans have conferred upon their chief executive formal "powers" regarding foreign relations, as students of the Constitution emphasize. But to use the word "powers" in this context is not strictly accurate. *Power cannot be conferred;* rather, power reflects a set of directive relationships achieved through manipulation of political resources, of which formally conferred authority is a chief one. The so-called strong presidents in American history are those who have created the most effective directive relationships, that is, those who have most effectively transformed authority into power.

A high correlation exists, moreover, between so-called strong presidents and their forceful employment of the foreign affairs authority to achieve a level of power. This is so because the constitutionally conferred authority of the president in foreign affairs is more specific and more complete than the authority conferred to him in other areas of government. Skillful use of constitutionally conferred presidential authority in the conduct of foreign policy has proved to be the most clear-cut path to power for an American president.

Every president since Franklin D. Roosevelt has made his deepest imprint on the body politic on the basis of his foreign affairs, not his domestic, "powers." Is Harry Truman remembered for his "Fair Deal" or for his decision to employ the atom bomb and to send American troops to Korea? Is Dwight Eisenhower remembered for the important steps he took toward equal rights or for the diplomacy of alliance so thoroughly developed by his secretary of state, John Foster Dulles? John Kennedy's thousand days in the White House were marked by crisis and confrontation—in Berlin, Cuba, and Vietnam—rather than by domestic programs. Even Lyndon Johnson who, in Aaron Wildavsky's words "de-fused domestic issues" by persuading Congress to enact "everything," is recalled for his role in Vietnam rather than for the program of domestic reforms embodied in his "Great Society." Few will deny that, whatever else Richard Nixon did, he transformed the foreign policy of the United States. Gerald Ford carries on the tradition. Despite the overwhelming defeat of his party in the congressional elections of 1974 and a broad dissatisfaction with his domestic initiatives, by 1975 President Ford had made a discernible impact on the presidential office in the exercise of his foreign affairs authority. After only five months in office he had met with both Brezhnev and French President Valery Giscard d'Estaing and had negotiated new strategic weapons parameters with the Soviets in Vladivostok.

Students of the American presidency have emphasized that persuasion, bargaining, and coalition-building are necessary skills of the effective chief executive. But each president since Roosevelt has demonstrated that he can make foreign policy, often with a minimum of bargaining and persuasion. That is possible because in foreign affairs the president holds many of the trump cards. Indeed, the practice of recent presidents has been to act first and to persuade and bargain after the fact Truman committed the nation to intervention in Korea and subsequently sought legitimization of the act. Eisenhower landed U.S. marines in Lebanon and justified his action later. Nixon mined Haiphong harbor without prior persuasion or bargaining, conducted a "secret war" in Cambodia without consultation outside the presidential subsystem, and mounted on behalf of Israel the most intensive airlift of arms and equipment in the history of the republic, in each case justifying his actions later.

American presidents *expect* to make foreign policy. Nixon, substantiating what other presidents have said, and perhaps speaking for the international foreign policy system as well, said in May 1974 that foreign policy "no longer is made by foreign ministers. It is made by heads of state."[2]

But presidents do not make foreign policy in a vacuum. Rather, they must make their decisions in an atmosphere of conflicting pressures—from Congress, the media, special-interest groups, the bureaucracies, and actors in the international system—which need to be sorted, considered, and assigned degrees of significance. The foreign policy system is designed to help the president resolve conflict about foreign policy arising from various sources, whether domestic or international, formal or informal. This book examines the structure and process of some of the principal bureaucratic subsystems formally charged with that task; the Department of State and its two principal subsystems, USIA and AID, comprise the major focus of concern.

It is unproductive to dwell excessively upon an alleged ascendancy or decline of the Department of State. Regardless of the department's position in the "pecking order" in the foreign policy process at any particular time, a functional subsystem for the conduct of foreign affairs is indispensable within the larger American political system. As long as that situation obtains, it is highly unlikely that the functionality of the Department of State will evaporate.

---

2 James J. Kilpatrick, "Nixon Emphatically Rules Out Resignation," *Los Angeles Times,* May 17, 1974, Pt. I.

INSIDE
FOREIGN
POLICY

THE FOREIGN POLICY SYSTEM

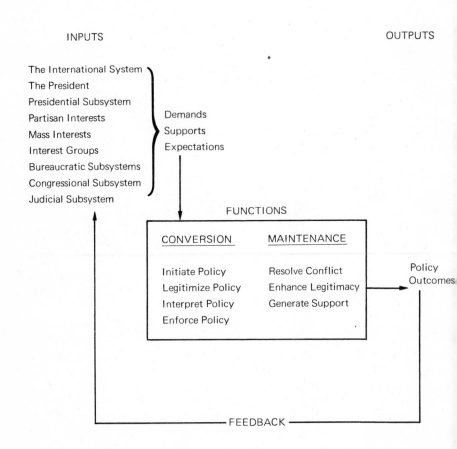

INPUTS   OUTPUTS

The International System
The President
Presidential Subsystem
Partisan Interests   Demands
Mass Interests   Supports
Interest Groups   Expectations
Bureaucratic Subsystems
Congressional Subsystem
Judicial Subsystem

                          FUNCTIONS

CONVERSION   MAINTENANCE

Initiate Policy   Resolve Conflict   Policy
Legitimize Policy   Enhance Legitimacy   Outcomes
Interpret Policy   Generate Support
Enforce Policy

————————————— FEEDBACK —————————————

CHAPTER 1

Parameters of Study

"You can't follow the game without a scorecard and lineup!" This cry to baseball fans from generations of program hawkers applies as well to foreign policy. The student of the foreign policy process can't follow the "game" unless he knows its terminology, its principal actors, and their roles.

The fact that political scientists have appropriated the terms of sports and the theater for use in analyzing political processes indicates, perhaps, an avid, but for the most part spectator, interest in foreign affairs as a game. This book is written, however, by two players involved in the game of foreign affairs for a combined period of over forty years in the hope that it will offer insights into the process from the playing field itself.

The foreign *relations* of the United States are of vast scope, ranging from events that alter the course of history to the most mundane exchanges of individual citizens. Each time the United States government interacts with a foreign government or international agency, it is contributing to the sum total of American foreign relations. These interactions may be page-one news, such as President Nixon's historic visit to China in 1972 or, less spectacular, the appointment of a new ambassador. Equally a part of U.S. foreign relations are the interactions between its citizens and foreign governments or agencies, as 1 well as those between foreign citizens and the United States government. They may be as routine as an American student applying for a visa to visit Japan or a foreign national applying to the U.S. Immigration and Naturalization Service for residence status, but each constitutes an aspect of U.S. foreign relations.

Another, and highly important, segment of foreign relations is the web of nonpublic relationships between groups or individuals in the United States and foreign groups or individuals abroad. Such *transnational* relationships are epitomized by the modern multinational corporation. If we were to explore the totality of the foreign relations of the United States, we would have to categorize almost ad infinitum.

PARAMETERS OF FOREIGN POLICY

The foreign *policy* of a nation is somewhat easier to conceptualize and to encompass. It is limited to official *governmental* acts and relationships involving other nations and international organizations. Obviously, every interaction between the United States government and the approximately 135 nations with which it has diplomatic, i.e., official-formal, relations is part of its foreign policy. But foreign policy also includes interactions between the United States and nations with whom it has no formal relationships. In 1973, during the Middle East Yom Kippur War, the United States was without diplomatic representation in Damascus, but United States-Syrian interactions directly affected both nations, as well as American relationships with every other state in the region.*

Interaction with international agencies comprises part of U.S. foreign policy, a prime example being membership in the United Nations. The United Nations and its specialized agencies in economic, social, cultural, educational, health, and related fields are units of a system of more than 130 intergovernmental agencies; the United States is associated with a great many of these units.

Foreign policy is not formulated in a vacuum. It is either an initiative or a response to another state's actions. In either case, policy is a means to an end. History suggests, and political science affirms, that the primary goal of any national political system is survival in a world environment of nation-states. Companion goals are to enhance its power, prestige, and security in order to increase its chances for survival. Thus a state's foreign policy—its behavior

* Incongruously, the United States may even have a foreign policy toward states that no longer exist! The United States has never recognized the absorption of Latvia, Estonia, and Lithuania by the Soviet Union during World War II, and for years representatives of those erstwhile states have resided in Washington and been accorded formal recognition.

toward other states—is the means employed to achieve these goals.

Within the nation-state system individual efforts to improve position vis-à-vis other states inevitably result in conflict. Conflict, in turn, is the essence of politics, which, in a classic definition, is concerned with who gets what, when, and how. A state's foreign policy will therefore reflect efforts to achieve its goals of survival and to increase its power, prestige, and security by successfully managing conflicts with other states. To gain the advantage, a state's internal resources must be marshaled—people, arms, capital, technology—and a foreign policy system and subsystems developed through which its political resources can be employed to secure the compliance of other states with its wishes.

The foreign policy subsystems of the United States government are numerous. Some forty institutionalized units carry out United States foreign policy by means of their activities and physical presence in countries throughout the world. Other elements operate entirely within the United States but have a major impact upon foreign policy. All make decisions about the allocation of national political resources to achieve foreign policy goals. For example, the setting of tolls for the Panama Canal by the Panama Canal Company or the adjustment of the prime interest rate by the Federal Reserve Board in Washington are as much foreign policy decisions as is the conclusion of a trade agreement between India and the United States by the Department of State. Together, all the mechanisms constitute a foreign policy system which is part of the American political system, itself a subsystem of the international political system.

SYSTEMS APPROACH TO POLICY ANALYSIS

Political scientists have borrowed the concept of *system* from biology and have used it as a research tool to help achieve an understanding of the complex reality of politics, i.e., the process by which resources are employed to achieve goals. As previously indicated, in the case of the nation-state the primary goal is that of survival. Analysts suggest that organizations, groups, and individuals within the polity interrelate with one another to perform functions necessary for survival of the polity—just as the parts of a biological system must interrelate to maintain life in an organism. In the words of one foreign policy analyst, "the concept of a system provides a means to reduce the complex reality to intellectually manageable proportions."[1]

Interrelationships among the actors or elements within a political system—in this case the foreign policy system—can be depicted by means of abstract models (see front table, "The Foreign Policy System") which show how the interactions make functional contributions to performance of the system as well as identify actors within the system whose continuing role-playing is necessary for maintenance of the system.

In applying the systems approach, one could speak of demands, expectations, and supports which affect a particular subsystem charged with foreign policy management. Demands, expectations, and supports are inputs converted within the system into policies, which are characterized as outputs. As a simplified example, the systems analyst might say of the original United States involvement in Vietnam that consensus about national security, expectations of success, and support for United States intervention on ideological grounds (anticommunism) were converted by the foreign policy subsystem (president, Congress, foreign policy agencies of the government, interest groups, media, political parties, and military establishment) into a policy of military action in that country. When support for the policy eroded beginning in 1966, feedback to the foreign policy system created new inputs which called for change.

One advantage of the systems approach is its consideration of a large number of variables, encouraging the scholar to look beyond the formal institutions of government to the vast number of informal actions which constitute the infrastructure of politics. In analyzing the foreign policy of the United States, a researcher could conceivably begin with the least complicated unit exhibiting system characteristics—for example, the personnel office which hires Filipino laborers to work at the U.S. air base outside of Manila—and proceed with analysis upward and outward through ever larger foreign policy subsystems to the entire American political system, and finally, to interaction between the American political system and the international political system. Or a researcher could begin by attempting to identify and describe the largest political system and work downward and inward through the numerous subsystems. But a task of this scope is well beyond the present state of empirical research in political science, even assuming consensus about research methods and techniques. Thus any analysis of the foreign policy of the United States will be incomplete at best.[2]

FUNCTIONAL FRAMEWORK OF THE AMERICAN POLITICAL SYSTEM

All of the institutions and actors which affect the foreign policy of the United States together constitute a functional framework within the American political system. The functions they perform in the conversion of inputs are those of initiating, legitimizing, and executing foreign policy. The functions they perform to assure system maintenance are those of resolving conflict, enhancing system legitimacy, and generating support for the system. Each element contributes to this end.

Actors in the foreign policy system are not confined to the three branches of the United States government. Interest groups, such as multinational corporations,* political parties, the mass media, and scholars, are additional sources of domestic inputs. These and other groups and individuals articulate electorate demands and expectations about foreign policy.

For example, broad popular support within the United States for Israel has consistently resulted in foreign policy favoring Israel. The external, or international, political system likewise imposes demands upon the American political system to which response must be made. The Arab oil boycott of 1973-74, for example, caused economic dislocation in the United States and speeded U.S. efforts to achieve national energy self-sufficiency. The overview which follows attempts to delineate only the functions of the three governmental branches of the American political system.

Initiation of Policy

The executive branch headed by the president is the principal vehicle for foreign policy initiation. The president initiates foreign policy when he engages in formal or informal interactions with other states, such as inaugurating the exchange of diplomatic representatives; making treaties, executive agreements, or other contractual obligations; and associating the United States with international organizations.

Legitimization of Policy

Much policy initiation requires specific expenditure of funds for which congressional approval, or legitimization, is necessary; and all treaties require the advice and consent of the Senate before they come into force. For example, the treaty establishing the North Atlantic Treaty Organization (NATO) had to be approved by the Senate and the obligations to commit funds and troops to NATO had to be funded by Congress.

Executive agreements do not require congressional approval, but if funds are necessary, Congress must provide them. U.S. air bases in Thailand are a

---

* The importance of these transnational actors can hardly be exaggerated. According to Thomas O. Enders, assistant secretary of state for economic and business affairs, "Since the Second World War, American enterprise overseas has been the most dynamic single agent of economic change in the world, consistently outperforming every national economy, including Japan's." *An Action Program for World Investment,* Department of State Publication 8780, September 1974.

product of executive agreement, and Congress tacitly approves or legitimizes these foreign policy initiatives when it votes funds to maintain them. Military aid to Israel, also an outcome of executive agreement, requires congressional appropriation of funds for implementation.

In its annual consideration of the federal budget, Congress has an effective means of reviewing the foreign policy initiatives of the executive branch. The budget, as presented to Congress by the president, is a reflection of his overall foreign policy priorities. By voting on monies for these ends, Congress legitimizes presidential priorities, reorders them, or denies them. The Vietnam War was a case in point. Despite repeated attempts by interest groups and individual senators and representatives to reorder presidential priorities, Congress voted funds to conduct the war and to support the South Vietnamese government until 1973. At that time Congress forced a presidential reordering of foreign policy priorities by threatening to cut off funds for further air strikes in Cambodia unless the president agreed to end military action by August 15, 1973, a condition which he accepted.

Congress may express its agreement or displeasure with executive foreign policy initiatives in other than monetary terms. For example, in 1919 the Senate refused to consent to the treaty, drafted and signed by President Woodrow Wilson at the Paris Peace Conference, to permit American participation in the League of Nations. In 1964, in contrast, Congress gave a stamp of approval to President Lyndon Johnson's policies in Indochina by adopting the Tonkin Gulf Resolution. In November 1973, over President Nixon's veto, Congress passed the War Powers Resolution to express its displeasure with the chief executive's Vietnam policy by limiting presidential war initiative. Paradoxically, in reasserting its constitutional power to declare war, Congress specifically limited that power by permitting the president to engage in armed conflict for sixty days on his own initiative, although limiting him thereafter.*

A third way in which Congress expresses agreement or disagreement with the president's foreign policy initiatives is its approval or disapproval of presidential appointments. The Constitution requires that the president

---

* Enacted into law November 7, 1973, over President Nixon's veto. "In addition to certain supporting requirements H. J. Res. 542 set a 60-day limit on any Presidential commitment of U.S. troops abroad without specific Congressional authorization. The commitment could be extended for another 30 days if necessary for the safe withdrawal of troops. Unauthorized commitments could be terminated prior to the 60-day deadline through Congressional passage of a concurrent resolution—a measure which does not require the President's signature to take effect." Congressional Quarterly Service *Weekly Report*, November 10, 1973, Washington, D.C., p. 2985. Another anomaly is that experts nearly unanimously believe that a nuclear weapons exchange would reduce the world to rubble long before the sixty-day limit when congressional approval becomes mandatory.

appoint "Ambassadors, other public Ministers and Consuls" with the advice and consent of the Senate. While that approval is usually given, striking examples of disagreement have occurred in recent years. When the Senate has declined to concur in a presidential appointment, it has usually been because the prospective appointee has been closely identified with some facet of foreign policy called into question by influential senators. In one such instance, in 1969, Senator William Fulbright, chairman of the Senate Committee on Foreign Relations, delayed the appointment of McMurtrie Godley as ambassador to Laos because of his dissatisfaction with Godley's ambassadorial role in the Congo crisis several years earlier. During the same period Fulbright also kept Ambassador-designate to Venezuela Robert McClintock in suspense for months, alleging that McClintock had been a key Department of State architect of Vietnam policy. On July 11, 1973, Godley again came before Fulbright's committee, which refused to confirm him as assistant secretary for East Asian and Pacific Affairs, a pointed rebuff to presidential foreign policy thrusts. Godley was eventually appointed ambassador to Lebanon.

Interpretation of Policy

The judiciary primarily interprets foreign policy. Judicial review of the foreign policy behavior of both the president and Congress is accorded the courts when cases involving that behavior are contested before them. Although its functions in the foreign policy area are less evident than those of the other two branches, the judicial branch nevertheless interprets both constitutional and statute prescription about foreign policy and has influenced foreign policy outcomes from the inception of the republic. Acceptance within the American political system of the concept that executive agreements have the force of law is the consequence of rulings by the United States Supreme Court.

Enforcement of Policy

Initiation and legitimization of foreign policy must necessarily be followed by execution of policy. The president and agencies of the executive branch administer the policies and agreements which have been adopted. Led by the Department of State, which by law was originally charged with conducting "all correspondence and business" with foreign nations, a panoply of executive branch agencies carry out thousands of foreign policy tasks. These range from political and military collaboration with treaty allies to stamping passports of American citizens traveling abroad; from administering multibillion-dollar foreign assistance programs to collecting customs duty from a returning citizen who bought a camera in Japan; and from electronic surveillance of all the continents by means of space satellites to horseback patrols along the United States-Mexican border to prevent the illegal entry of aliens.

Multiplicity of Functions

Most of the functional units—the president, Congress, and the courts—actually perform several secondary functions in addition to their primary one.

While the president is chief initiator, he is also a legitimizer of foreign policy because acts of Congress, except in the unusual case where his veto is overridden, require his approval for enforcement. The president is also a rule maker. The executive agreements which he concludes with other countries have the force of law; he has wide latitude in setting tariff schedules under general statutes; he determines, through his budget formulation, the mix of foreign aid programs; he decides whether to recognize changes of government in other nations and whether to receive diplomatic officials from them. The list is long.

The president, through the executive branch, also performs judicial acts which affect foreign policy. He interprets treaties and executive agreements; he makes administrative determinations which interpret general statutes, such as immigration and naturalization laws; and his interpretation of his powers as commander-in-chief of the armed forces has a major impact on the conduct of foreign policy.

Congress is an initiator of foreign policy in addition to being a legitimizer of executive foreign policy initiatives. Its control over appropriations is such that the "markup" of a foreign aid or military authorization bill in effect determines the level of the program, a level, and therefore a program, which may be quite different from that envisaged by the president. Congressional demands in 1974 for better treatment of Soviet Jews as a precondition to trade development between the United States and the Soviet Union is an example of such policy initiation. Another was the introduction in 1974 of a number of bills to control foreign investment in the United States in consequence of the concern of some congressmen that foreign interests—particularly Arab oil producers who were estimated to hold $50 billion in liquid capital—could take over key sectors of the American economy.

When American courts in cases before them interpret international law and its applicability to the United States, they are making rules in addition to interpreting law. American courts, for example, make judgments about U.S. claims to jurisdiction over the resources of the continental shelf, the use of the territorial sea by other nations, as well as whether bays and inlets are national waters. American courts make rules concerning the relations of the United States with foreign states, organizations, and nationals when such cases are brought before them.

EXECUTIVE BRANCH SUBSYSTEM

Among the three governmental branches, the Constitution assigns the dominant foreign policy role to the executive branch. The president is given the authority to make treaties, to nominate and receive ambassadors, and to be commander-in-chief of the armed forces. In short, the president of the United States is assigned responsibility by the Constitution for *making* foreign policy.

While the president and the subsystem for foreign affairs which he heads are paramount in mounting policy initiatives, the president also formally heads the entire national bureaucracy—the cabinet departments and agencies comprising the remainder of the executive branch—which also makes foreign policy inputs.

In terms of statutory authority, the Department of State and its subsystems are charged with the task of *conducting* American foreign relations to achieve American foreign policy goals. The Department of State is a major functional unit of the executive subsystem. It initiates many foreign policy inputs; it enforces presidential and congressional policy legitimizations by acting in accord with them; and it interprets broad presidential and congressional foreign policy mandates.

Role of the Department of State in Foreign Policy

Whatever criteria are employed in choosing appropriate elements for study in an attempt to explain the foreign policy process in the United States, the Department of State political system and its subsystems must be a central focus. Together they perform more foreign policy roles than any other actors in the American political system.

Secretary of State Henry A. Kissinger's perception of the role of the Department of State leaves little doubt that he considers it a primary one: "The work done in the Department of State has to be so outstanding that the issue of who is the principal adviser to the President does not arise as a bureaucratic problem, because if the work is of the requisite quality, then inevitably the Department of State will be the organization for decision-making."[3]

TABLE I THE GOVERNMENT OF THE UNITED STATES

THE CONSTITUTION

LEGISLATIVE

THE CONGRESS

Senate   House

Architect of the Capitol
General Accounting Office
Government Printing Office
Library of Congress
United States Botanic Garden
Cost Accounting Standards Board

EXECUTIVE

THE PRESIDENT

Executive Office of the President

White House Office
Office of Management and Budget
Council of Economic Advisers
National Security Council
Office of Economic Opportunity
Energy Policy Office
Council on Economic Policy
Federal Property Council

Office of the Special Representative for Trade Negotiations
Council on International Economic Policy
Council on Environmental Quality
Domestic Council
Office of Telecommunications Policy
Special Action Office for Drug Abuse Prevention
Council on Wage and Price Stability

JUDICIAL

The Supreme Court of the United States
Circuit Courts of Appeals of the United States
District Courts of the United States
United States Court of Claims
United States Court of Customs and Patent Appeals
United States Customs Court
Territorial Courts
Federal Judicial Center
Administrative Office of the United States Courts
United States Tax Court

DEPARTMENT OF STATE

DEPARTMENT OF THE TREASURY

DEPARTMENT OF DEFENSE

DEPARTMENT OF JUSTICE

DEPARTMENT OF THE INTERIOR

DEPARTMENT OF AGRICULTURE	DEPARTMENT OF COMMERCE	DEPARTMENT OF LABOR	DEPARTMENT OF HEALTH, EDUCATION AND WELFARE	DEPARTMENT OF HOUSING AND URBAN DEVELOPMENT	DEPARTMENT OF TRANSPOR- TATION

INDEPENDENT OFFICES AND ESTABLISHMENTS

Administrative Conference of Energy Research and Development Adminis- tration

Civil Aeronautics Board

Commission on Civil Rights

Consumer Product Safety Commission

District of Columbia

Economic Stabilization Program

Environmental Protection Agency

Export-Import Bank of the U.S.

Farm Credit Administration

Federal Communications Commission

Federal Deposit Insurance Corporation

Federal Home Loan Bank Board

Federal Maritime Com- mission

Federal Mediation and Conciliation Service

Federal Power Commission

Federal Reserve System, Board of Governors of

Federal Trade Com- mission

General Services Adminis- tration

Interstate Commerce Commission

National Aeronautics and Space Administration

National Foundation on the Arts and the Humanities

National Labor Relations Board

National Mediation Board

National Science Founda- tion

Railroad Retirement Board

Securities and Exchange Commission

Selective Service System

Small Business Admin- istration

Smithsonian Institution

Tennessee Valley Authority

U.S. Civil Service Commission

U.S. Information Agency

U.S. Postal Service

U.S. Tariff Commission

Veterans Administration

Adapted from United States Government Manual, 1973-74

Within both statutory and organizational frames of reference, the Department of State and its subsystems enjoy exclusive authority from Congress to conduct foreign policy. No other units of government possess equal, formally conferred, legitimacy in the foreign affairs area. Literally scores of other governmental agencies and departments make inputs into the foreign policy system, participate in the legitimization of those inputs, and help enforce policy outputs. But these also play extensive, complex domestic roles not shared by the Department of State. Demands and expectations regarding subsystems with clearly mandated domestic roles differ from inputs to subsystems without them.

Much contemporary literature about foreign policy outcomes stresses the enormous influence of the Department of Defense (DOD) or the intelligence community. The Department of Defense, however, employs more personnel and utilizes more resources *within* the United States than it does abroad. It is thus subject to domestic demands which are more parochial—and often more intense—than the demands placed upon it in the discharge of its foreign policy roles. Answerable to a vast domestic constituency, this department experiences pressures ranging from demands of the multibillion-dollar defense-related industry to expectations of American labor unions which influence Department of Defense personnel policies at hundreds of domestic military installations. The Central Intelligence Agency, despite wide popular interest in its foreign operations, functions principally in Washington to evaluate intelligence regarding national security from *both* foreign and domestic sources.

By contrast, the Department of State has few direct-line relationships to nonofficial domestic constituencies; it is mainly answerable to the presidential subsystem and to Congress. Foreign policy demands from the nation's diverse interest groups are largely filtered through the executive and legislative subsystems rather than exerted directly upon the department.

The department performs each of the functions associated with the functional approach to the foreign policy process. When the department prepares a position paper to be used as a basis for discussion by its representatives at a conference on the law of the sea, it is *initiating* policy. When AID, as a Department of State subsystem, prepares an agenda for economic assistance to third-world nations, it is also initiating policy. When the department approves a course of action toward Guyana recommended by the American ambassador posted there, it is *legitimizing* foreign policy. The U.S. Information Agency subsystem's publications, press releases, and commentaries on policy which are distributed overseas are *interpretations* of policy. When the American ambassador to Tanzania explains United States policy positions to and negotiates with that country's foreign office, he is *executing* foreign policy.

The Department of State political system consists of the Washington-based bureaucracy headed by the secretary of state, who is by law the senior member of the president's cabinet; the network of diplomatic and consular posts—i.e., diplomatic missions which include embassies, consulates-general, consulates, and consular agencies—maintained in nation-states throughout the world; and the Foreign Service corps of the department, which staffs the posts in various countries.

The subsystems of the Department of State are (1) the Agency for International Development (AID), which is organizationally linked to the department in a solid-line relationship but quasi-independent in practice; (2) the United States Information Agency (USIA), a separate agency carrying out informational and cultural roles abroad through the United States Information Service, which is under the supervision of the chief of the United States diplomatic mission; (3) the Arms Control and Disarmament Agency, a separate agency whose director reports to the secretary of state and who serves as principal adviser to the secretary and to the president on arms control and disarmament; and (4) the Peace Corps, an element of ACTION, which is a separate multipurpose agency whose foreign operation—the Peace Corps—is under the jurisdiction of United States diplomatic missions.

Other Executive Branch Actors in the Foreign Policy System

As the United States expanded its role in the international political system following World War II, other executive departments and agencies became increasingly important and visible within the American foreign policy system. More important ones include (1) elements of the presidential subsystem involved in foreign policy, especially the National Security Council subsystem; (2) the Department of Defense; (3) the intelligence community, comprising the Intelligence Resources Advisory Committee, the Central Intelligence Agency, and bureaucracies controlled by or associated with the Department of Defense; (4) the Energy Research and Development Administration; (5) the National Aeronautics and Space Agency; (6) the Department of Treasury; (7) the Department of Commerce; (8) the Department of Agriculture; (9) the Immigration and Naturalization Service; (10) the Bureau of Customs; (11) the Federal Bureau of Investigation; and (12) the Drug Enforcement Administration. Well over forty departments, agencies, commissions, and services with foreign policy roles physically maintain personnel abroad.

Rather than attempting to analyze all of the subsystems which together comprise the foreign policy system of the United States, and whose roles and significance vary widely, this volume focuses on the "three foreign affairs agencies," as they are informally categorized within the federal bureaucracy: the Department of State and its subsystems, the United States Information Agency, and the Agency for International Development. The Department of State and its subsystems are significant because the department influences *all* U.S. foreign policy outcomes—political, national security, economic, and social.

We shall first present an overview of the foreign policy roles of principal bureaucratic subsystems other than the Department of State, specifically the presidential subsystem, the Department of Defense subsystem, and the intelligence community. After the parameters of these roles are delineated, we shall analyze in some detail the operations, both in Washington and abroad, of the Department of State, the United States Information Agency, and the Agency for International Development.

The objectives of this volume are threefold: (1) to acquaint students of foreign policy with the role of the Department of State system and its subsystems in foreign policy decision-making; (2) to provide insights into the internal relationships of the three foreign policy agencies; and (3) to provide students of the American political system with data concerning a major area of public administration.

Presidential Subsystem, Department of Defense, and the Intelligence Community: Major Foreign Policy Elements

The phrase "crisis diplomacy" is so widely used in contemporary foreign affairs as to lose some of its impact. Yet few other terms so aptly describe U.S. foreign policy since World War II. From the Berlin blockade of 1948 through the de facto partition of Cyprus in 1974, crises within the international political system have assailed U.S. policy makers in dramatic succession. Specific examples are numerous.

When the People's Republic of China in 1954 began bombardment of islands held by the Republic of China on Taiwan, President Eisenhower asked for and received from Congress permission "to employ the armed forces of the United States as he deems necessary for the specific purpose of securing and protecting Formosa [Taiwan] against armed attack."

In 1958, in response to a request from the Lebanese president for immediate military support, President Eisenhower dispatched some 14,000 American marines to Lebanon. After the landing, Eisenhower stated that the mission of the troops was to protect Lebanon from communism and to thwart the tactics of the United Arab Republic.

15

On April 30, 1970, President Nixon told the American people that North Vietnamese and Viet Cong troops were turning Cambodia into a vast enemy staging area which was creating an extremely difficult military position for American and South Vietnamese forces in South Vietnam. In consequence, Nixon announced he had launched a combined United States-South Vietnamese military operation against enemy operations in Cambodia.

Two years later, expressing concern about North Vietnam's offensive across the demilitarized zone in South Vietnam, President Nixon made public on May 8, 1972, his decision to mine all entrances to North Vietnamese ports to shut off supply channels by sea.

United States behavior in each of these crisis chapters in foreign policy was initiated by the president as a result of inputs to him from his advisers in the presidential subsystem and executive branch bureaucracies directly concerned with national security, especially the Department of State, the Department of Defense, and the national intelligence community.

As Morton H. Halperin and Arnold Kanter suggest, "The predominant sources of a nation's behavior in the international arena are the organizations and individuals in the executive branch who are responding to opportunities for, and threats to, the maximization of their diverse interests and objectives."[1] An examination of the presidential subsystem, the Department of Defense, and the intelligence community will therefore afford insights to an understanding of the foreign policy process and will provide a setting for subsequent closer examination of the role of the Department of State and its subsystems in the foreign policy system.

Bureaucracy means literally rule by bureau. In a broad sense, the foreign policy bureaucracy is the sum total of foreign policy actors in the executive departments, independent agencies, and commissions which perform foreign policy roles, such as the Department of Defense and the Central Intelligence Agency. A useful distinction can be made between the regularized statutory subsystems which constitute the bureaucracy and the flexible, particularistic presidential subsystem, which is also engaged in foreign policy role-playing.

Departments, independent agencies, and commissions performing foreign policy roles *administer* programs which serve widely varying interests. The role of the Executive Office of the President, which is the principal component of the presidential subsystem, is primarily to *advise* and *assist* the president. Bureaucracies must satisfy relatively broad demands and expectations to survive, while demands upon the presidential subsystem at any given time tend to be confined to those of the president it serves. The interests of the bureaucracies and those of the presidential subsystem may, therefore, differ.

TABLE II   THE PRESIDENTIAL SUBSYSTEM AND THE NATIONAL BUREAUCRACY

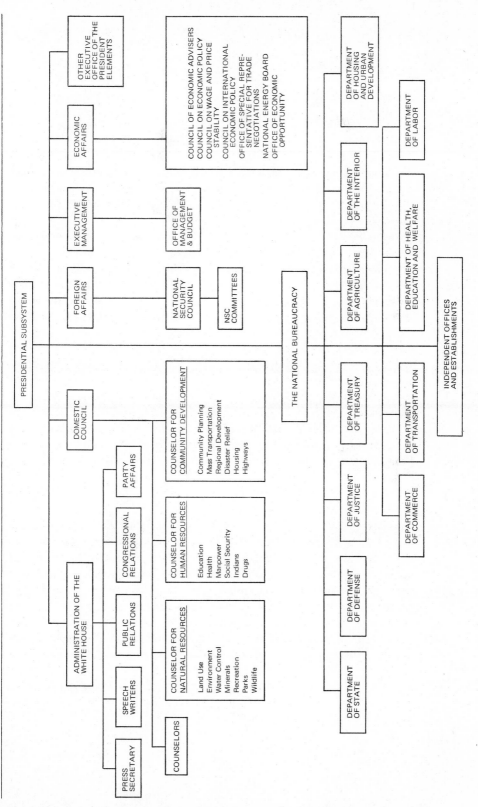

PRESIDENTIAL SUBSYSTEM:
A WEB OF PERSONAL RELATIONSHIPS

Individuals with foreign policy roles in the presidential subsystem act in close relationship to the president. Because they are appointed by the president, they tend to share his attitudes about foreign policy substance and goals. Since they are not associated with executive department bureaucracies, their allegiance is not divided between departmental and presidential interests, but given wholly to the president.

In the widest sense, the presidential subsystem overlaps other subsystems; in the narrow sense, as used here, the presidential subsystem includes only those organizations and individuals who, within a specific directive relationship to the president, assist him in resolving conflict. These are (1) the officials of the White House office, including presidential counselors and presidential assistants,* (2) the heads of statutory offices and councils which together form the Executive Office of the President, (3) the ad hoc commissions and task forces appointed by the president to advise him, (4) the cabinet—i.e., the heads of the eleven executive departments, and (5) unofficial presidential advisers.

The Executive Office of the President is the major element within the presidential subsystem involved in the foreign policy process. Within the Executive Office, the National Security Council (NSC) is the advisory body to the president for national security affairs. National security affairs are practically synonymous with foreign policy considerations.

National Security Council (NSC)

When Congress created the National Security Council in 1947, it was responding to perceived national security problems associated with the cold war. Prime Minister of the United Kingdom Winston Churchill had delivered his famous speech observing that "an iron curtain" had descended over Soviet-controlled Europe, and the Truman Doctrine for bolstering Greece and Turkey with military and economic assistance had been announced. American perspectives of the international system included a perceived need for institutionalization of the broad new role of the military establishment in the foreign policy process which World War II had conferred upon it. The

* In mid-1974 there were 510 White House Office positions. Sixty-five of them were "executive grade" positions, with salaries equaling or exceeding the maximum civil service pay of $36,000 a year. Fourteen of the 65 executives received salaries of $42,500 annually. On June 25, 1974, the House of Representatives voted to reduce the top-paid level from fourteen to five by attrition. This action is indicative of congressional attempts to restrain the executive branch of government.

National Security Council was therefore created as a means of relating military resources to foreign policy objectives.

Chaired by the president, the statutory members of NSC include the vice president and the secretaries of state and defense. The director of the Central Intelligence Agency (CIA) and the chairman of the Joint Chiefs of Staff (JCS) are designated as advisers. Other executive branch officials may be invited to attend NSC meetings. The actual role of the NSC has varied under different presidents, but none have felt themselves bound by NSC recommendations. President Truman, who participated in creation of the NSC, is quoted as saying, "Everybody on the National Security Council predicted the world would come to an end if we went ahead [with economic and military aid to Greece]. But we did go ahead and the world did not come to an end."[2] In his memoirs President Eisenhower commented that the NSC is "only advisory in action. Its duty is to advise the President but he can use it, ignore it, meet with it personally or not in whole or in part, and can add, as he sees fit, any number of people to its membership."[3]

Nevertheless, because the most important foreign policy decisions since World War II have pertained to national security, all chief executives have perceived a need for some form of consultative procedure to utilize inputs from both military and civilian subsystems.

Eisenhower: The Committee System President Eisenhower set up an elaborate committee structure within the presidential subsystem which led to the expansion of the NSC secretariat, the creation of an Operations Coordinating Board, and a provision for regularized inputs to the presidential subsystem from the Joint Chiefs of Staff of the military services. In the view of some students of the presidency, Eisenhower institutionalized and compartmentalized his office to the point where a president was scarcely needed! Eisenhower's subsystem reflected his lifelong experience with military staff patterns.

Kennedy: A Personal Staff When President Kennedy succeeded Eisenhower in 1961, he appointed McGeorge Bundy to the revamped and expanded position of special assistant to the president for national security affairs and chief of the NSC staff. Kennedy used the formal NSC as an umbrella under which he could develop a strong presidential foreign policy staff, headed by Bundy, nominally associated with the NSC but actually located in the White House. Following the Bay of Pigs fiasco, Kennedy became ever more wary of institutionalized procedures and further centralized national security policy—and thus foreign policy—formulation in the White House. He depended largely upon his personal advisers and their informal advice, especially during the Cuban missile crisis of 1962.[4]

Johnson: The Tuesday Lunch Bunch Lyndon Johnson inherited the informal Kennedy-White House foreign policy crisis managers. Their names became household words for many Americans during the Vietnam War. Robert McNamara, McGeorge Bundy, Dean Rusk, Maxwell Taylor, Richard Helms, Walt Rostow, and Earle Wheeler were the "architects" of American policy in Vietnam. Johnson consulted them through a regular but informal meeting which came to be known as the "Tuesday Lunch."[5] Walt Rostow recalls that "the only men present were those whose advice the President wanted most to hear."[6] The "Tuesday Lunch," referred to by Rostow as the "heart of the many-sided NSC process," largely superseded the formal meetings of the NSC, although Johnson in his memoirs frequently alluded to inputs from the NSC.[7]

Walt Rostow, who succeeded McGeorge Bundy in 1966 as special assistant for national security affairs and chief of the NSC staff, advocated using the NSC for in-depth study of important matters requiring a presidential decision, not in the immediate but in the foreseeable future. Johnson approved this role for the NSC, and Rostow felt that the twenty or more such "anticipatory meetings" between 1966 and early 1969 proved useful in forcing the bureaucracies to present a "coherent picture of a problem and the alternatives confronting the president." Even more important, according to Rostow, it permitted the president to make an early input into staff thinking.[8]

Nixon and the NSC President Nixon initiated changes of major importance, promising to restore the NSC to its preeminent role in national security planning and requiring that it present him with dispassionate, fully staffed options on all policy decisions under consideration. He appointed Henry A. Kissinger as his assistant for national security affairs and chief of the NSC staff.

Philip Odeen, director of program analysis on the NSC staff during the Nixon administration, contrasted the NSC subsystems under his three predecessors with the quite different one of President Nixon.[9] The Eisenhower NSC system focused on compromise among the members and agencies. The NSC members in the Kennedy and Johnson administrations both held and expressed advocate views at NSC meetings. Secretary of Defense Robert McNamara, for example, according to Odeen, expected his advocate point of view to prevail in defense policy and would not tolerate NSC, or even White House, intervention in decision-making affecting the military establishment.

The Nixon approach was designed to bring all policy options to the table for *subsequent* consideration by the president and, above all, to maintain flexibility for the president. Thus beginning in 1969 the NSC *staff*, headed by Kissinger, assumed particular importance since it was this staff which prodded the statutory members of the NSC, the foreign policy bureaucracies, and the interdepartmental NSC committees to explore and develop options. In actual fact, however, President Nixon's avowed intentions to utilize the NSC in a meaningful and regularized fashion proved to be more rhetoric than reality. Alexander Haig, who served as one of the president's closest advisers, characterized the formal NSC role in the Nixon administration as that of a mere resource for the president. "On a knotty issue, he will very patiently elicit the views of the statutory members, or special guest members, if they have a special interest in the subject. He then will go to his own counsel. He doesn't take a vote. It is not a consensus. I have known of several key decisions in which he reversed what was the strong consensus of the council."[10] The peripheral role of the NSC is suggested in the procedures Odeen described for developing policy recommendations about an appropriate U.S. posture in the event of detente between its ally, South Korea, and North Korea, heretofore considered an enemy. First, a national security study memorandum from Kissinger to appropriate agencies and ad hoc groups was issued, calling for assessments and options. The Senior Review Group, characterized as the most important of the NSC committees, then considered, initially rejected, and eventually approved revised options, which were finally forwarded to the president. A full NSC meeting on the matter did not take place.

During preparations for SALT II (the second stage of the strategic arms limitation talks), Odeen described the steps involved in the input of the NSC subsystem, an input that again was largely the product of NSC committees and working groups:

1. Following the signing of, and publicity concerning, the SALT I agreements, Kissinger brought together the Verification Panel (a committee of six to eight persons from the NSC system) for extended sessions about what additional forms of Soviet arms limitation the United States would be able to verify should the U.S.S.R. accept them.
2. Kissinger issued a "consensus paper" based on the panel's assessments and proposed possible next steps.
3. Other NSC committees set forth all possible arms control measures which the United States might pursue with the Soviets.
4. The NSC committees (it should be noted that these are interagency in composition, including representatives from all appropriate executive branch elements, e.g., State, Defense, intelligence community, Atomic Energy Commission, etc.) were pressed to define a whole series of objectives such as: (a) enhancement of the survivability of U.S. strategic offensive systems, (b) stabilization of strategic offensive systems of both sides, (c) reduction of strategic offensive systems by each side.

5. The Verification Panel was convened anew to test the measures proposed against the capability of the United States to verify Soviet compliance with them.

6. Proposed measures which survived the verification test were then forwarded through the NSC to the president.

Other major Nixon-Kissinger foreign policy initiatives were shared little, if at all, with the NSC.* Odeen flatly declared that "current China policy was not evolved through the NSC system." Nor, it should be noted, was this policy objective shared to any significant degree with any of the foreign affairs agencies. Kissinger's original journey to Peking in mid-1971 was camouflaged by having him become "ill" in Pakistan and thus out of circulation for the time required to complete his China visit. Following the Kissinger trip and until Nixon's official visit to China in February 1972, Department of State officers were instructed not to discuss nor to speculate about the impending visit.

Again, the worldwide alert of American military forces on October 25, 1973, in response to the perceived threat of Soviet military intervention in the Middle East, was *announced*, not discussed, by Kissinger at an NSC meeting which he chaired in place of the president, who is formal chairman of the council.

As the foregoing discussion suggests, the impact of the formal NSC on policy determination is almost entirely a reflection of what a particular president decides it should be. Except for countenancing advocate views of strong NSC members such as Robert McNamara during the Kennedy-Johnson years, presidents have tended to limit formal NSC inputs to ratification of decisions made elsewhere. It is also clear that many significant decisions have emerged following presidential interaction with informal groups, such as President Kennedy's White House staff of personal advisers, or the more broadly recruited "Tuesday Lunch Bunch" of President Johnson. When President Nixon came into office in 1969 he saw in the NSC subsystem as it was then structured an opportunity to exert more effective institutionalized White House control of all aspects of foreign policy.

NSC Committee System   The NSC committees mentioned by Odeen pro-

* The *New York Times* broke the story in January 1974 that a Navy yeoman had been stealing highly classified documents for the chairman of the Joint Chiefs of Staff from the Washington Special Actions Group, a unit within the NSC committee system. The reason, according to the press, was that Kissinger was keeping from the military materials which had formerly been available through the NSC. It was believed that Kissinger felt he needed to exclude from his confidence "traditional cold war warriors" in order to bring about basic foreign policy changes. *Facts on File*, January 19, 1974, Facts on File, Inc., New York.

vided the foundation for the presidential subsystem for foreign policy during the Nixon administration. Skillful manipulation of resources by President Nixon and Henry Kissinger succeeded in reversing directive authority. Both the NSC and the foreign policy bureaucracy became, in effect, subservient to the *NSC committee system.*

To explain the evolution of the phenomenon, it is helpful to review developments beginning in 1966. At that time, and at the urging of General Maxwell D. Taylor, President Johnson created a Senior Interdepartmental Group (SIG) chaired by the under secretary of state. Interdepartmental Regional Groups (IRGs) chaired by assistant secretaries of state were created which reported to the Senior Group. By placing Department of State officials in the chair positions, it was reasoned, the department's primacy in foreign policy, which had been adversely affected during the Kennedy years, would be reasserted. Moreover, representatives of the Department of Defense, the Joint Chiefs of Staff, AID, USIA, and the White House were included at both levels of the tier to ensure that diverse interests would be represented.

However, the portion of the presidential subsystem for foreign policy which centered in SIG and IRG soon fell into disuse. At least two reasons for the decline may be advanced: (1) Secretary of State Dean Rusk considered himself primarily a staff officer of the president rather than the executive head of a functional subsystem, the Department of State; (2) President Johnson and Secretary Rusk became preoccupied with problems of the Vietnam War which were increasingly being addressed through the medium of the Tuesday Lunch meetings, and they tended to neglect the new system.

During his 1968 election campaign President Nixon demonstrated his strong interest in foreign policy and promised to "call the turn" in foreign policy formulation. He seized upon the NSC system as a vehicle for regularizing and centralizing policy formulation in the White House. The network of interdepartmental committees was shuffled and the IRGs redesignated as Interdepartmental Groups (IGs). USIA and AID were removed from formal membership in these groups. SIG was abolished in favor of an Under Secretaries Committee (USC). Department of State assistant secretaries continued as chairmen of the IGs and the under secretary of state (now deputy secretary of state) continued to chair the USC. But instead of reporting to each other at the two levels, as they had under Johnson, they reported to a new Senior Review Group, an NSC committee chaired by Kissinger. I. M. Destler, a close student of organizational politics in the United States foreign policy system, remarks of this development that "State officials vociferously protested this breach of their departmental chain of command but the subordination of the committees to the review group did resolve one serious problem in the SIG-IRG system—its lack of any strong link to the Presidency."[11]

Emergence of the Kissinger Fiefdom　The Senior Review Group which was established by President Nixon to control the foreign policy bureaucracies in turn facilitated the rise of the Kissinger fiefdom.

First, in his role as special assistant for national security affairs, Kissinger also became chief of the NSC staff, a position which he converted into a kind of de facto chairmanship of the NSC. He scheduled NSC meetings and sometimes has presided at them.

Second, the rationale for the Senior Review Group—that of eliciting from the foreign policy bureaucracies the policy options insisted upon by Nixon—has enabled Kissinger as de facto chairman of the NSC to determine the role of the Senior Review Group and that of the Interdepartmental Groups and Under Secretaries Committee which report to it. Kissinger's national security study memoranda from the Senior Review Group to the other committees define problems and request recommendations, as in the case of the two Koreas already alluded to. The foreign policy bureaucracies in consequence are forced into competition with one another to produce meaningful policy options for presidential consideration. Their time is thus spent in developing policy papers rather than in exercising operational coordination.

Third, beginning in 1969, a series of ad hoc NSC committees, all chaired by Kissinger, were created to deal with specialized problems. The so-called "Forty Committee" (named after the presidential memo that authorized it) is responsible for authorizing and coordinating covert intelligence activities. The Vietnam Special Studies Group coordinates Vietnam policy. The Defense Programs Review Committee acts as a budgetary and substantive check on the Department of Defense. The Verification Panel noted earlier is active in the continuing strategic arms limitation talks with the Soviets. A Washington Special Actions Group is concerned with contingency planning and crisis management.

Fourth, Kissinger became chief of the NSC's internal staff, a group of more than 100 persons—three times as many as in previous administrations. These actors, youthful and intensely devoted to Kissinger, began zealously pressing the bureaucracies to recommend thoroughly staffed policy positions.

Fifth, President Nixon added another dimension to Kissinger's role when by executive order of January 5, 1973, he designated Kissinger as presidential assistant for foreign affairs, a role broader than national security affairs and located within the White House Office.

Sixth, when he was appointed secretary of state in September 1973, Kissinger emerged in yet a wider role, and undisputed primacy in foreign policy was thus restored overnight, through the person of the secretary of state, to the Department of State. By mid-1974 Kissinger's personal role was literally perceived as indispensable, first by a harassed and vulnerable Richard

Nixon, and subsequently by President Gerald Ford, a comparative novice in foreign affairs.

Nixon was heavily indebted to Kissinger for the latter's successes in negotiating military disengagements in 1974 between Israel and the United Arab Republic and between Israel and Syria, as well as for successfully arranging Nixon's final visit to Moscow despite what appeared to some as Soviet reservations about Nixon's credibility arising from his domestic political problems. Kissinger achieved a degree of personal invulnerability in the Nixon administration which permitted him while in Europe en route to the Middle East publicly to threaten resignation unless Congress completely exonerated him in connection with alleged wiretapping activities in earlier years. Congress, led by Senator Fulbright, the long-time nemesis of secretaries of state, immediately complied.

Upon accession to office, President Ford's first act was to request Kissinger to remain as secretary of state. The *Los Angeles Times* reported on September 17, 1974, that Ford's presidential transition team recommended limitation of Kissinger's authority by relieving him of his dominance over the NSC committee structure. Within hours, however, the White House vigorously denied the story and Ford personally assured the secretary that his dual role would continue. To demonstrate the depth of his conviction, Ford specifically alluded in his first address at the United Nations General Assembly to Kissinger's role in his administration and subsequently presented Kissinger with an autographed copy of the speech!

Whether the power personified by Kissinger will accrue to the department's *bureaucracy*, as distinguished from a small coterie of confidants within the department, is not clear. The secretary brought his top aides with him from the NSC staff rather than depending on the careerists in the department. During his first year as secretary of state he managed the department out of his suitcase because of his incessant, although spectacular and successful, "shuttle diplomacy."* A consequence is that his contact vertically within the department is more limited than that of his predecessors.

President Ford's strong endorsement of Kissinger's dual role—the role within the White House where, significantly, he retains his old NSC office and uses it regularly, and the other role as chief of the principal bureaucracy concerned with foreign policy—lends credence to a thesis expounded by Aaron Wildavsky. Accepting the premise of theorists of public administration that large bureaucracies are largely impenetrable and therefore unchangeable, Wildavsky argues further that contemporary public issues are largely insoluble.

* From September 1973 to June 1974 Kissinger's "shuttle diplomacy" took him to the Middle East repeatedly, as well as to China and the Soviet Union. One hundred days of his first 260 days in office were spent outside the United States.

Therefore, by bureaucratizing the White House, i.e., including the secretary of state on his personal staff, a president can associate himself with foreign policy successes and assign accountability to the Department of State and other foreign affairs bureaucracies for foreign policy failures.

Office of Management and Budget: A Foreign Policy Tool

President Nixon shaped another powerful tool within the Executive Office of the President when in 1970 he reorganized and expanded the role of the fifty-year-old Bureau of the Budget. The new Office of Management and Budget (OMB) is no longer a neutral arbiter for the large executive departments which compete for limited funds. Instead, the management role conferred upon OMB has been perceived within the presidential subsystem as a lever which the president can use—since he appoints the principal managers —to ensure priority consideration for foreign policy financial requirements and to ensure that specific foreign policy programs will be carried out. The new OMB concept of "management by objective" not only appends priorities to objectives but permits the management element within it to assign priorities to some programs at the expense of others. Management thus becomes "management advocacy" in the interests of the presidential subsystem.[12] When Gerald Ford acceded to the presidency in mid-1974 the acute national economic problems he faced guaranteed continuation of some version of management by objective. Ford immediately announced that the government would take the lead in fighting inflation by cutting the budgets and personnel of all of the executive departments, a task which certainly requires management by objective as well as a reordering of priorities in domestic as well as foreign affairs.

Certainly it is not difficult to envisage the value to the president of an advocate OMB for facilitating foreign policy implementation. In addition to helping to meet the ongoing costs of foreign policy that are reflected in defense expenditures, the price tag for maintaining the large U.S. intelligence community, and the funds required for economic and military assistance to other countries, advocacy on behalf of the presidential subsystem within OMB assures presidential ability to meet the costs of ad hoc diplomacy. Only a "managed" budget process can accommodate such totally unforeseen developments as the sudden decision to provide a nuclear reactor for Israel or to give Egypt a $2-million helicopter!

DEPARTMENT OF DEFENSE:
THE MILITARY AND FOREIGN POLICY

The National Security Act of 1947 created the National Military Establish-

TABLE III DEPARTMENT OF DEFENSE

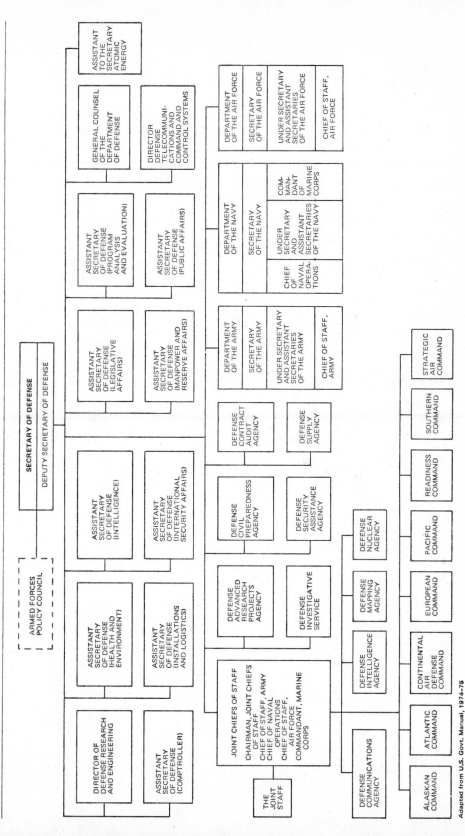

Adapted from U.S. Govt. Manual, 1974-75

ment by combining the War and Navy departments. In 1949 the name was changed to the Department of Defense (DOD). The 1947 act legitimized a permanent, institutionalized role for the military establishment in the foreign policy system, specifically with respect to national security policy. Since 1948, there have been frequent allegations that a "military-industrial complex" (a term coined by President Eisenhower in the closing days of his administration) dominates foreign policy decision-making. Moreover, it is a fact that only in the United States and the Soviet Union (and Israel), among the developed nations, is the military establishment maintained as the single largest feature on the political and economic landscape.

But it would be a mistake to assume on the basis of present evidence that the military dominates U.S. foreign policy. According to an analysis by the *New York Times*,[13] Department of Defense views in 1971 were rejected as often as they were accepted. And one might add that at no time can the military establishment be more powerful than the commander-in-chief allows it to be.

It was Franklin D. Roosevelt who expanded the foreign policy role of the military during World War II. He assigned major roles to the armed forces in formulating surrender terms and occupation policy, and he invited inputs from the military about the newly forming United Nations. His successors, however, have repeatedly shown skepticism toward major military involvement in foreign policy. Students of the Truman administration have suggested that Truman instinctively distrusted the military because of the red-tape difficulties he had experienced as a National Guard officer. But undoubtedly his greatest distrust was as a result of his experiences during World War II as chairman of the Senate Committee to Investigate the National Defense Program (the so-called Truman Committee), which was established to keep an eye on military expenditures.* President Eisenhower, himself a military product, was careful not to seem the pawn of his former colleagues.

President Kennedy may have been the single exception in the post-World War II years. Whatever else history eventually says of Kennedy, this coldest of cold war warriors laid the foundation for military intervention in Vietnam and used military threats as a basis for United States foreign policy toward the Soviet Union in both the Cuban and Berlin crises. President Johnson had fewer options regarding military inputs into foreign policy because, essentially, he was entrapped by the foreign policy initiatives of Kennedy.

* Truman's attitude toward the military was forcefully expressed by President Truman himself in the interviews he gave Merle Miller during the years 1961–62. When asked why he fired General MacArthur, President Truman is quoted as saying, "I didn't fire him because he was a dumb son of a bitch, although he was, but that's not against the law for generals. If it was, half to three-quarters of them would be in jail." Merle Miller, *Plain Speaking: An Oral Biography of Harry S. Truman* (New York: Berkley Publishing Corporation, 1973), p. 287.

Speaking from his long experience on the Senate Armed Forces Committee, however, Johnson once said, "The generals know only two words—'spend' and 'bomb.' "

Both Truman and Johnson were criticized by the military for waging "limited wars" for "limited ends." The objective of both the Korean and Vietnam wars was to restrain and contain the opposing forces. In neither case was the avowed objective to occupy the North or to force unconditional surrender. The issue of "limited" versus "total" war was the crux of Truman's troubles with General MacArthur.

Nixon's foreign policy coincided with military views in important instances—support for the Cambodian incursion of 1970 and the Laos invasion of 1971, as well as the "Christmas bombing" in Vietnam of 1972. But Nixon also overruled the military. He insisted upon destruction of stocks of biological weapons, and he proceeded counter to military views in the SALT arms limitation agreement with the Soviet Union in 1972. Moreover, his détente with both the Soviet Union and China was the antithesis of brinkmanship and military confrontation.

Department of Defense Input

Political resources of the Department of Defense for making effective inputs into the foreign policy decision-making process are formidable. In addition to its enormous size, the organizational framework of the department is dominated by military officers who demonstrate a high degree of goal-sharing and a technological expertise which tends to legitimize their views in the eyes of many laymen. Pentagon planning, management, and budget officials maintain continuing, in-depth relationships with congressional committees, especially the Armed Forces and Appropriations committees. Members of Congress, industrial leaders, media representatives, educators, students, as well as groups and individuals throughout American society, are subjected to sophisticated public information and persuasion campaigns.[14] The CBS television special, "The Selling of the Pentagon," first shown on February 23, 1971, shed considerable light on the promotional techniques used by the military establishment to influence the input process.

The influence of DOD on foreign policy formulation was strengthened during the 1960s because the most formidable foreign policy problem of that decade—Vietnam—was also a military problem. Capable, aggressive actors such as Secretary of Defense McNamara and the "whiz kids"* he placed in

* The "whiz kids," many of them in the Office of International Security Affairs, DOD, or in close relationship to Secretary McNamara—e.g., Adam Yarmolinsky, his special assistant—were analysts and efficiency experts. According to James A. Donovan many of these young men "came from Eastern schools and had impressive records of advanced

senior DOD positions actively searched for challenge and thrived on crisis management. The U.S. military commitment in Southeast Asia gave them extraordinary opportunities to contribute to policy formulation. Secretary McNamara's reports to the president following his periodic visits to Vietnam, documented in *The Pentagon Papers*, reflect such input. Bigger defense budgets gave DOD officials more opportunities to demonstrate policy-related skills in management, coordination, and, above all, persuasion.

A comprehensive examination of the foreign policy roles of DOD is beyond the scope of this volume. It would include an analysis of the character and amount of military inputs to the presidential subsystem through the NSC structure, the enormous impact of DOD lobbying activities in Congress, and the close relationships DOD maintains with the chairmen of congressional committees, especially the Armed Forces and Appropriations committees of each House. It would also involve the study of interactions about national security policy among the several military services,[15] and detailed examination of the inputs of prominent presidential military advisers, such as those of General George C. Marshall concerning China in 1946 and of General Maxwell D. Taylor regarding Vietnam during the 1960s.

For the purposes of this volume, a short overview of the role of the Joint Chiefs of Staff and the Office of International Security Affairs of the Department of Defense will suffice to underscore the breadth of military inputs into the foreign policy process.

Joint Chiefs of Staff as Input Channels

The Joint Chiefs of Staff is a body comprised of the chief of staff of the army, the chief of naval operations, the chief of staff of the air force, and, as a practical matter, the commandant of the marine corps. The chairman is appointed from the officers of the regular components of the armed forces by the president with the advice and consent of the Senate. The Joint Chiefs are the senior military advisers to the president. They are also responsible for providing strategic direction to the armed forces of the United States. Their inputs are made to the secretary of defense and through him to the NSC, or they may be made directly to the president.

As senior advisory and planning role players, the Joint Chiefs assess the

---

degrees and intellectual performance. They were eager to exercise power, and in contrast to most older civilians and civil servants who work in the Department of Defense they were not overawed by the military rank." James A. Donovan, *Militarism, USA* (New York: Charles Scribner's Sons, 1970), p. 127. See also John C. Donovan, *The Cold Warriors: A Policy-Making Elite* (Lexington, Mass.: D. C. Heath and Company, 1974) for extended discussion of Department of Defense actors who influenced national security policy.

capability of the armed forces to achieve foreign policy ends. As participants (by delegation of the secretary of defense since 1958) in the chain of operational command running from the secretary of defense to field commanders, they implement U.S. foreign policy thrusts which involve the armed forces. Since the organization of the JCS in 1947 under the National Security Act (the JCS actually came into practical being in 1942 during World War II), their impact on foreign policy has been highly significant. Beginning with the establishment of the North Atlantic Treaty Organization in 1949, through the Korean War, the recurring Middle East crises, the several Cuban crises, the U.S. military intervention in the Dominican Republic, and the massive military involvement in Southeast Asia, the record has been one of continuing need for military input into foreign policy decisions.

The quality of the JCS input to, and impact on, national security policy has varied. When President Kennedy called General Maxwell Taylor out of retirement to head the JCS in 1961, it was because Kennedy was disillusioned with the quality of advice he had received, particularly concerning the ill-fated Bay of Pigs invasion of Cuba that year.[16] James A. Donovan has suggested that JCS problem-solving routines were clumsy, time-consuming, and ritualistic, enabling the McNamara-recruited civilians "to seize power from the professionals."[17] The Joint Chiefs, for example, had not been prepared for Secretary of Defense McNamara's program-planning-budgeting-system (PPBS), a concept based on cost-effectiveness criteria which McNamara introduced from the business world; this was one factor that contributed to their temporary semi-eclipse.

The decline in JCS influence that characterized the McNamara years (1961-67), during which civilians controlled DOD, was arrested when Melvin Laird became secretary of defense in the first Nixon administration. Laird had dealt with the military services extensively during his years as a congressman and established rapport with the JCS by seeking their advice. His successor once removed, James R. Schlesinger, has continued to give full recognition to JCS counsel.

Whatever its faults, the JCS consistently considers the implications of using raw military power as it approaches a problem and will sometimes be a restraining influence as a result. For instance, the JCS reportedly cautioned restraint in early 1969 when an unarmed U.S. reconnaissance plane was shot down off the coast of North Korea, and again in 1970 when hundreds of Syrian tanks invaded Jordan.[18]

ISA: A "Little State Department"

A major bureaucratic input channel to the foreign policy process within the

Department of Defense is the Office of International Security Affairs (ISA). During the years of U.S. military involvement in Vietnam a succession of able assistant secretaries of defense for international security affairs, including William P. Bundy and John T. McNaughton, expanded the ISA staff to more than 300, and its inputs into the foreign policy system became significant. The "whiz kids" of Secretary of Defense McNamara transformed ISA into a "little State Department." Their brief but thorough position papers in the military manner focused directly on issues in contrast to the rambling, inconclusive documents for which the Department of State has been criticized.

ISA demonstrated that it could marshal sufficient political resources to influence national security policy not only in favor of escalating United States intervention, but, subsequently, toward deescalation of American involvement. *The Pentagon Papers* record that during the Vietnam buildup period, John McNaughton, who headed ISA from mid-1964 to mid-1967, took a stronger Vietnam "line" in ISA than did his Department of State counterpart and ISA predecessor, William Bundy. By 1967, however, when McNaughton became disillusioned about the war, ISA analysts and planners were exerting their influence in favor of deescalation. According to McNaughton's principal deputy, Townsend Hoopes, the value of ISA is that of "an alternative source of staff support in the consequential area of foreign-military affairs—an independent counterpoise able to test JCS positions and propose different ones."[19] The crux of Hoopes's account of how the Johnson policy of escalation in Vietnam was reversed is that ISA convinced Secretary of Defense Clark Clifford that military victory in Vietnam could only be achieved at unacceptable costs, both domestically and in the international system, and that Clifford persuaded President Johnson to the same view in March 1968.

Veterans of the United States Foreign Service can recall pre-World War II years when the departments of State, War, and Navy occupied the same nineteenth-century Gothic building at Seventeenth Street and Pennsylvania Avenue in Washington. They recall quiet, broad corridors, high-ceilinged splendor, and secretaries of state who rarely deigned to talk to members of the military services. Franklin D. Roosevelt and World War II changed this situation dramatically. A permanent military role in the foreign policy process emerged from the war, a role that was institutionalized by the National Security Act of 1947. The importance of military input has been constant ever since because military alliances, assistance, and intervention have been consistent policy ingredients in much U.S. post-World War II foreign policy. The influence of the Joint Chiefs of Staff has varied depending on how large a role was assigned to them by the president currently serving as commander-in-chief and the degree of counsel sought by individual secretaries of defense. The Office of International Security Affairs exerted major influence on foreign policy during the period of the war in Vietnam, but was less prominent during the Nixon administration because the Nixon-Kissinger procedure of demanding foreign policy options from all the foreign affairs agencies forced the "little State Department" at DOD into an arena of intense competition. Bureaucracies struggle to survive, however, and during the first year of the Ford administration ISA carved out new roles for itself, notably respecting national security aspects in law-of-the-sea negotiations.

THE INTELLIGENCE COMMUNITY: AN ADVISORY ROLE

According to Harry Howe Ransom, a leading authority in the literature on intelligence, "The pivotal importance of intelligence, whatever its form, in a rational system of decision making probably cannot be exaggerated."[20] Among intelligence categories, military intelligence has long ranked first in importance, and during World War II its activities were extensively broadened. After the war the need to centralize and coordinate intelligence activities of the several military services led to provision for the establishment of the Central Intelligence Agency (CIA) under the National Security Act of 1947. National security concerns, however, extend beyond military intelligence to political, economic, and scientific intelligence gathering. It was the CIA's responsibility to keep the NSC informed of intelligence activities conducted by elements of the executive branch, together with its mandate to coordinate all overseas U.S. intelligence activities, that quickly catapulted the agency into prominence.

The Central Intelligence Agency is not the gargantuan organization often depicted. Indeed, it is smaller than at least three of the intelligence agencies whose activities it is charged to coordinate. Senator William Proxmire (D-Wis.) estimated in 1973 that the CIA employs a work force of 15,000 and operates on an annual budget of $750 million. Estimates by Proxmire for other arms of the intelligence community include: (1) the National Security Agency, assigned to breach the communications security of other nations by deciphering codes and to monitor world electronic communications—20,000 employees and a $1 billion budget; (2) the Defense Intelligence Agency, created in 1961 to coordinate military intelligence programs—5,016 employees and a budget of $100 million; (3) army intelligence—38,500 employees and a $775 million budget; and (4) air force intelligence—60,000 employees and a $2.8 billion budget. The National Reconnaissance Office, which is associated with the air force, spends much of the $2.8 billion linked by

TABLE IV CENTRAL INTELLIGENCE AGENCY

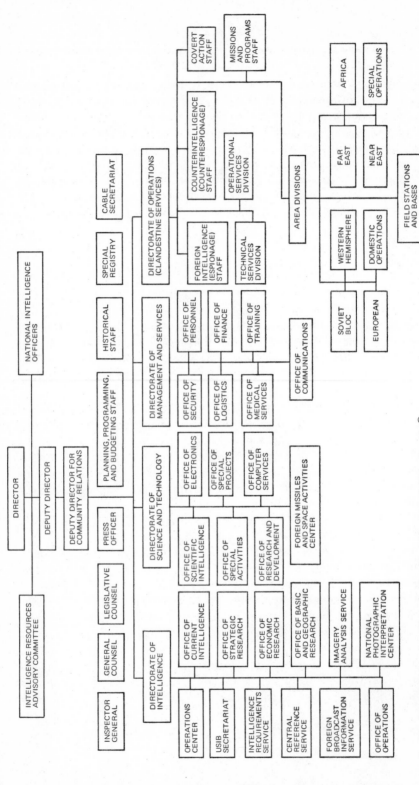

From *The CIA and the Cult of Intelligence*, by Victor Marchetti and John D. Marks. Copyright ©
1974 by Victor L. Marchetti and John D. Marks. Reprinted by permission of Alfred A. Knopf, Inc.

Proxmire to air force intelligence for aircraft and satellite reconnaissance. To this list should be added the Energy Research and Development Administration (successor to the Atomic Energy Commission), whose principal intelligence roles are to estimate Soviet nuclear capabilities, to assess nuclear test-ban proposals, and to monitor radioactivity in the atmosphere. The total intelligence community, according to Proxmire, employs some 148,000 persons and spends approximately $6.2 billion annually. The total figure reflects added "coordination" costs.[21]

Impact on Foreign Policy Formulation

Intelligence data if correctly evaluated and effectively used can have an important influence on foreign policy decision-making. In 1962 the detection of Soviet-supplied offensive missiles in Cuba led President Kennedy to demand their withdrawal; in 1968 intelligence inputs indicating the superiority of North Korean air power during the *Pueblo* incident dissuaded President Johnson from retaliatory action; U.S. officials negotiating with the Soviets during the strategic arms limitation talks of 1972 were provided with a precise catalogue of numbers, deployment, and characteristics of Soviet missiles, nuclear submarines, and aircraft.

But intelligence data are not always correctly evaluated or, if correctly evaluated, successfully utilized. The last two Middle East wars offer excellent case studies. American intelligence apparently correctly evaluated the 1967 Middle East situation that culminated in the Six Day War, but political action based on that evaluation was unable to avert Israeli "preventive attacks" against Syria, Egypt, and Jordan. In the case of the Yom Kippur War of October 1973, faulty evaluation by the intelligence community resulted in a U.S. failure even to foresee the outbreak of hostilities. Secretary of State Kissinger stated that three times during the week prior to October 6 he had asked for special assessment of the American and Israeli intelligence evaluation that the Egyptian and Syrian military buildup was *not* preliminary to an all-out war. "There was the unanimous view that hostilities were unlikely to the point of there being no chance of its [attack] happening," Kissinger reported at a press conference on October 12, 1973.[22]

CIA Mission and Foreign Policy

The Central Intelligence Agency was created under provisions of the National Security Act of 1947 to collect and evaluate information affecting the security of the United States from whatever sources. The agency is authorized to coordinate all U.S. overseas intelligence and counterintelligence activities and to perform services of "common concern" to other elements of the government as ordered by the National Security Council. The latter mandate is the CIA "charter" for covert actions such as the air reconnaissance over the Soviet Union in 1960 which ended with Soviet detection and destruction of an American U-2 aircraft and capture of the American pilot.

According to Harry Rositzke, who was employed for many years in operations with the CIA, covert political actions have played only a marginal role in American foreign policy since 1948, although the full record is not available either to Congress or to the public.[23] When CIA covert political actions are revealed, as was the case in 1974 when the director of CIA admitted that $8 million had been expended to influence politics in Chile, public expression of moral outrage inevitably is strong. In the Chilean case public outcry may have magnified the actual importance of the action. Speaking of the disclosures, Manuel Trucco, Chilean ambassador to the Organization of American States and a longtime career diplomat, said "The CIA could not have destabilized the Allende government for $8 million. It's ridiculous. I have no idea if the $8 million was earmarked [by the CIA to overthrow the Salvador Allende government] or not, but if so it wasn't enough even to get one spool moving."[24]

In practice, the foreign policy role of the Central Intelligence Agency is confined principally to collection and evaluation of data for use by the foreign policy system. Moreover, it is estimated that about half the daily flood of intelligence information comes from open sources—newspapers, periodicals, reports, statistics, radio monitoring—a third from satellites and telemetry, and only ten to fifteen percent from agents.[25] The covert political actions to achieve policy ends that former Secretary of State Dean Rusk once described as "dirty tricks" amount, according to Rusk, to no more than five percent of CIA actions, and decision makers are aware of and authorize all of them.[26] The principal task of American intelligence for the decade of the 1970s, according to Richard Helms, former director of the CIA, is the ever more precise determination of the accuracy of Soviet missiles.[27] This is a role for electronic surveillance rather than "secret agents."

Politicization of Intelligence

Under terms of an administrative reorganization ordered by President Nixon in 1971, an Intelligence Resources Advisory Committee (IRAC) replaced the United States Intelligence Board as coordinator of all national intelligence activities. Under the new arrangement, the director of CIA was to chair the new IRAC as he did the previous board. Moreover, the major agencies of the intelligence community were now required to clear their budgets with the IRAC, a practice aimed at reducing duplication and promoting integration of intelligence roles.

The 1971 administrative reorganization, however, introduced other changes which could lead to greater politicization of the output of United States intelligence agencies. A Net Assessment Group (NAG) was established *within the NSC staff* to review and evaluate *all* intelligence products. At the same time an NSC Intelligence Committee, chaired by then Presidential Assistant for National Security Affairs Henry Kissinger, was formed "to give direction and guidance on national intelligence needs." In short, the reorganization appeared to center intelligence evaluation within the White House rather than in the hands of professionals trained to make evaluation. The changes evoked criticism from members of Congress and elsewhere on the grounds that intelligence evaluation should be divorced from the political environment of the White House.

Demands for Change

The centralization of intelligence management and the politicization of intelligence evaluation in the presidential subsystem, and especially within the National Security Council staff; the Watergate disclosures of CIA participation in domestic political activities; and the perfection of modern electronic and surveillance systems requiring sophisticated equipment rather than personnel are among developments which have raised demands that CIA and other elements of the intelligence community shed their secrecy and limit their roles. In 1973 Senator Proxmire urged that the government's entire intelligence budget be made public. In 1974 on Proxmire's initiative the Senate voted to insert the word "foreign" before every reference to intelligence in CIA's charter and to direct the agency to report to Congress on all duties assigned to it by the National Security Council.[28] Proxmire's objective was to ensure that the CIA would henceforth be concerned exclusively with foreign intelligence.

However, intelligence activities by their very nature require secrecy. Information collection includes espionage—a practice as ancient as government—which means "to observe secretly." Counterintelligence is concerned primarily with the protection of information or agents and likewise, of course, is conducted in secret. Covert political actions undertaken to protect or enhance the security of the United States are by definition secret, but, according to Ransom, "labeling them as 'intelligence' is a distorted use of the term."[29] Distorted use of the term or not, covert political actions are carried out under the aegis of the intelligence community.

Intelligence agencies whose budgets would become public record, as advocated by Senator Proxmire, would no longer be able to carry out their roles effectively. If the targets of intelligence programs knew in advance the volume and mix of a national intelligence effort, they could adapt to counter it. If the CIA will be required to report to Congress on all duties assigned to it by the NSC, as the Senate voted in 1974, it is hard to see how congressional news leaks can be avoided. Moreover, if the CIA is restricted to foreign intelligence, domestic threats to national security, such as the assembling of a nuclear weapon by a fanatical group within the United States, could be undertaken with far greater assurance of success.

On the other hand, if the White House were to dictate intelligence evaluation on the basis of what it perceived as political necessities, the role of intelligence in rational foreign policy formulation could be diminished—as could national security.

CHAPTER 3

Department of State Power Structure: Formal and Actual

Harry Truman remarked tersely at one point in his presidential career, "The buck stops here." As chief of state he recognized that the organizational framework of government laid ultimate responsibility at the door of the Oval Office. However, below the Oval Office on a descending ladder are levels of responsibility and opportunities for inputs. One bureaucrat's input may differ from that of his predecessor, but his power and maneuverability are clearly circumscribed by his position on the ladder.

In recent years behavioral studies in political science and public administration have tended to ignore the formal structures of an organization in favor of probing the underlying currents which affect policy decisions. This approach is useful, but by disregarding formal structures an important area of bureaucratic conflict in decision-making has been ignored. As James W. Davis, Jr., says, "In the attempt to discover what lies beneath the surface, the surface has been ignored."[1]

This chapter attempts to provide the student of foreign policy with practical guidelines about how the department operates, characteristic relationships among actors and organizational elements, and most importantly, it attempts to indicate the relationship between the importance of a decision 39 and the level where it is made within the department. It looks at the department primarily during the decade of the 1960s when the international political equilibrium was severely disturbed for a long period by the war in Vietnam. While Vietnam affected U.S. policy on a worldwide basis, its impact was, of course, most clearly felt on U.S. policy in Asia. The chapter, therefore, focuses principally on departmental actors and elements concerned with Asia.

Few would argue with the thesis that organizational structure is a reflection of the formal allocation of power, of rights and responsibilities, and of authorizations and limitations. If, as John C. Ries indicates, a certain power relationship obtains "when one party gives in to another because of a threat of a sanction,"[2] the men who possess formal powers have an advantage. By showing who has access to whom, at what level, and under what limitations, organizational arrangements clearly delineate information networks. Finally, organizational structure pinpoints precise areas in the organization for assigning accountability—who did what, and why.

What, then, are the *formal* power relationships in the Department of State, and what clues can these provide toward an understanding of *actual* power relationships? Who most influences State Department inputs in foreign policy decision-making?

FLOOR HIERARCHY

In April 1974 the Department of State employed 7,154 Americans in the United States and 5,587 Americans abroad. Of the latter, 3,300 were Foreign Service Officers. In addition, 10,801 foreign nationals were on its payrolls overseas.

The department has its headquarters in an eight-story complex of four square blocks, completed in 1961, which is located between Virginia Avenue and C Street, and 21st and 23rd streets, in Washington, D.C. It is shared with the semiautonomous Agency for International Development and the U.S. Arms Control and Disarmament Agency. It becomes immediately apparent at department headquarters that, like a Christmas tree, the brighter lights are at the top. This deference to rank arises from protocol orientation, the influence of traditional hierarchy, as well as the dictates of Washington bureaucracy.

The building's crowning glory is a series of elegant eighth-floor public rooms with spacious balconies overlooking the city. These include the private dining room of the secretary of state and three gracious reception rooms, the largest of ballroom size. The eighth floor is used primarily for representational and diplomatic functions.

The seventh floor, synonymous with departmental authority and exten-

TABLE V DEPARTMENT OF STATE

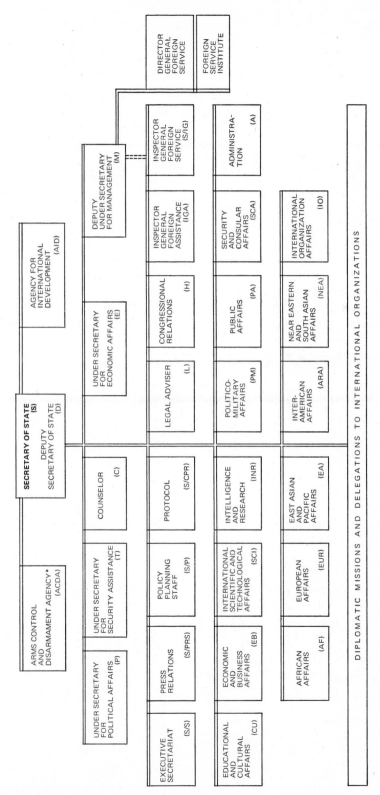

SECRETARY OF STATE (S)
DEPUTY SECRETARY OF STATE (D)

ARMS CONTROL AND DISARMAMENT AGENCY* (ACDA)

AGENCY FOR INTERNATIONAL DEVELOPMENT (AID)

UNDER SECRETARY FOR POLITICAL AFFAIRS (P)

UNDER SECRETARY FOR SECURITY ASSISTANCE (T)

COUNSELOR (C)

UNDER SECRETARY FOR ECONOMIC AFFAIRS (E)

DEPUTY UNDER SECRETARY FOR MANAGEMENT (M)

DIRECTOR GENERAL FOREIGN SERVICE

FOREIGN SERVICE INSTITUTE

EXECUTIVE SECRETARIAT (S/S)

PRESS RELATIONS (S/PRS)

POLICY PLANNING STAFF (S/P)

PROTOCOL (S/CPR)

LEGAL ADVISER (L)

CONGRESSIONAL RELATIONS (H)

INSPECTOR GENERAL FOREIGN ASSISTANCE (IGA)

INSPECTOR GENERAL FOREIGN SERVICE (S/IG)

EDUCATIONAL AND CULTURAL AFFAIRS (CU)

ECONOMIC AND BUSINESS AFFAIRS (EB)

INTERNATIONAL SCIENTIFIC AND TECHNOLOGICAL AFFAIRS (SCI)

INTELLIGENCE AND RESEARCH (INR)

POLITICO-MILITARY AFFAIRS (PM)

PUBLIC AFFAIRS (PA)

SECURITY AND CONSULAR AFFAIRS (SCA)

ADMINISTRATION (A)

AFRICAN AFFAIRS (AF)

EUROPEAN AFFAIRS (EUR)

EAST ASIAN AND PACIFIC AFFAIRS (EA)

INTER-AMERICAN AFFAIRS (ARA)

NEAR EASTERN AND SOUTH ASIAN AFFAIRS (NEA)

INTERNATIONAL ORGANIZATION AFFAIRS (IO)

DIPLOMATIC MISSIONS AND DELEGATIONS TO INTERNATIONAL ORGANIZATIONS

* A separate agency with the director reporting directly to the Secretary and serving as principal adviser to the Secretary and the President on Arms Control and Disarmament.

From *Organizational Directory* of The Department of State, September 1974

sively referred to in that context by the press and department personnel, houses the handsome offices of the secretary of state; the deputy secretary; the three under secretaries for Political Affairs, Economic Affairs, and Security Assistance; and the deputy under secretary for Management. It also contains the offices of the counselor of the department (a high-ranking officer whose position description is purposely ambiguous), the executive secretary of the department, a number of special assistants, the Director of Planning and Coordination, the assistant secretary for Congressional Relations (the only assistant secretary housed on this floor), the director of the Bureau of Politico-Military Affairs, and the director general of the Foreign Service.

These officials and their staffs, with the exception of the special assistants who are not in "line" units, comprise in the aggregate the significant policy-making mechanism of the department. Their location in the building is directly related to their importance.*

Below them on the sixth floor are the offices of eleven assistant secretaries of state, including one for each of the five geographic or regional bureaus—Africa, Europe, Inter-American Affairs, Near East and South Asia, and East Asia and the Pacific—who are "responsible" for relationships with the various regions of the world. The other seven assistant secretaries on this floor (like the lone assistant secretary on the floor above) head functional, as distinguished from geographical or regional, bureaus. These are the bureaus of Public Affairs, Economic and Business Affairs, Educational and Cultural Affairs, International Organization Affairs, Administration, and Oceans and International Environmental and Scientific Affairs. The sixth floor also houses the inspector general of Foreign Assistance, the inspector general of the Foreign Service, the legal adviser, the director of the Bureau of Intelligence and Research, and the administrator of the Bureau of Security and Consular Affairs. The title "director," as it refers to persons domiciled on the *sixth* or *seventh* floors (e.g., the director of the Policy Planning Staff on the seventh floor and the director of Intelligence and Research on the sixth floor), is equivalent to "assistant secretary." Otherwise the term "director" refers to an office director, who is usually responsible to an assistant secretary and is invariably located on the *fifth* floor. The term "administrator" equates with the assistant secretary level or higher. Thus, the administrator of the Bureau of Security and Consular Affairs is the equivalent of an assistant secretary and is on the sixth floor. The administrator of the Agency for International Development (AID) is clearly at the under secretary level; he is in an

* Interestingly, among seventh-floor *offices*, as distinguished from *officers*, the executive secretariat, which is presumably not involved in policy-making, is the largest office, with more than 100 employees, exceeding the secretary of state's office force of ninety-six persons and dwarfing that of the under secretary for economic affairs, whose staff numbered six employees in 1974.

adjoining building where his floor location does not involve the pecking order in State!

Rank-order also pertains *within* the sixth-floor hierarchy. The assistant secretaries of the regional bureaus (e.g., the assistant secretary for African affairs) are normally considered *primus inter pares* in relation to functional assistant secretaries (e.g., the assistant secretary for the Bureau of Educational and Cultural Affairs). Substantive cables, for example, must be cleared through the *regional* assistant secretary's office by a *functional* assistant secretary since the former is the coordinator as well as the regional authority for the area.

The relationship between hierarchical status and the physical location of offices is not as clearly visible below the sixth floor, mainly because certain of the regional and functional bureaus are so large that their personnel are dispersed among several floors. However, some space on the more prestigious fifth floor is available to all offices of approximately equal rank in the pecking order. As on the sixth floor, country directors in the regional bureaus—officers responsible for an individual country—are held to supersede in rank office directors of the functional bureaus.

The fourth and lower floors are occupied primarily by specialized bureaus outside the main power structure. For example, the fourth floor houses the office of the deputy assistant secretary for communications, the security assistance planning staff, the media services, personnel offices, and various staff units of the regional and functional bureaus.

The department library, an outstanding research tool, occupies much of the third floor, along with most of the staff of the Bureau of Economic Affairs and the Bureau of Inter-American Affairs. In these cases the physical locations of bureau personnel do not correspond to the normal pattern. Only lack of space on the fifth floor relegates them to the lower level, not the relative importance assigned to their functions.

The Office of Press Relations has offices both on the seventh floor, for the convenience of the secretary, and on the second floor, to provide easy access for the scores of newsmen who visit it daily. Medical services, security, and some office units of the director general of the Foreign Service are also located on the second floor, in addition to lounge facilities and personal services for Foreign Service Officers.

The first floor houses the protocol office with its various units, including an office with a sign on its door requesting foreign embassies to "Deposit Diplomatic Notes Here." The office of International Conferences is located on the first floor near the large conference rooms. The office of the deputy assistant secretary for Operations and the office of Special Consular Services are also on this floor.

A number of other elements are located in various "annexes" in Washington and Virginia. The Foreign Service Institute occupies an entire high-rise office building in Rosslyn across the Potomac River. Other units situated at a distance from the main State building include the Passport Office, the Historical Office, the Office of Foreign Buildings, some personnel offices, and various offices of the Bureau of Educational and Cultural Affairs.

MICROANALYSIS

Generalizations about political subsystems stress their performance of *functions* by means of *structures*. Rather than referring merely to a table of organization, the term "structure" is applied to recurring patterns of interaction among role players in the subsystem. The larger political system determines what is to be the appropriate distribution of power within the subsystem, as well as the appropriate functions and behavior of the units and individual actors whose duty it is to discharge those functions. The structures are the consequence of determinations made by the larger political system. In other words, structures reflect the values of a political culture and will vary from one political culture to another. In spite of these variations, the functional requirements of all political subsystems are identical—that is, to convert input demands and supports into outputs which are sufficiently responsive to demands and expectations for the survival of the political subsystem.

It is necessary, therefore, in examining a particular political subsystem, to supplement generalizations with specific and precise descriptions. In the words of Ries,

> A more microscopic examination of subsystems, their particular institutions and activities, will permit a refining of the concept of executive position. It will allow us to understand better what an executive is expected to do by providing an idea of the activities in which the unit of government where he is located engages.[3]

SEVENTH FLOOR: LOCUS OF POWER

It is almost a cliché to describe the "seventh floor" as the locus of power in the Department of State. Memoirs of men who have operated from the seventh floor use the term as a synonym for the decision-making center.*

* For example, *The View from the Seventh Floor* is the title of Walt W. Rostow's account of his sojourn as chairman of the Policy Planning Council, Department of State.

Official department literature describing the Program Analysis and Resource Allocation (PARA) system adopted in 1971 uses the term "seventh floor" repeatedly in ascribing roles to the department's top decision makers in the management and planning process. Journalists use the term constantly.

But the literature is meager about what actually happens on the seventh floor in terms of how its occupants spend their time, how they interrelate with one another, or the degree and character of their inputs to policy formulation. The writings of ex-occupants of the seventh floor, or of persons who held equivalent positions in the Department of State before the present headquarters was built, abound with observations about the policies that originated there, but these observations tell little or nothing about how the policy decisions were made.[4] It is difficult, therefore, to document seventh-floor policy inputs, but deductions can be made from such sources and from presidential memoirs. Inferences can also be drawn about high-level executive behavior from the expectations and supports generated by sixth-floor actors—the regional assistant secretaries.

Department of State executives, like executives in any governmental department, are subject to numerous role-playing and organizational demands, and these demands are characteristic of the subsystem in which they operate. Behaviorial characteristics of seventh-floor officials, regardless of differing work styles from incumbent to incumbent, are determined by demands which are relatively constant in nature. The most basic of these demands are those associated with operational responsibilities.

In the case of the secretary of state, a major claimant on his time is the department itself, personified by the five officials with whom he interacts in a straight-line directive relationship: the deputy secretary (whose role has been enhanced recently owing to Secretary Kissinger's prolonged diplomatic journeys abroad), the three under secretaries, and the counselor of the department, who is a kind of "free agent" in the service of the secretary. Other demands on the secretary derive from his role as the senior member of the president's cabinet. In an era when bureaucratic foreign policy formulation is increasingly a multidepartmental process, and when foreign policy decision-making has been drawn inexorably to the White House, the secretary's energies necessarily are extended outward, rather than downward, in ever greater proportion.

In addition, many demands of a symbolic nature are imposed on the secretary. These range from formal daily staff conferences (at which few real decisions are made), through interminable rounds of appointments with foreign and American officials, to the social and protocol chores of his office. The secretary must also keep himself fully informed. This is accomplished by means of information supplied him in abbreviated form—either verbal or written—by his corps of assistants, and by his daily, nightly, and weekend "reading" (as it is termed in the department), namely, the written materials marked for the secretary's attention.

Each of the other chief actors on the seventh floor daily faces a similarly compartmentalized (or perhaps jumbled) work experience. Every under secretary must respond to the demands of the functional areas for which he is responsible. If the deputy secretary can be considered for discussion purposes as the alter ego of the secretary, the most important remaining positions, in terms of role-playing demands, are those of under secretary for political affairs and the deputy under secretary for management.

The under secretary for political affairs is the ultimate "clearance level"* for significant policy messages to be transmitted to the field. The under secretary finds a stack of these messages on his desk at the end of the day, each of them researched, coordinated, cleared horizontally within and without the department, and cleared vertically to his level. Final initialing by the under secretary authorizes their transmission to the field, an action which commits the department to a policy position. This action is frequently taken on the advice of an assistant secretary, or after consultation with an especially articulate or knowledgeable staff expert.

The deputy under secretary for management is under equally heavy pressures in the administrative area. He faces daily a large volume of clearance-required administrative documents, messages, and position papers. In mid-1974 approximately 2,000 Department of State employees were engaged in administration and management. John Franklin Campbell, special assistant to under secretaries George Ball and Nicholas Katzenbach, alleges that "the Secretary of State probably pays less attention and has less a personal role in formulating his own department's annual budget than does any other cabinet officer."[5] As Campbell points out, administration—encompassing management of all kinds and degree—is the single largest activity of the entire department and is left almost entirely to the deputy under secretary concerned.

In addition to their constituencies, or functional areas, the principal seventh-floor actors are subjected to the demands of the secretary's office, other cabinet departments (especially Defense), the White House, the intelligence community, Congress, the media, interest groups, and their "clients," who are the approximately 135 countries with whom the United States has official relationships. They must meet much the same time-consuming schedule of conferences, meetings, and representational activities as the secretary himself, and they must keep themselves informed in much the same manner.

---

* Clearance is the process of securing written agreement of other actors to a proposed action or position.

SIXTH FLOOR: EXPERTISE

Because of the extensive field experience of almost all regional assistant secretaries and the deputies and country directors who make up their staffs, the offices of the assistant secretaries of state for the geographic bureaus are the linchpins of the department. Their area expertise has a centripetal effect on other departmental elements (e.g., economic, cultural, or United Nations affairs) concerned with countries of their particular geographic area. Moreover, since the 1960s, directives both from within the department and from the White House have consistently stressed the coordinating and directional roles of the geographic bureaus. The key role of the regional bureau was reinforced in 1966 when the traditional "country desk officer" of middle-grade Foreign Service Officer level was elevated to "county director" at senior Foreign Service Officer level.

The backgrounds of key officers in the Bureau for East Asian and Pacific Affairs in 1969-70 suggest the quality of preparation and experience deemed desirable for occupants of senior positions in a regional bureau. Assistant Secretary William P. Bundy, brother of President Johnson's adviser McGeorge Bundy, came to the department from a career in intelligence activities with an emphasis on Asia, although he had never served in the field. The senior deputy assistant secretary, Winthrop G. Brown, was a career minister and a former ambassador to Laos and Korea. G. McMurtrie Godley, another deputy assistant secretary, had extensive diplomatic experience in France and Cambodia and previously served as an ambassador (to the Republic of the Congo). Godley later became ambassador to Laos and then ambassador to Lebanon. The third deputy assistant secretary, Philip C. Habib, had previously served in Korea and had been chief of the political section of the very large American mission in Saigon. He later became operational head of the American delegation to the Paris peace talks with North Vietnam and then ambassador to Korea. By 1970 Bundy had been succeeded by Marshall Green, an Asia expert who played a key role in Korea and had been ambassador to Indonesia. In 1974 Habib himself became the assistant secretary. This typical staffing pattern in the East Asian Bureau is duplicated in the four other regional bureaus. It reflects formidable expertise as well as a game of musical chairs.

Regional Assistant Secretaries and Decision-making

Both observation and the table of organization of the department suggest that decision-making—decisions that affect policy content—begins at the regional assistant secretary level, rather than lower in the hierarchy. In the regional bureau U.S. goals in various countries within the region must be weighed; for example, in regard to the Middle East, U.S. desires for the security of Israel must be balanced against needs to secure and maintain the friendship of the Arab nations. The sometimes conflicting interests of the Department of Defense, AID, and USIA must be defined in the regional bureau, and it is at this level that partisan political influence is most likely to be brought to bear and the pressures of private interest groups are most keenly felt.

Recommendations of the regional bureau also become inputs to the significant decisions which face the department's principal decision makers—the secretary and the under secretaries—who in formulating policy must weigh regional interests vis-à-vis one another and in terms of U.S. global goals. When the region is a crisis-stricken one—and few geographic regions have not been crisis-stricken much of the time since World War II—pressures on the regional bureau become intense.

Department of State regional bureaus operate normally with three deputy assistant secretaries under the supervision of the assistant secretary. Only the latter normally has unrestricted access to seventh-floor principals, who can in turn devote only limited time and energy to regional problems. Problems of significant proportion are usually managed on the seventh floor.* While some problems are brought to the seventh-floor principals by an assistant secretary, others have already been under scrutiny on the seventh floor because of their special importance. As soon as a problem reaches significant status, it is taken out of the hands of the regional assistant secretary, who is, in essence, a problem manager on the periphery of significant decision-making. He normally does not possess sufficient power resources to manage or coordinate a significant problem because of the inevitable intervention of other interests over which he has no control. He is not, for example, privy to all the verbal communications, much less to all the nuances, that pass between his seventh-floor principals and the White House or the Department of Defense. Although the under secretary for political affairs, or even the secretary himself, may brief the regional assistant secretary, subtleties may be lost in the retelling.

On the other hand, the regional assistant secretary may possess more *facts* about a problem affecting a particular region than do his principals. Quite likely the regional assistant secretary has already had significant field experience upon which he can draw in assessing a regional problem. He is also

* A rough distinction between a *significant* and a *routine* decision is offered by how the clearance of a cable to the field is handled. Transmission of cabled (i.e., radioed) instructions to U.S. diplomatic missions abroad must be "cleared" within the department. Minor decision cables are usually cleared at the country director level, routine decision cables at the regional assistant secretary level, and significant decision cables at higher levels. It is estimated that from 1700 to over 4000 incoming and outgoing cables are processed daily by the department.

thoroughly familiar with the "traffic" concerning a problem—the reports and views of ambassadors, the intelligence community, the military, and his own country directors. It would not be physically possible for his generalist superiors—except those who might also have had appropriate field experience and, more importantly, a continuing interest in the region—to acquire as much specific information as the regional assistant secretary can provide. Moreover, all problems originate in one or another geographic region. The ultimate decision makers—whether they be on the seventh floor, in the White House, the military, the intelligence community, or even in Congress—need the informational fund of the assistant secretary as well as his assessment and judgment. But the regional assistant secretary cannot move toward basic problem resolution without the input, assessment, and sanction of his own principals and those of other agencies. He may propose but he may not dispose.

The principals, however, rarely write position papers which reflect the decisions they have made. Rather, they make decisions—incomplete as they might be—and leave to the regional bureau the burden of interpreting and committing to written form what they have decided. It is this task which is a major function of the assistant secretary. He attempts not only to reflect the actual decision but to convey the rationale upon which it is based. The drafting of the position paper, the question of whether or not to disclose the full policy rationale to his regional bureau staff, the preparation of cables to the field concerning the position or decision and its public information implications—all these are the direct responsibility of the assistant secretary. However, he must frequently return to his principals for corroboration and agreement.

Such circumstances tend to personalize policy issues for the assistant secretary. He is expected to assume operational responsibility for the decisions, even though he has participated only peripherally in making them. The greater the issue, the more likely he is to develop a proprietary interest; and the more personal his involvement, the less likely he is to share it fully with his own subalterns.

The Vietnam issue, which towered over everything else in the East Asian regional bureau during the entire decade of the 1960s, is a textbook example of the tendency to personalize. Vietnam was the *least* discussed issue in regular regional bureau staff conferences throughout that period. While a vast preponderance of all staff business during that decade concerned Vietnam to some degree, principal policy decisions and thrusts were conveyed, even to the regional bureau political officers directly working on Vietnam, largely by osmosis.

At the regional bureau staff meetings the assumption seemed to be that if subordinate political officers or directors of East Asian functional bureaus were not somehow inherently aware of decisions and content, it was for good reason. A kind of natural law of disclosure, the "need to know" security classification (an actual operational security category), was apparently invoked although never enunciated.

Assistant Secretary William P. Bundy and Vietnam

Assistant Secretary of State William P. Bundy's performance during the U.S. military involvement in Vietnam offers a striking case history of role-playing by a regional assistant secretary in a crisis situation. His activities were highly visible and well documented. Moreover, the author was in a position, in the field and in Washington, to observe him as the drama unfolded.

Bundy became assistant secretary of state for the Far East (the bureau name was later changed to East Asian and Pacific Affairs) in March 1964, having transferred from the Department of Defense and following a decade of service with the intelligence community. He was immediately immersed in the Vietnam problem, which soon totally consumed his energies. During his initial year at the Department of State Bundy began a series of periodic trips to Saigon, stopping at U.S. missions en route for briefings on Asian affairs. Briefings were usually confined to matters concerning the war and discussions on how a particular embassy in the region could assist the Indochina effort.

Bundy's concentration and dedication were infectious. U.S. ambassadors along the route to Saigon perceived the magnitude of the growing U.S. commitment and geared their mission operations accordingly. This was especially true in the case of the Philippines, where Clark Air Force Base and the Subic Bay Naval Base were fundamental to the logistics of intervention, and in Thailand for even more cogent reasons—Thailand's proximity to the fighting and the willingness of the Thai government to devote facilities and resources to the American forces. Policy cables *to* and *from* Saigon (copies to American embassies in Manila, Vientiane, Bangkok, etc.) began to reflect Bundy's style and even his language.

Bundy also played a major role among his Washington principals as rapporteur. As earlier suggested, top decision makers often make decisions in informal meetings, with little or no record of what they actually say to each other.[6] Moreover, conscious that they occupy prestigious positions, unwilling to appear uncooperative, eager to convey impressions of intimate knowledge about the problem in question, and caught up in the easy spirit of old friends meeting together, decision makers often seem to agree, or even pretend to agree, when in fact they do not.* The regional assistant secretary in whose

* Irving Janis invented the word "groupthink" to describe the process. See his *Victims of Groupthink* (Boston: Houghton Mifflin, 1972).

area the problem is centered has the continuing task of determining whether or not the principals have in actuality agreed to a policy course. He accomplishes this, even though he may not physically have been present at the decision-making meetings, by committing to writing what he *perceives* the consensus to be. By offering his version to the principals as their presumed consensus, he quickly learns the extent of agreement.

Not only did Bundy show skill in fathoming the intentions of his principals, but he had an ability to weave qualifying points of view into joint position papers on Vietnam that might otherwise have been dominated by the military. In a memorandum of August 26, 1964, for example, the Joint Chiefs of Staff recommended "counteroperations" against North Vietnam which "must be greater than the provocation in degree, and not necessarily limited to response in kind against similar targets."[7] Following discussions by the principals of this and other proposed plans of action, Bundy, in a memo of September 8, recorded "the consensus reached in discussions between Ambassador Taylor and Secretary Rusk, Secretary McNamara and General Wheeler, for review and decision by the President." In the memo, Bundy specifically recommended *against* the Joint Chiefs' argument that responses "must be greater than the provocation," and recorded the principals as believing "such deliberately provocative elements should not be added in the immediate future while the GVN [Government of Vietnam] is still struggling to its feet."[8] All the steps outlined by Bundy as reflecting the consensus of State, Defense, and White House thinking on subsequent courses of action were approved by President Johnson in a national security action memorandum of September 10, 1964.

Bundy also found himself responsible for proposing certain actions. When summaries of his proposals were forwarded to the Pentagon, the Commander-in-Chief, Pacific (CincPac), Saigon, and Vientiane, however, it frequently happened that the basic philosophies he was trying to enunciate were significantly altered in editing. For example, in a memorandum of August 11, 1964, Bundy proposed "Next Courses of Action in Southeast Asia." *The Pentagon Papers* revealed that the full draft of that memorandum was edited in the office of Assistant Secretary of Defense John T. McNaughton, and in the process deletions and insertions were made that considerably hardened the tone of the document. Refinement and restatement of Bundy's proposed course of action by Admiral Sharp, Pacific Commander, Honolulu, went further than McNaughton's redrafting. Bundy had set out to examine "the courses of action the U.S. might pursue, commencing in about two weeks ... [since] we have agreed that the intervening period will be in effect a short holding phase. . . ."[9] When Admiral Sharp responded to the document on August 17, he objected that "the proposed two weeks suspension of

operations is not in consonance with desire to get the message to Hanoi and
Peiping."[10] His rejection of Bundy's "short holding phase," and of the basic
assumption behind it, undermined the logic of the remainder of Bundy's
memo. Might Bundy not have proposed different "next courses of action"
had he realized the issue of the advisability of a "holding phase" had not been
resolved?

Throughout most of his tenure as regional assistant secretary (1964–69),
Bundy continued in his role as a kind of general rapporteur concerning
Vietnam policy proposals originating in the State and Defense departments.
At the same time he was faced with conflicting pressures in his own department, ranging from the hawkish views expressed by Policy Planning Chief
Walt Rostow,* who, according to *The Pentagon Papers*, repeatedly called for
air attacks and commitment of ground forces, through the more moderate
views of Secretary Rusk, to the deescalation advice of Under Secretary
George Ball. Bundy's task was complicated personally by the fact that his
brother, McGeorge Bundy, was President Johnson's national security adviser
and, in effect, secretary of the National Security Council. Often one Bundy
found himself speaking for the military while the other spoke for the political
operators.

Implications of the William Bundy Saga   Bundy obviously played a unique,
multifaceted role in political interaction concerning Vietnam. He was both a
principal initiator and a prime processor of inputs. At times, especially during
portions of the period 1965–68, Bundy's direct input to the actual decision
makers was an important resource and, without it, incremental decisions
would have been more difficult to make. He participated in that highly elite
subsystem the "Tuesday lunch bunch," the group of ad hoc advisers to the
president which was the focal point of Johnson's emerging informal structure
for attempting to manage the crisis. Bundy was, moreover, a fount of
knowledge about Vietnam for his own superior, Secretary of State Dean
Rusk, who of course was formally charged with executing foreign policy. As
rapporteur, Bundy had a limited mandate to be a broker** within the presidential subsystem—a go-between for the various political, military, and
intelligence interests. Since he drafted many of the crucial memoranda,
however, he could shade the tone and interpretation of what the principals
were agreeing about, or thought they were agreeing about (as Secretary of
State Acheson once said, "In a memorandum of conversation the author

* Walt W. Rostow served as counselor of the Department of State and chairman of the
State Department's Policy Planning Council from 1962 until 1966 when he became
President Johnson's national security adviser.

** The role of broker does not necessarily imply complete objectivity or passivity. See
Ries, pp. 105-6.

never comes off second best"). In short, Bundy was at the vortex of decision-making.

In a great many respects Bundy's role in Vietnam policy formulation was by no means typical of bureaucrats of his rank. Assistant secretaries of state normally do not play as broad a role regarding basic policy over so long a period of time as Bundy did respecting Vietnam. Moreover, Bundy was highly conspicuous throughout the period, and this too was atypical. His inputs to policy are documented in *The Pentagon Papers* and are repeatedly discussed by David Halberstam in his encyclopedic but undocumented book, *The Best and the Brightest*. President Johnson in his memoirs, *From the Vantage Point*, repeatedly lists William Bundy as a participant at Johnson's famous "Tuesday luncheons," as well as at numerous other ad hoc work sessions on Vietnam.[11] In these respects Bundy's performance throughout was more like that of a seventh-floor actor—and an important one—than that of a sixth-floor regional secretary.

He was not totally free of the normal restraints of his position, however. Despite the fact that he operated within a structural framework that afforded him extraordinary opportunities for exercising an effective executive role, Bundy still functioned mainly as a catalyst of inputs, a reliable provider of ideas about a chronic crisis that required constant response. His position afforded him only limited ability to resolve conflicts among principal actors, and his direct influence on actual policy outcomes—even minor incremental ones—was slight.

Another way to analyze Bundy's role is to consider it within the framework of "political acts," as these are defined in the work of John Ries. In his perceptive volume, *Executives in the American Political System*, Ries suggests that all political actions fall within three broad categories: symbolic interactions, acts of exchange, and acts of compliance. Let us examine Bundy's "political actions" in these terms. Certainly he was required to conform to the wills of other actors—presidential advisers, cabinet and agency heads, military role players, and superiors in his own department. Certainly he engaged in exchange actions, that is, he traded with others in the sense that he submerged his own views—his concerns about military escalation at one point, and, later, his misgivings about disengagement from Vietnam—in return for continued acceptance by his superiors of his unique role among the assistant secretaries of state.

Finally, throughout the entire period he was performing symbolic acts and gestures as he attempted through his memoranda and recapitulations to project an appearance of in-house unity among decision makers. Ries believes that much of the action of executives really consists of this kind of activity— symbolic gestures to reduce anxiety among constituencies: "A great deal of what political [or bureaucratic] leaders do falls into this category—more than most people realize," he states.[12] In Bundy's case, his "clients" were elite decision makers headed by President Johnson, and much of Bundy's energy was expended in efforts to reduce anxieties among them by articulating rationales for the kinds of decisions they were contemplating.

Eugene V. Rostow's analysis supports the notion that Bundy played a "reassuring" role. Further, Rostow, who was under secretary of state for political affairs, points out how Bundy's memoranda to his principals were similar to public opinion in the United States about the Vietnam War, and how memoranda and public opinion were mutually reinforcing. "These opinions [official and public] would have been the same, I am convinced," he says, "if the memoranda of . . . William Bundy had been printed in the papers every morning on the day they were typed to supplement the columns about their ideas which appeared regularly all over the country and the world."[13]

Regional Bureaus: Demands and Inputs

A regional assistant secretary travels daily to the seventh floor to meet with one or another of his principals, or with groups of them. He also meets constantly and informally with his several deputy assistant secretaries; he normally meets several times a week with his country directors in the "smaller staff meeting," and he confers weekly at the "larger staff meeting" with his country directors and with various functional specialists from AID, Cultural Affairs, United Nations Affairs, USIA, and military liaison, among others.

When the assistant secretary meets with his deputies, it is often to discuss intradepartmental themes such as the state of the bureau's relations with the seventh floor, to trade information concerning regional and departmental policy on operational matters, and to formulate positions to be taken in presenting policy recommendations to the seventh floor. It is also at these meetings that bureau budget, management, and personnel decisions are made.

The "smaller," or country directors', staff meeting promotes intimacy and an open expression of viewpoints. The group of country directors—from six to twelve—is small enough that all the directors can sit around a conference table with the assistant secretary and/or one or more of his three deputies. All of the country directors are, technically at least, equal in the hierarchy, and all are basically concerned with political problems, often with the same problem if it is a regional one.

At these smaller meetings the assistant secretary can brief country directors on the results of his private sessions with seventh-floor principals about problems in which the directors are involved: Will the military procurement request for Thailand be pared down in the budget process? Will the department support an initiative to increase the number of FBI operatives attached to the embassy in Tokyo? Should the country director for Indonesia encourage the American ambassador in Djakarta to assure the Indonesian foreign minister that tariff schedules will not be altered?

It should be noted that none of these issues is of overwhelming policy importance to the United States government. Each of them, however, involves interest representation—and a recommendation—by the assistant secretary to his seventh-floor principals, and a response from those principals reflecting not only their personal views but inputs to them from the larger political system (i.e., cabinet departments, Congress, independent agencies) of which they are a part.

Frequent ad hoc conferences with individual country directors are an important tool in the conduct of bureau affairs. Such conferences center on the "clients" of the country director, namely, "his" country and the U.S. mission in that country. Discussions may range from recommendations about routine personnel changes to admonishing the country director not to encourage a particular line of action because the ambassador who resists it may shortly be transferred and the proposed action can wait until after his departure.

During individual conferences with country directors the assistant secretary or his deputy may also encourage the country director to give a comprehensive personal assessment of how well the field mission is performing. As a result of such conferences the country director may be asked to convey his superior's views about an internal mission problem to the ambassador in the field, frequently by "official-informal" personal letter which receives no distribution at the field post and very limited distribution in the department.

As director of the Office of East Asian and Pacific Programs of the Bureau of Educational and Cultural Affairs, the author regularly attended from August 1965 through December 1969 the weekly "larger staff meetings" over which Assistant Secretary William P. Bundy presided. The author also attended numerous ad hoc smaller meetings chaired by officers at the deputy assistant secretary level. The following discussion of what occurred at the meetings is based upon the author's systematic notes each week. Of necessity, observations are limited to activities of one political bureau, the Bureau of East Asian and Pacific Affairs. However, almost five continuous years of observation throughout the Department of State, and detailed interviews and discussions with officers at various levels in other political bureaus, convince the author that basically similar procedures and similar levels of substantive discussion obtain in all the regional bureaus.

At the larger staff meetings an unenunciated but very real "pecking order" obtains. The country directors, because they are concerned with actual political issues, occupy seats around a conference table with the assistant secretary. The functional specialists sit in a concentric ring near the walls, removed from the conference table, inconspicuous but alertly present, since this is their principal opportunity to learn what issues and business currently occupy the political operators.

Substantive discussion at regional assistant secretary staff conferences may roughly be divided into three categories: (1) major problems arising from policy thrusts, which are discussed mainly in terms of how these thrusts affect various countries, and how messages should be drafted to assist field posts in dealing with problems arising from them; (2) briefings by the assistant secretary, one of his deputies, or a country director on developments in other regions which affect major policy thrusts; (3) reports on diverse subjects of general interest, either from country directors or from functional specialists in attendance.

At larger regional bureau staff conferences issues of substantive importance are seldom mentioned specifically and substantive decisions are never made. For example, during the years 1965 to 1970, when there was a great deal of *public discussion* concerning the issue of Chinese Communist representation at the United Nations, that subject was never discussed at the larger staff meetings of the Bureau of East Asian and Pacific Affairs, nor was the issue of U.S. policy vis-à-vis Prince Sihanouk in Cambodia. Similarly, U.S. fears about the validity of elections in Vietnam never surfaced in the discussions. The department positions on all of these were presented as ready-made policy thrusts to the regional staff conferences. The only "issue" involved was determining what could be suggested to the field posts, via messages to be drafted by country directors, to solicit support for the U.S. position from host countries.

Problems encountered in *execution* of policy, however, receive a great deal of attention at such meetings. The overriding problems throughout the decade of the 1960s related, as might be expected, to Vietnam. In 1965 attention centered on how to publicize for field use newly uncovered evidence of Viet Cong atrocities and how to blunt rising discontent on university campuses at home. The American student problem involved domestic as well as foreign policy pressures on the political system and, uncharacteristically, one meeting was devoted almost entirely to consideration of how to respond to a threatened University of Michigan "sit-in" at which "managed violence" was expected.

By 1966, with the tempo of conflict escalating, it appeared important that the conferees mount efforts to reflect support for Vietnam policy among U.S.

allies. Thus, when Japanese press and government reaction to the U.S. bombing of oil installations near Hanoi was unexpectedly and gratifyingly mild, discussion emphasized the need to communicate this fact to field posts for use in justifying U.S. policy to host country officials.

By 1967, as academic input to foreign policy formulation became a major concern, discussions at staff meetings reflected general frustration over scholarly inattention to what bureau officials considered a correct and reasonable Vietnam policy. Almost poignantly it was pointed out that "not a single paper on Vietnam was delivered at the International Congress of Orientalists" held in the United States that year. Difficulties with Congress were also discussed, with great attention being paid to Senator Mansfield's increasingly dove-like statements. At one meeting, conferees characterized one of Mansfield's speeches as "unclear," and went on to suggest that the bureau might therefore be able to find facets of the statement that it could "live with," the implication being that ambiguity could be used to the bureau's advantage. Meanwhile, bureau officials, led by Bundy, kept to an exhausting schedule of speeches throughout the United States to underscore alleged Viet Cong aggressive intentions as revealed by captured documents. The documents were reproduced in the *Department of State Bulletin* and country directors were urged to read them as their "homework."

Execution of Vietnam policy and problems arising from its outcomes were the central substantive matters occupying the bureau until the 1968 policy modifications which began with President Johnson's dramatic speech of March 31 and the subsequent agreement with North Vietnam to commence talks in Paris. Other substantive problems—not issues, but problems encountered in carrying out policy thrusts—included, in descending order of importance, relationships with Japan, with Cambodia and Laos, and with the remaining countries of Asia.

Even in 1965 great stress was being placed on economic talks with the Japanese, as well as on urging a sharing of the burden of economic aid to countries in the region. For example, it was suggested that Asian countries request assistance directly from Japan, for, as one country director commented, "The Japs can't say no to Asians; the Koreans get more out of the Japs directly than if we helped." During 1965 the importance of a favorable civil air agreement with Tokyo was emphasized. In 1967 Prime Minister Sato's visit to the United States—how to handle it and its implications—was a matter for major discussion. In 1968 the desirability of Japanese restraint on steel exports was a favored topic, and in 1969 President Nixon's personal session with Foreign Minister Aishi was discussed; it was duly noted that this constituted "the exception to Nixon's policy of personally seeing only presidents and chiefs of state."

Relationships with countries in the Indochina group other than Vietnam were particularly difficult since Laos was officially neutral and Cambodia was led by the volatile and unpredictable Sihanouk, with whom the United States had no diplomatic relations. Border incidents and allegations of territorial violations of Cambodia by U.S. forces claimed emergency consideration more than once and were the subject of innumerable map-study sessions to *reinforce* the policy determination that Sihanouk's protests about border violations were invalid. In no case was a policy *issue* injected; rather, the question was how to cope with the consequences of policy.

Compared to Japan and Indochina, remaining countries in the East Asian sphere received comparatively little attention at the meetings. The Caltex Oil Company's "hopefulness" about the new government in Indonesia following the overthrow of Sukarno in 1965 was noted. The demands and expectations of the Philippines about continued preferential trade treatment following expiration of the Laurel-Langley Agreement in 1974 were repeatedly discussed, as well as the perennial question of U.S. versus Filipino jurisdiction over "incidents" on U.S. military bases in the Philippines. The widely publicized *USS Pueblo* affair of early 1968 and the "Flying Pueblo" incident of early 1969 (the former involving North Korean seizure of a U.S. communications vessel and the latter involving North Korean destruction of a U.S. patrol plane) enjoyed surprisingly brief exposure at the meetings. Again, the unwritten guideline was to raise only matters peripheral to basic policy concepts; the concepts themselves were never considered, whatever the country or the policy.

Regional bureau staff meetings frequently include briefings, as distinct from discussions, on various bureau-related matters. Such briefings may range from position statements to speculation about the *consequences* of policy changes. A political briefing in mid-1966, for instance, depicted Thailand with a "booming economy," a country aware of the insurgency situation in the northeast and middle south, and having a police system "far ahead in security and intelligence over four years ago." Budgetary shifts, changes in personnel levels, and restructuring of program emphases are frequently the subjects of briefings. In 1968, for example, a briefing was given on the policy decision to effect a 10 percent cut (BALPA)* at all missions with 100 or more Americans—"Vietnam is excepted and we don't know about Bangkok or Vientiane"—and on a possible voluntary reduction in the size of the U.S. military assistance group in Thailand. In 1969 a briefer reported that the AID program in Thailand had been heavily critized in a report from the General Accounting Office, and that a congressional subcommittee would shortly visit

* The multipronged effort of the foreign policy subsystem to reverse unfavorable U.S. balance of payments accounts.

Bangkok, a remark which prompted forewarning cables to every field mission in Asia having an AID program.

Summary of Sixth-Floor Procedure

Obviously U.S. foreign policy is not formulated at regional bureau staff conferences. Equally obviously, policy problems of a significant nature are not resolved by the regional assistant secretary. As previously emphasized, issues of significant proportion are referred to the foreign policy managers at the seventh-floor level and also usually involve other actors at similar levels in other bureaucracies, the presidential subsystem, and elsewhere.

But a degree of week-to-week decision-making about shifts in policy emphasis and policy recommendation does take place at the level of the regional assistant secretary. The substantive issues which regional assistant secretaries actually resolve are addressed at ad hoc meetings between the regional assistant secretary, his deputies, and the appropriate country director. When agreement has been achieved, the decision is committed to writing, usually by the country director who may act as rapporteur at the meeting. The written draft of the decision—whether a paper or a cable—is again reviewed by the regional assistant secretary and, after his clearance, prepared for review by, and concurrence of, seventh-floor principals.

The regional assistant secretary knows from experience which of his policy decisions require review by seventh-floor principals before transmission to the field. Seventh-floor principals, either personally or through their staff assistants, are normally already aware of the particular policy problem and are monitoring developments. The regional assistant secretary will already have assessed the degree of seventh-floor interest in the matter and will seek or not seek concurrence accordingly. In many cases, the final concurrences must be obtained outside the department at Defense, the White House, or within the intelligence community. After final clearance, the document which emerges becomes a statement of policy. The assistant secretary tends to act in conformity with theory on bureaucratic behavior, namely, conservatively by proposing incremental rather than marked change, and safely by "clearing" with the seventh floor so that responsibility is diffused.[14]

FIFTH FLOOR: RESOURCE PEOPLE

Each regional bureau is subdivided along country lines, with country directors designated to coordinate day-by-day relationships with individual nations in the area. Some country directors are responsible for several countries. Since 1966, when the position was upgraded, all country directors are senior Foreign Service Officers.

Constraints

In theory, the country director coordinates *all* U.S. interests regarding "his" country. But in practice, a proliferation of foreign policy interests of bureaucracies outside the department, particularly the Department of Defense, precludes his carrying out this role. Many country directors are forced to devote more time to keeping abreast of developments within the bureaucracies which affect "their" countries than in coordinating foreign policy thrusts. The country director, above all else, must keep informed. He must be—but often is no more than—a resource person for his superiors in the regional bureau.

Besides external bureaucratic pressures, departmental procedures also inhibit the country director. The requirement for clearance of outgoing messages is an administrative device that practically guarantees the director cannot perform to the level of his formally assigned responsibilities. Only minor messages prepared by the country director's assistants—who usually number three or four relatively junior officers—may be transmitted over the country director's initials alone. Since these communications are normally reproduced for broad distribution throughout the departmental hierarchy, they tend to be bland or equivocal so as not to infringe on anyone else's interests. Most other messages to field missions originating with the country director require clearance at the assistant secretary level, or, conversely, the country director prepares messages upon the instruction of the assistant secretary, who subsequently reviews them. While in most instances clearance is eventually achieved, the process is time-consuming, authority-deflating, and often unnecessary.* Indeed, clearance procedures are so cumbersome, and reproduction and distribution of incoming and outgoing cables so broad, that country directors traditionally have tried to control sensitive interaction with field missions by employing the device of "official-informal" personal letters which are not distributed beyond the addressee, or by assigning a limited-distribution category to cables and other messages.

---

* The *New York Times* has noted that "an instruction to an ambassador can require up to twenty-seven signatures for clearance before it is dispatched. One new officer recently managed, by nagging everyone concerned to put a moderately important cable through to an embassy in Southeast Asia in a week's time. He was astonished when more experienced colleagues applauded." Terence Smith, "Foreign Policy; Ebbing of Power at the State Department," *New York Times*, January 17, 1971.

Representational Responsibilities

The country director has an operational as well as a symbolic role in relation to the diplomatic representatives of "his" country who are accredited to the United States. He is the principal point of contact between a foreign ambassador and the U.S. government after the ambassador has paid an initial representational call on the president and the secretary of state. Unless issues between his country and the United States reach problem proportions, the ambassador may never again converse with the secretary—except at social functions—until he makes his farewell call upon departure.

The country director also performs the role of liaison between the U.S. diplomatic mission to "his" country and the Washington bureaucracies whose personnel are represented at the mission. At the Department of State he is the surrogate of the American ambassador to the country. As a result of this role-playing, he tends to become an advocate of "his" country within the American foreign policy system, often to the point of defending it. He also tends to perceive broader U.S. interests in "his" country than are seen by other foreign policy actors.

The behavioral characteristics of the American ambassador whom he services affect the quality of input made by the country director within the Department of State. An egocentric or secretive ambassador who consistently bypasses the country director by communicating directly with the assistant secretary through "official-informal/eyes only" letters will adversely affect the usefulness of the country director. An American ambassador who is lax about meeting the department's political and economic reporting requirements becomes a problem for the country director, as does the ambassador who expects special attention for "his" country.

Many an ambassador learns to appreciate the role of the country director when he comes to Washington for consultation and witnesses the efforts of the country director on his behalf within the total U.S. diplomatic framework of some 135 nations. Washington consultation may also have an adverse effect on an ambassador's vanity: the prestige he enjoys at his field post suddenly vanishes. In Washington he is merely one of more than 100 chiefs of mission. His "office" is a desk temporarily claimed from some junior officer in the country director's office, where he sits awaiting summons from the sixth floor, exactly as does his Washington surrogate and department contact, the country director.

Inputs

Country directors are focal points in relations between "their" countries and the United States in direct proportion to the degree they keep themselves informed of government-wide communication, planning, and discussion affecting their area of concern. By so doing they become useful resource persons for their superiors at the assistant secretary level.

The goal of every country director—to influence actual policy outcomes— is not impossible. Despite limitations on his authority imposed by clearance hurdles, the proliferation of other agency interests, the tight rein of the assistant secretary's office, and the avalanche of information he must absorb, the country director possesses greater political resources than do his competitor-counterparts in other bureaucracies of the government. As a formally designated government-wide coordinator of U.S. interests, he is kept informed by his counterparts in other government bureaucracies of their agency initiatives and responses affecting foreign policy, including matters about which formal consultation may be unnecessary. At the very least, inputs of an experienced and skillful country director will not be disregarded, and, at the other end of the spectrum, they may become rationales upon which subsequent significant policy positions may be based.

Obviously it is difficult to define precisely the parameters of a country director's role. What he can and cannot do will depend in part on the role his immediate superiors expect him to play. He will be expected, as Richard Snyder *et al.* have postulated about executives, to respond to "cues from above," but he may also be encouraged to be a free spirit—a brainstormer. If so, however, his license to brainstorm will have limits that he himself can plainly understand. For example, it would be appropriate for the country director for the Philippines to suggest a more generous wage and benefits policy toward the thousands of Filipinos employed at the U.S. naval base at Subic Bay. The increased cordiality in U.S.-Philippine relations which might result could conceivably help, in the short run, to deter Philippine authorities from invoking further restrictions on American investment. Moreover, the continuing receptivity of the Filipinos to operation of U.S. military bases on Philippine soil is important to successful conduct of contemporary U.S. foreign policy in the western Pacific. The country director's input in such circumstances, though modest in concept, might have long-range results.

On the other hand, it would be highly inappropriate for the Philippine country director to offer proposals concerning the mission and deployment of the U.S. Seventh Fleet stationed in the Philippines. Such an initiative by the country director would far exceed the role his superiors expect him to play.

Moreover, the input of a country director is limited by the information to which he has access. It could be hypothesized that his input is in inverse ratio to the urgency of a problem, or, in other words, to the significance of a decision. The Middle East crisis of 1973-74 is an extreme example. A country director could not possibly be privy to important variables perceived only by such on-the-scene participants as President Nixon and Secretary of State Kissinger. In this case the input of Middle East country directors in decision-making could be no more than as resource people. If, however, at the other extreme, the ambassador to India should ask the Department of State (i.e., the country director for India) for speech-making themes to promote a greater degree of cordiality between the two countries, the country director might offer the ambassador his own views.

DECISION-MAKING AND THE DEPARTMENT OF STATE

If one reviews decision-making in the Department of State in terms of a continuum of five decision categories—minor, routine, significant, fundamental and critical—it is clear, first, that country directors are engaged principally in *minor* decision-making, although they make resource inputs to routine and significant decision-making concerning "their" countries. Second, assistant secretaries are limited principally to *routine* decisions affecting their geographical areas, although they make resource inputs to significant decisions involving their areas and, occasionally, other geographical areas through inputs which propose alternative policy positions. Even the highly significant role of Assistant Secretary of State William Bundy in Vietnam policy formulation was not an exception. Evidence suggests that Bundy, rather than managing the Vietnam problem, was himself largely managed by the actual decision makers both within and outside the Department of State. Third, few *significant* decisions are made below the level of the seventh floor, and many significant decisions—probably the bulk—are made in consequence of interactions with the White House (the presidential subsystem) and the bureaucracies of other foreign policy agencies. Fourth, all *fundamental* and *critical* foreign policy decisions involve the White House.

In a perceptive comment on the bureaucratic role in post-World War II foreign policy, Robert J. Art suggests that the strength of the "bureaucratic paradigm" lies in its relevance to policy *implementation* rather than to policy *formulation*.[15] It is the author's conclusion, following some twenty years of observation of structure and process in the Department of State and the United States Information Agency, that Art is correct. To understand the interactions through which policy is implemented is to understand the role of the Department of State in the foreign policy process. However, policy positions per se have only limited impact upon the international geopolitical environment which all nations seek to influence. Rather, policy implementation, that is the specific actions taken in pursuance of decisions, provides the impact. In the American political system the Department of State has an implementation role concerning *all* foreign policy decisions, both through its interactions in Washington and through U.S. missions abroad.

CHAPTER 4

The United States Diplomatic Field Mission: A Cluster of Power Centers

Jean Jules Jusserand, a French diplomat and scholar who was ambassador to the United States from 1903 to 1925, reportedly told an American audience that diplomacy is "the art of bringing home the bacon without spilling the beans."[1] Jusserand's amusing remark is also a perceptive one. Diplomacy is politics in its purest form, and politics, according to Harold Lasswell's famous definition, is who gets what, when and how. The *Oxford English Dictionary* states that diplomacy is "the management of international relations by negotiation: the method by which these relations are adjusted and managed by ambassadors and envoys; the business or art of the diplomatist." Diplomacy stresses *method*. It is concerned with the *skill* with which the diplomat can carry out the instructions of his government.

The term diplomacy is derived from the Greek word *diploma*, which in French came to refer to the license or privilege which one sovereign accorded the envoy or messenger of another sovereign to safeguard the envoy's security so that he might convey messages and enter into negotiations on behalf of his king. By the fifteenth century permanent diplomatic missions began to be established in Europe headed by *ambassadors* (a word of Italian origin), and 65 their licenses or privileges were legitimized by custom and practice as diplomatic immunity. Subsequently, international agreements (such as those emerging from the Congress of Vienna which established a rank-order list for diplomatic titles) and judicial interpretation have produced a vast body of international law regarding diplomats and diplomatic practice.

It cannot be overemphasized that diplomatic missions in whatever country are privileged subsystems, fundamentally distinct from the national political system of the host countries in which they operate. Their interactions with the national political system differ significantly from those, for example, of overseas American corporations, which are also subsystems that interact with national political systems.

The United States Constitution specifically recognizes the special status of ambassadors as representatives of one sovereign to another. Article II specifies that the President "Shall nominate, and by and with the Advice and Consent of the Senate, shall appoint Ambassadors, other public Ministers and Consuls. . . ." An *agrément* must be obtained from the host country, which thereby agrees to accept the specific individual proposed as ambassador. Upon accreditation by the host country, the American ambassador becomes the *personal* representative of the president of the United States in the host country. The ambassador and his *official* staff enjoy diplomatic immunity as long as they are accredited. An ambassador or official who is no longer acceptable to the host country may be declared *persona non grata* and must leave forthwith.

While the Constitution addresses in a single phrase "Ambassadors, other public Ministers and Consuls," international law distinguishes between diplomatic and consular roles. Diplomatic officers are concerned with formal binational, mainly "political," interactions. The role of consular officers is to facilitate commerce involving citizens of the nation they represent and to protect their rights in the host country. In 1924, following British precedent established several decades earlier, the United States Congress passed the Rogers Act, which merged the consular and diplomatic services into a single Foreign Service with interchangeability of consular and diplomatic *assignments* for Foreign Service Officers.

However, distinctions between consular and diplomatic *roles* appear to be minimal in contemporary U.S. practice. The Department of State announced in February 1973 that the forty-seven Foreign Service Officers assigned to Vietnam to "serve in the Embassy [and] in the four newly established Consulates General . . . will carry out classic diplomatic duties."[2] In a sense, U.S. consulates, which were originally designed to assist American traders and to protect American citizens, have become "little embassies" where role-playing parallels that in embassies. In practice, consular posts are designated as consulates general, consulates, or consular agencies, in descending order, on the basis of their size and importance in foreign policy role-playing. They perform political, economic/commercial, administrative, and consular roles, and often include AID, CIA, USIS, and Peace Corps role-playing as well.

For purposes of this study, the term *diplomatic mission* refers to the total, *formal* United States government presence in a host country. The word *embassy* actually means the residence of an ambassador, and the term *chancery* refers to his office. In popular practice, however, *embassy* is customarily used to refer to the chancery and to the employees of the United States government who are formally *accredited* as diplomatic and consular officers to another nation. Embassy, in the latter context, equates with the *traditional* components common to diplomatic missions of the United States prior to World War II—political, economic, consular, and administrative officials, plus specialists such as military, commercial, and agricultural attachés and, since 1946, *non-traditional* elements which have expanded significantly in number and size—intelligence officers (CIA), cultural and information officers (USIA), and administrators of the various economic assistance programs (AID).

Other governmental departments and agencies may be represented within the *mission*—as distinguished from the embassy with its formally accredited officers. The Immigration and Naturalization Service, the Public Health Service, the Treasury Department, the Department of Commerce, the Peace Corps, and especially the Department of Defense may, subject to agreement by the host country, maintain a physical presence within the mission.* U.S. military elements at diplomatic missions, aside from officers accredited to the host country as military attachés, can be numerous and their activities complex. Their roles depend in part upon treaty and other contractual arrangements with the host country and usually pertain to host country national security.

The term *chief of mission* normally refers to the ambassador, who is nominated by the president, confirmed by the Senate, and formally appointed to represent the president in a particular country. In the absence of an ambassador, the Department of State may designate a *chargé d' affaires.* The term *national* or *host country*, as used herein, refers to the foreign state to which the U.S. chief of mission is accredited.

* The *New York Times* identifies thirty-four agencies with resident overseas personnel, and the *United States Diplomatic Mission to Thailand Telephone Directory Bangkok, Thailand, July 1970,* lists seven others.

DIPLOMATIC MISSIONS:
MICROPOLITICAL SYSTEMS

Functions

Within the political systems framework, U.S. diplomatic missions discharge functions common to all political systems. The mission serves as an important first link in the chain of communications from the host country's political system. A request from Jordan to the United States for economic assistance would be an example of such an input. In reverse, the foreign policy system in Washington makes its inputs to the host country through the mission—for example, an instruction to the ambassador to the Philippines to convey the American position on sugar quotas to that government. When these inputs have been registered within the diplomatic mission and communicated to the host country, conflict may occur about their significance, the appropriate level and tone of response to Washington, or related choices. In the process, the inputs may undergo conversion before an appropriate mission response, or output, is made. Mission responses are subsystem outcomes which, in turn, become inputs to the larger foreign policy system in the United States.

The case of the Dominican Republic in 1965 is a good example of how a mission converts inputs into behavioral outputs. On Tuesday, April 27, provisional President Molina requested the American ambassador to assume a direct role in negotiating between his rebels and the regular military forces who were advancing on Santo Domingo. In line with Washington's general guidance and policy of nonintervention, Ambassador W. Tapley Bennett, Jr., declined to act and urged instead that an accord be achieved "by Dominicans talking to Dominicans." By the next day the Molina group had collapsed and a new governing junta had emerged. When Pedro Benoit, leader of the junta, asked the United States to land 1200 marines "to help restore peace in the country," Bennett transmitted the request to Washington but advised against such action.

Two hours later the mission reassessed the situation and cabled Washington that events were "deteriorating rapidly," and that "American lives are in danger." The ambassador stated that the country team, composed of the senior political, economic, and information officers and the military attachés, had unanimously concluded that "the time has come to land the marines." In consequence of this recommendation by the U.S. mission, President Lyndon Johnson subsequently ordered 20,000 troops and some forty ships and helicopters to the island to evacuate American citizens and other foreign nationals, to establish a neutral zone between battling Dominican factions, and to prevent a communist takeover of that country.[3]

Roles

In simplest terms, the formal role of a U.S. diplomatic mission is to interact with the foreign affairs system of the host country—principally through its ministry or department of foreign affairs—in order to achieve U.S. foreign policy goals respecting the host country. Traditional diplomacy is the sum total of the techniques the diplomat utilizes—persuasion, bargaining, negotiation, sanction, and reward—to achieve ends. However, it would be a gross error to conclude that the mission's role is limited to traditional "diplomatic" interactions between the ambassador and the host country foreign office or chief of state. On the contrary, U.S. diplomatic missions engage in a variety of specialized interactions, largely informal, at different levels within the national political system. Important changes in the composition, size, and especially the roles of U.S. diplomatic missions have taken place since World War II as the result of an increasing number of specialized interactions between the U.S. and host countries. So many more actors within the mission are involved in role-playing that resemblance to the traditional pre-World War II diplomatic mission is almost coincidental, and certainly much of this role-playing has little in common with traditional concepts of diplomacy.

Varying roles in a diplomatic mission can be linked to the several organizational units within it. In terms of traditional diplomacy, the ambassador is the principal role player. It is he who literally conveys and receives communications between the United States government and the host government. He delivers "diplomatic notes" to the host country foreign office, often accompanying delivery with a verbal message in accordance with his instructions. He may be instructed to negotiate a treaty or an agreement on behalf of the president (a task which may require years to complete), or he may be requested to elicit from the host-country foreign office its views on a subject of immediate interest to the United States.

Similarly, the foreign office of the host country delivers its diplomatic communications to the American ambassador and summons him when it wishes to discuss, negotiate, or complain. An ambassador must always respond to the summons.

The symbolic acts of the ambassador, termed representational functions by the United States Foreign Service, are numerous. He officially conveys greetings or messages from the president of the United States to the chief of state of the host country. Upon his arrival in the host capital he formally presents his credentials to the chief of state amidst appropriate and often elaborate ceremony. He must observe, ceremoniously and appropriately, American Independence Day and attend the national-day celebrations of the host country and of every other diplomatic mission to the host capital. The ambassador is expected to attend many official functions of the host government and to make frequent public appearances.

Since his principal role is to engage in official *political* interaction, the ambassador utilizes the political section of his mission as a resource unit to help him assess political relations with the host country and to interpret changes in them. The political section, together with the economic section and the intelligence unit of the mission, serves as a collective listening post for the ambassador; on the basis of these inputs he reports regularly to the Department of State. All official communications from a U.S. diplomatic mission which are prepared by the traditional embassy elements—i.e., the political, economic, consular, and administrative sections—are transmitted to Washington over the signature of the ambassador or of the deputy chief of mission.

Non-traditional mission elements which have evolved since World War II also contribute to role-playing, but their contributions are of a different nature. Most new, or non-traditional, elements are engaged in the operation of programs, rather than in negotiating, communicating, and reporting. Among traditional mission elements only the consular section engages in activities of a program nature: it provides assistance to U.S. nationals and issues visas for entry of host-country nationals into the United States. The major programmers are the administrators of the economic and military assistance programs, the joint security operations, the propaganda and cultural programs, and, for want of a more precise term, the quasi socio-humanitarian program of the highly publicized Peace Corps.

Economic and military assistance programs are the political resources that the mission can use in bargaining and persuasion. They are administered respectively by the mission staff of the Agency for International Development (AID) and the mission-attached military advisory and/or assistance element, usually called the Joint United States Military Advisory Group (JUSMAG). In Latin American countries where a U.S. military advisory program operates, it is usually in consequence of a contractual arrangement and is known by the acronym MilGroup. In the case of assistance to any ally engaged in physical conflict with other powers, or with insurgents as in Thailand, a United States Military Assistance Command (MAC—for example, MACTHAI) may operate. Politico-military role-playing may also extend to joint physical security arrangements involving operation of military bases on host-country soil, thus generating another set of inputs. The United States Information Service (USIS)—the mission element of the United States Information Agency—conducts cultural relationships with the host country and administers information programs via mass media channels to assist in achieving U.S. objectives in the host country. Since the late 1960s USIS programs have also been mounted to promote commercial, investment, and trade objectives of the United States.

The chart on page 72 depicts a typical large U.S. diplomatic mission.

DIPLOMATIC MISSIONS: INTERNAL COMPETITION

Although elements or sections within the diplomatic mission perform formally assigned tasks under the titular authority of the ambassador, their actual roles are conditioned by differing interests which may disturb system equilibrium. A number of mission elements are actors in external executive branch subsystems (i.e., non-Department of State) such as USIA, DOD, CIA, and are accountable to these Washington-based subsystems as well as to the ambassador at the mission. Perception of national goals by such elements may differ from those of the chief of mission and of mission elements which are integral to the Department of State.

As a consequence, a diplomatic mission is a cluster of subsystems, each a center of power within the mission. Power in this context equates with the ability of actors or elements to influence the behavior of others. In ascertaining where power can be identified within the mission, a simplified application of Harry Eckstein's concept of authority patterns may be useful. Eckstein defines an authority pattern as "a set of asymmetric relations among hierarchically ordered members of a social unit that involves the direction of the unit."[4] In short, a clue to power relationships would be the identifiable patterns of behavior in which direction and compliance are present. The power of a particular element of the mission can be judged on the basis of how well it succeeds in convincing other elements of the mission of the legitimacy and necessity of its proposed course of action.

Factors· within the mission which influence establishment of power bases include (1) the Foreign Service personnel system, which was designed for an elite corps of Foreign Service Officers (FSOs) who would manage the mission, and to which has been added since 1946 a melange of subsidiary officers and staff personnel who are usually not considered by FSOs as their equals; (2) the character of the political environment in the host country; (3) the size of the mission;[5] (4) the directive *quality* of the chief of mission's leadership (i.e., directions which, in Eckstein's terms, activate perceptions of legitimacy); and (5) the relative abilities of the mission's various sections to convert inputs pertaining to their specialist areas into political resources which will enhance the legitimacy of that section of the mission, and the character and style of that section chief.

TABLE VI   UNITED STATES DIPLOMATIC MISSION

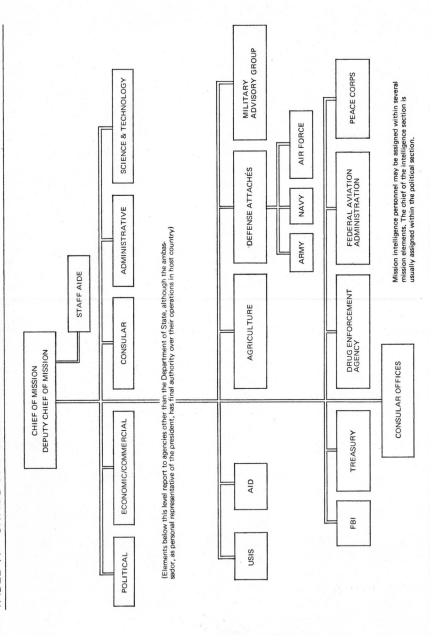

CHIEF OF MISSION
DEPUTY CHIEF OF MISSION

STAFF AIDE

POLITICAL

ECONOMIC/COMMERCIAL

CONSULAR

ADMINISTRATIVE

SCIENCE & TECHNOLOGY

(Elements below this level report to agencies other than the Department of State, although the ambassador, as personal representative of the president, has final authority over their operations in host country)

USIS

AID

AGRICULTURE

DEFENSE ATTACHÉS

ARMY

NAVY

AIR FORCE

MILITARY ADVISORY GROUP

FBI

TREASURY

DRUG ENFORCEMENT AGENCY

FEDERAL AVIATION ADMINISTRATION

PEACE CORPS

CONSULAR OFFICES

Mission intelligence personnel may be assigned within several
mission elements. The chief of the intelligence section is
usually assigned within the political section.

Impact of Rank

Rank is important in a mission, not only because it determines an individual's representational role in the host country—his place on the diplomatic list vis-à-vis diplomats of all states maintaining missions in the host country—but also because it constitutes a formal allocation of status within the mission and confers perquisites both within the mission and in the host country.* Rank (i.e., minister, counselor, first secretary, second secretary, third secretary, attaché**) and Foreign Service Officer class (8 to 1 in ascending order) establishes a precise order of precedence within the embassy. For example, if two Foreign Service Officers each hold the rank of counselor, the one in the higher class, or longer in that class, takes precedence over the other according to embassy protocol. (And the foreign service class of an officer immediately communicates to all mission employees the officer's salary.)

In addition to formal rank, a most precise, albeit informal, status is assigned to officers depending upon the category to which they are appointed—Foreign Service Officer, Foreign Service Information Officer, Foreign Service Reserve Officer, or Foreign Service Staff Officer.

Foreign Service Officers (FSOs) are career officers in the Department of State Foreign Service. They usually occupy the highest places in the formal role-playing order, as well as in the informal pecking order. They tend to be assigned to the traditionally more visible, and by implication more significant, sections of the embassy—staff officer positions in the ambassador's office and in the political and economic sections. These sections have role counterparts in the diplomatic missions of most other countries and are responsible for most of the reportage required by the Department of State in Washington. Officers assigned to these sections carry out "diplomatic" roles in the classical sense and, in practice, often manage to relate their roles to almost all mission activities. In effect they participate in most decision-making within the mission.

Military personnel at the level of general officer equate with the senior Foreign Service Officers heading the traditional sections. These officers enjoy a particular prestige among other military officers and the civilian employees whom they supervise. Perquisites such as military aides, assigned automobiles, and personal flags are status symbols. Lesser military officers, other than attachés on the ambassador's staff, are important *within* their military command or advisory group but are hardly consequential to traditional mission operations.

* Rank is carried to an amusing extreme in Manila, where the Philippine government issues to a diplomatic official an automobile license plate identifying his embassy and his precise rank within it.
** An attaché's rank-order on the diplomatic list is determined solely by his salary.

The Foreign Service Information Officer (FSIO) is a new category, created in 1968 when Congress by law accorded diplomatic rank and career status to selected officers of the United States Information Agency. An FSIO and FSO are equal in rank, but within a diplomatic mission an FSIO does not enjoy the same status. Instead, the primacy of the "political" over the "functional" prevails at the mission exactly as it does in the Department of State. The FSO is presumably involved with political/economic affairs; the FSIO is involved with cultural/educational/media affairs.

Foreign Service Reserve Officers (FSRs)—except for the most senior officers of the AID element who usually are FSRs—and Foreign Service Staff Officers (FSSOs), who are usually senior technical specialists, have even less hierarchical standing. The former are not career personnel, and the latter are not generalists, two criteria which historically have characterized the American diplomatic service. FSRs normally have diplomatic status; FSSOs may or may not.

Senior civil service employees supervise offices of U.S. agencies associated with the mission at large posts—e.g., Internal Revenue Service, Immigration and Naturalization Service, Treasury Department. They do not have diplomatic rank nor are they included in the embassy hierarchy.

Host Country Political Environment

The more receptive the host country political environment is to U.S. programs and perceived interests, the more numerous are the opportunities for mission elements to utilize the environment as a political resource to strengthen their positions. In congenial political systems mission elements tend to have greater access to power centers in the national community and freer forums for carrying out operational programs such as AID, USIS, and intelligence activities. In consequence, each mission element has the means, stemming from relationships with important subsystems in the national community, to build influence for itself within the mission proper.

Occasionally elements within the mission literally become the official U.S. presence to host country military, economic, cultural, intelligence, or other subsystems. Examples of this phenomenon are found in Cambodia and Thailand, where the obvious advantage enjoyed by U.S. military assistance commands and advisory groups with their national counterparts ensures them a predominant role in the American mission. And in these countries the military is the predominant actor in the national political system.

In some instances Peace Corps volunteers or individual cultural attachés have enjoyed wider acceptance in a host country than other mission elements, and in developing nations the AID director is sometimes more important to host country decision makers than the American ambassador.*

Simply stated, status and influence accrue to those elements which most successfully penetrate the national organizational environment in which the mission operates. The penetration is reflected in numerous ways, even extending to varying privileges accorded by national authorities to some mission elements and not to others (e.g., permitting importation of tax-free personal items). The most important criterion, however, is what subsystem the mission element can influence in the host country and to what degree.

Missions which operate in an optimal political environment—an environment sympathetic to U.S. foreign policy aims, where the outlook for achievement of mission goals is most positive—are most likely to experience a high degree of competition among the various internal mission power centers.

An optimal political environment is one characterized by (1) clear short- and long-term perceived American interests, which are also perceived and accepted by the host country; (2) the perception by host country decision makers that their foreign policy interests parallel those of the United States in the geographical region; (3) military, political, economic, and cultural links and alliances between the host country and the United States; (4) willingness of the host country to accept establishment of regional U.S. agency headquarters in the country (for example, regional Federal Bureau of Investigation offices, Voice of America transmitters); (5) English as the *lingua franca;* and (6) a history of host country friendliness toward the United States.

Exemplifying an optimal political environment is Thailand, which is strongly anticommunist, an active ally of the United States in Southeast Asia, and deeply concerned about its rebellious, procommunist northeastern provinces. Thailand's economy is heavily dependent upon a continuing infusion of American military and economic assistance. It has permitted American military and civilian agencies to set up headquarters on its soil. Its citizens generally find empathy with Americans, and Thai "service industries" such as hotels, tourism, crafts, and clothing manufacturers were developed for the American trade. Moreover, English is the western language spoken by most educated Thais.

Internal mission conflict tends to be less intense where, as in the Soviet Union, the national political system is essentially closed to the United States and thus virtually beyond the power of the American mission to influence. As

* Sheldon Appleton records that in 1965 rebels in the Dominican Republic stated they would release six captured U.S. Marines if a *Peace Corps* representative was designated as an intermediary. (Sheldon Appleton, *United States Foreign Policy* [Boston: Little, Brown and Company, 1968], p. 186); Robert Kennedy noted in 1967 that the AID director in some missions had greater influence than the ambassador, and in many Latin American countries the military element of the U.S. mission was dominant (Robert Kennedy, *Thirteen Days* [New York: Signet Books, 1967], pp. 114-15.).

a result, mission elements are confined to the mission proper and forced to greater cooperation among themselves. The directive authority of the ambassador is thereby strengthened.

Size and Diversity of Mission

The size of a mission is of obvious importance in considering internal power structure and conflict. In a small mission such as Somalia, where in 1974 the mission consisted of two officers in the executive section (the ambassador and the deputy chief of mission), one officer in the political section, one economic-commercial officer, four administrative officers, and two USIS officers, the ambassador has an opportunity to achieve close professional and social relations with all of his officers, and he can, with relative ease, exercise effective supervision over his staff.

An ambassador's awareness of, and control over, the activities of the various elements decreases, however, as the size of the mission increases. The problems of managing a large mission are obvious as agencies and personnel proliferate and as interests multiply.

The U.S. diplomatic mission in Thailand, with 325 assigned foreign service personnel, was among the largest of the 119 U.S. missions in the *Foreign Service List* of February 1974. The list is confined to the field staffs of the Department of State, U.S. missions to international organizations, AID, the Peace Corps, USIS, and the United States Department of Agriculture. Excluded are all military personnel except armed forces attachés. Only about one-fourth of the 325 mission personnel listed were Department of State employees.

As early as 1970, the *Telephone Directory of the United States Diplomatic Mission to Thailand* listed thirty-one U.S. government agencies with employees resident in Bangkok and a total of 1203 American mission employees residing in Thailand. The directory did not list most personnel below the level of principal officer at agency branch offices and subposts throughout Thailand, although it listed adults residing in Bangkok who were dependents of personnel assigned outside the city. (A completely separate telephone directory for United States Armed Forces listed principal military personnel at major U.S. military bases outside the capital.) Thus, the ratio of personnel representing traditional embassy elements (over which the ambassador has specific supervisory control) to the personnel of the total mission (over which the ambassador has nominal control) was about one to four.

Ambassadorial Leadership

An ambassador, like any executive, is largely what the values of the system permit him to be in terms of his own character and style. His leadership is judged from superior to unsatisfactory according to how well he fulfills system expectations. The degree of individuality displayed by ambassadors depends in part on their personalities and widely varying experiences, as well as on the differing political environments in which their missions operate. Widely experienced career ambassadors usually develop styles which are recognizable and predictable. For example, Ellis Briggs in Latin America always strove for economy; Raymond Hare in the Middle East sought accommodation with the Arabs. Non-career ambassadors, who in the post-World-War-II era have seldom exceeded twenty-five percent of the total number of U.S. representatives, predictably bring with them aspects of their pre-diplomatic life styles. For example, Chester Bowles, a former governor of Connecticut, was noted when he was ambassador to India for his informality and the politician-common man approach.

Non-career ambassadors, whether they have held previous government appointments (like Shirley Temple Black, the ambassador to Ghana who was previously U.S. delegate to the United Nations; and John Volpe, ambassador to Italy, formerly secretary of transportation) or come from business (like the wealthy political campaign contributors traditionally assigned to certain major European capitals because the cost of "representation" is beyond the means of an FSO who normally has to live on his government allowances), or from academe (e.g., Edwin Reischauer, Harvard scholar and ambassador to Japan) are assigned highly experienced senior Foreign Service Officers as deputy chiefs of mission. The leadership styles in such cases are frequently a compromise between the style of the ambassador and that of his deputy.*

In addition, the several regional geographic bureaus of the Department of State vary in what they expect of ambassadors. Some regional assistant secretaries insist upon a greater degree of guidance from, and control by, the regional bureau than do others. An ambassador's behavior within the mission subsystem will reflect all of these factors.

Increased complexity of operations and ever larger staffs have characterized U.S. missions ever since the dramatic initial expansions of the post-World-War-II years which accompanied the expanded U.S. role in world affairs. As a result, in 1961 President Kennedy felt compelled to clarify and restate the role of the ambassador as the supreme U.S. authority at overseas missions. Worldwide instructions were issued, reinforcing the ambassador's authority over all mission civilians. The ambassador's authority was extended

* Walter Annenberg stated that during his tenure as ambassador to Great Britain "he had spent between $200,000 and $250,000 yearly beyond his government allowance of $25,000 to operate the residence" in London. He was also reported to have "kept his public speeches here to a minimum [and] relied heavily on his embassy staff for advice." Yankee Doodle Spent to London, *Washington Star-News*, October 15, 1974.

to the military area by President Johnson in March 1966 when, in consequence of a recommendation by General Maxwell Taylor, Johnson ordered
the secretary of state "to assume responsibility to the full extent permitted
by law for the overall direction, coordination, and supervision of interdepartmental activities of the United States Government overseas."[6]

The ambassador has the formal authority but not necessarily the tools to
manage conflict successfully within the mission. He may by firm direction
reinforce his executive role, but competition and conflict are inevitable
within and among units of any organization. Size, diversity, and technical
complexity of the mission sections multiply the ambassador's problem of
exerting effective control. Prospects for mission sections to pursue advocate
interests regardless of the ambassador's supervisory authority are inherent
because non-Department-of-State elements have the prerogative to communicate directly with their Washington headquarters.

The military, CIA, USIS, AID, and other units are expected to "clear"
with the chief of mission all communications with their own headquarters,
whether they be foreign service despatches (the classical written report),
airgrams, operational memoranda, or cables (actually radio messages). While
clearance procedure is normally complied with, it does not necessarily extend
to "official-informal" letters from, for example, the chief of USIS to his
superior in Washington. Nor does it extend to so-called "back channel"
messages of the military or CIA. Although similar to "official-informal"
letters, the latter are transmitted over the mission's electronic communication
system, which is often operated at U.S. missions by the CIA and/or the
military, not by Department of State personnel. Moreover, no official record
is maintained of "back channel" messages.*

The ambassador utilizes the same communications techniques to
strengthen his own position. In our contemporary electronic age the cable has
eclipsed the foreign service despatch, the traditional pre-World War II procedure for reportage and transmission of policy recommendations. Easy to
prepare and quickly transmitted, the cable is heavily used by ambassadors
because it is more likely to survive the communication overload in Washington than is the formal written communication. Moreover, chiefs of mission
can assign to their outgoing cables a "limited distribution" or "no distribution" category which will automatically prevent circulation of copies
within the embassy. Thus policy considerations which the ambassador feels

---

* In May 1974 the United States Senate by voice vote approved an amendment to the
Department of State authorization bill "which would limit the freedom of CIA station
chiefs and military attachés abroad to operate without the knowledge of the ambassador
and the State Department bureaucracy." See "The Fulbright Loss and Foreign Policy,"
Washington Star-News, May 29, 1974, p. 1.

should be "closely held" may be concealed both from other mission units in the field and from non-Department of State agencies in Washington. The ambassador's ultimate device for reinforcing his role through the communications tool is to combine limited circulation of messages with their personalization, that is, to address messages for the attention of specific decision makers in the Department of State.*

Staff Meetings: Control Techniques   Just as large business corporations have executive committees to ensure more effective management control, U.S. missions since the 1950s have been directed by presidential and departmental instructions to establish country teams.** The purpose of a country team is to enable the ambassador to coordinate all elements of the mission more effectively. The country team consists of the chiefs of the principal elements within the mission, both traditional and non-traditional. In large missions, such as Paris, Bonn, Bangkok, Manila, and Saigon, non-traditional elements exceed in size and number the traditional elements.

The regularly scheduled country team meeting is a formal control mechanism whose value to the ambassador tends to be in inverse proportion to the number and size of the non-traditional mission elements with which he must cope. Among these, the military, AID, and Peace Corps elements are often numerically larger than the traditional mission sections and are functionally and operationally remote from the chief of mission. While neither the United States Information Service (USIS) nor the Central Intelligence Agency (CIA) is a traditional mission element, their roles are closely related to those of the traditional sections. The intelligence unit is, in effect, an extension of the political section. The public affairs role of USIS is closely identified with ambassadorial interest in achieving a favorable U.S. image within the host country.

At some missions, usually the smaller ones, the country team meets weekly with the chief of mission as a cabinet or inner council, where the interrelationship between the group and the ambassador approximates the concept intended. At other missions the ambassador meets with the section chiefs of the traditional embassy elements, plus CIA and USIS, at least weekly and often daily, while the full country team meeting is a less frequent

* The value of a confidential cable is questionable in the contemporary era when "leaks" of official documents are widespread. A confidential cable from Graham Martin, U.S. ambassador to South Vietnam, to Secretary of State Henry Kissinger was obtained and made public by Senator Edward Kennedy. It caused immediate public outcry against the ambassador. *See Los Angeles Times* editorial, "Misgivings about an Ambassador," April 4, 1974.

** The department's revamping plans announced in mid-1971, which have not been implemented, suggest a task force management concept, even at embassy level.

and more formal management procedure. If the country team was conceptualized as a harmonious forum where parallel interests would reinforce one another, it hardly achieves that distinction at many large missions where interests of mission elements, especially those of the military, are often not parallel. Instead the team often reflects such diverse advocate points of view that the ambassador and his immediate staff consider it expeditious to prepare carefully in advance for the periodic country team sessions. These meetings can become confrontations between the ambassador's senior *embassy* staff, who advance his point of view, and representatives of non-traditional *mission* units, especially, again, the military.

In addition to providing a focal point for management control, the country team meeting is intended to serve as a forum for open discussion of points of view concerning policy emphasis, policy change, and mission responses to Washington-initiated questions. Few ambassadors, however, even if they disagree with the AID director or the chief of the military assistance command, are willing to voice open disagreement in a country team setting with an admiral, a general, or an AID director who holds the diplomatic rank of minister. Frequently the direct, terse, even simplistic, military point of view is difficult to challenge without broaching subtler policy implications which are meaningful only in a context where all participants are equally conversant with all relevant issues and relationships between the host country and the United States. A dubious illusion of unanimity is, therefore, more common. Nonetheless, the country team procedure is one of the few control techniques available to the chief of mission to establish and maintain directive authority over mission elements which have separate budgets, separate administrators, and highly diverse substantive programs; it must be fully exploited if ambassadorial leadership is to prevail.

Ambassadors achieve more effective management within a conference framework comprising only the traditional embassy elements plus CIA and USIS. At smaller, frequent staff meetings responsibilities can be assigned, action agreed upon, and procedures for follow-up adopted. One widely used practice is the weekly, unstructured staff conference; country team meetings usually have a formal agenda. These conferences are devoted to round-the-table verbal reports from the traditional embassy chiefs of section plus CIA and USIS. Since staff meetings are by definition confined to staff, military chiefs of section and/or military commanders are not normally in attendance. Defense attachés of the embassy (army, navy, air force), as distinguished from representatives of autonomous military commands, attend.* At embassies

---

* Defense attachés possess one unique power resource. The Department of Defense, not the Department of State, owns the aircraft that may be assigned to larger embassies, and the ambassador must request permission of the air or naval attaché to use such transportation. The attaché, in turn, must secure clearance from Washington and from the host

where a formal American military presence—a military command as in Bangkok or a military assistance group as in Manila—is not found, but where American military concern is evident—as in Egypt before the 1967 Six Day War—defense attaché input can be significant.

In addition to weekly meetings with their staff officers, chiefs of mission often conduct daily morning meetings with staff section heads. Such meetings are short and informal, concerned with briefings and operational discussions. For example, at the American embassy in Cairo the counselor of embassy for public affairs (chief of USIS) was responsible for presenting orally a daily summary of the Arabic language press to the ambassador, the political and economic section chiefs, and the CIA station chief. Candid opinions about sensitive issues are encouraged at these within-the-family conferences and strict confidence is observed.

Emphasis on confidentiality has been underscored since the late 1960s by the addition of physical measures to protect communication security. At that time many embassies were supplied from Washington with portable metal rooms in which to hold staff meetings and conferences. These acoustically controlled rooms are fitted inside a chancery room and are designed to prevent electronic eavesdropping. The electronic "cages" are guarded by United States marines assigned to the embassies.

Changing Concepts in Diplomacy   Individual U.S. diplomatic missions are greatly affected by ambassadorial conceptions of how to practice diplomacy. Since World War II career officers have been appointed to fill, on an average, about three-fourths of the chief of mission positions. The remainder have been filled by political appointees, including such notable ones as Chester Bowles, John Kenneth Galbraith, Daniel P. Moynihan, and Edwin O. Reischauer. Very few political appointees could be termed failures despite recent disclosures linking appointments with political contributions. Almost all career chiefs of mission through the early 1970s have been in the foreign service for several decades and were nurtured in traditional diplomacy. To many of them diplomacy is an art, not suitable to any "scientific" approach, and good political judgment is a gift, not learned. Political analysis rather than modern management is their major concern. Because they share major interests and concerns, these mission chiefs tend to favor their subordinate career *political* officers, despite recent departmental efforts to popularize other career "cones," such as consular and administrative.* Thus the political

---

country before the flight can take place. Large embassies have both an air force and a naval aircraft.

* "Cone" is a contemporary term increasingly used by the Department of State to describe functionally related positions. There are administrative, political, economic/commercial, and consular cones.

officers often constitute an elite within the mission, responsive to the ambassador and highly conscious of the closed circle in which they operate. This conception of diplomacy tends to narrow the ambassador's operational scope to that of traditional reporting and representational roles, handicapping him in his relations with non-traditional mission elements. Older ambassadors often have had neither expertise in, nor even a complete understanding of, some of the non-traditional mission programs.

The shortcomings of traditional ambassadorial leadership prompted the department to issue the admonition in 1970 that:

> The traditional reliance of Foreign Service Officers on experience and intuition is no longer good enough. The diplomacy of the seventies requires a new breed of diplomat-manager, just as able as the best of the old school, but equipped with up-to-date techniques. . . . [7]

As younger officers are succeeding to ambassadorial posts and as modern management techniques become more widespread, leadership conceptions of chiefs of mission are changing. Senior Foreign Service Officers increasingly are exposed to modern management practices at the Foreign Service Institute, the teaching arm of the department in Washington. The emphasis upon management as "the key to the new diplomacy" is accompanied by new program management concepts being carried to the field by ambassadors, which will have increasing impact.

One new concept is the Policy Analysis and Resource Allocation System (PARA), introduced in 1971 to assure "a more systematic policy dialogue among the Department's top leadership, the operating bureaus, and the embassies."[8] The system imposes a policy review by the "Seventh Floor Management Team"* of an ambassador's political judgment as reflected in the mission's annual country analysis wherein the ambassador "identifies United States interests and objectives, and establishes priorities among them."[9]

Between preparation of a country analysis by the ambassador and his staff and its top-echelon review in Washington, intermediate-level offices in the department now also review the document, including the appropriate regional bureau and the department's Policy Planning Staff. The "PARA Study" which eventually reaches the seventh floor reflects more points of view than formerly when an ambassador's perception of short-term policy initiatives toward a host country was practically unchallenged on the supposition that the in-country chief knew best.

---

* Members of the "Seventh Floor Management Team" are the deputy secretary, the under secretary for political affairs, the under secretary for economic affairs, the under secretary for security assistance, the deputy under secretary for management and the counselor for the department.

The PARA is ultimately reviewed by the Senior Review Group, an appendage of the National Security Council, which may also contribute further points of view. When and if the Senior Review Group approves the study, its content becomes government-wide policy. The final product may or may not be entirely compatible with the original document submitted by the embassy. In any case, it is likely to be widely comprehensive and highly detailed, the product of inclusion of inputs from many advocate interests both within the department and throughout the executive branch.

If the PARA system is employed as conceived, the ambassador's program management and his leadership must perforce emphasize strategy and tactics not necessarily his own. And, by implication at least, the PARA system may limit his "traditional reliance on experience and intuition."

As the foregoing suggests, one thrust of the department's new foreign affairs management concepts is toward facilitating and regularizing interdepartmental participation in foreign policy formulation. The PARA system, or variations of it which involve interdepartmental participation, is likely to continue.

The Senior Review Group is an agent of the National Security Council, itself an element of the Executive Office of the president. The latter, in turn, tends to be dominated by the White House Office through a network of presidential counselors and assistants who may occupy positions in several subsystems.* The expansion in numbers and roles of presidential assistants and counselors which characterized the Nixon administration is also a hallmark of the Ford administration. A broadly perceived need for swift new thrusts in economic policy, both foreign and domestic, practically guaranteed that Ford would make maximum use of, and even expand, the presidential subsystem he inherited. Interdepartmental review of country policy thrusts, whatever the forum in which it occurs, guarantees inputs from the several executive departments as well as from the White House. Input from such widely differing sources is bound to reflect the ebb and flow of domestic political pressure. Behavioral outcomes may be significantly affected by domestic political considerations, as the case of Burma suggests.

Burma lies within the so-called "Golden Triangle" (Burma, southernmost China, Thailand, and Laos) which produces an estimated seventy percent of the world's supply of the opium poppy, the material base for heroin.

* An executive order of January 5, 1973, created a number of cabinet member-counselors and presidential assistants with dual functions. Henry A. Kissinger became presidential assistant not only for national security affairs but also for foreign affairs in general. In September 1973 he was appointed secretary of state, retaining the other role and title as well. When Kissinger became secretary of state he also became a statutory member of the National Security Council in addition to being chairman of the Senior Review Group which reports to the NSC!

Smuggling of opium-related drugs from Burma into Thailand in 1971 and their availability to the 45,000 U.S. servicemen there, as well as to the hundreds of thousands of servicemen in Vietnam, had reached serious proportions. As part of a worldwide anti-drug campaign mounted in response to domestic political demand, the Nixon administration instructed American ambassadors to offer U.S. financial and technical assistance to host countries which would initiate concerted programs to reduce production of drugs.

Ambassador Edwin W. Martin was appointed to Burma in 1971 with special instructions from the White House via the Senior Review Group to convince the government of Burma of the desirability of a drug control program. A cooperative anti-drug effort was a short-term objective of U.S. policy in Burma and was a principal facet of the country analysis of U.S. goals in Burma, which itself was the product of interdepartmental and White House inputs. Achievement of this particular goal had significant domestic political value for the Nixon administration, but the Burmese, who had been growing the opium poppy for 300 years without adverse results, perceived no reason for curbing production.

By mid-1973 the situation had changed. Drug addiction in Burma, a spin-off from the Thai and Vietnamese situation, had suddenly become widespread. When the government of Burma announced it was ready to accept the U.S. offer of assistance, the ambassador found that interest in Washington had waned to such a degree that he was unable to make a satisfactory response to the Burmese. The "tough-minded, aggressive White House group" which spearheaded the campaign, ensuring that the objective would have high priority in the country analysis, had been swept from office by the Watergate scandals. In the changed military situation and the ensuing interagency scramble for budget dollars the financial resources for assisting Burma had been drained away, although the goal remained as a written priority in the country analysis.[10]

RELATIVE POLITICAL RESOURCES
OF MISSION ELEMENTS

Each element within the mission plays a role in the internal political process which determines what priorities and supports will be given to programs and policy thrusts. With each mission element seeking to generate support for its particular position and programs, conflict inevitably arises and is largely resolved by the number and kinds of political resources available to each element. Among the political resources are control of financial and/or physical assets, the status accorded to actors by the hierarchy in which they play roles, and the symbolic importance which foreign service or military rank confers upon them. It may be hypothesized that mission programs which are most tangible and visible—or dramatic—and which involve the largest numbers of personnel, tend to provide advantages for the mission element which possesses them. Analysis of the roles of the various mission elements within this framework suggests that a fairly predictable rank-order hierarchy can be identified in most missions. Analysis also provides an insight into the nature and substance of mission interactions. For purposes of this study, the model is that of a large mission comprising all major mission elements—the traditional embassy elements, the military, AID, CIA, USIS, and the Peace Corps.

Military Interaction with the Embassy

Military elements—Joint U.S. Military Advisory Group (JUSMAG), Military Assistance Advisory Group (MAAG), contractual military personnel (Mil-Group) or Military Assistance Command (MAC)—are found at missions in every geographic region. At missions in European nations within the NATO alliance, military liaison offices are maintained. The role of the military varies widely. In Thailand it conducts military operations; at other missions it delivers military equipment and advises or helps train national armed forces. In each case the military element has a role related to the national security of the host country and is present as the result of invitation, treaty, or other contractual arrangement.

By operating programs which are visible and physical, which utilize relatively larger numbers of personnel than other programs, and which produce tangible results, such as increased military preparedness of a host country, military elements within a mission possess obvious political resources. Senior military actors also enjoy the prestige associated with military rank, the elite symbolisms accorded flag-rank officers, and a rank-order precedence within the mission hierarchy. Random analysis of country-team meetings of the mission in Manila over a protracted period will provide an insight into the substance of mission concerns and the relative importance of the military element vis-à-vis other mission elements within a subsystem formally managed by the Department of State.

Case Study in Military Preeminence: The Philippines   In Manila, as in other large missions with military elements, such as Bangkok, Bonn, Saigon, and Phnom Penh, the Department of Defense is a dominant intramission element. As a military ally of the United States, the Philippines permits the United States to maintain extensive military installations on its soil. Subic Bay Naval

Base is the headquarters of the U.S. Seventh Fleet. Clark Air Base is the headquarters of the U.S. Thirteenth Air Force. A separate but significant military contingent—the Joint United States Military Advisory Group (JUS-MAG)—also carries out security assistance programs.

A careful review of agenda items in Manila at a number of representative mission-wide country team meetings during 1963—a pre-escalation year in the developing Vietnam struggle—demonstrates that military matters, many of them minimal in substance, accounted for almost *all* country team agenda items. While specifics have changed, the basic themes and similar levels of substance have persisted in subsequent years. The agendas which follow are complete and typical.

Meeting of March 13, 1963

1. Arrangements for briefing U.S. National War College students arriving in the Philippines on a study tour.

2. Recommendations of U.S. Thirteenth Air Force in connection with fire fighting activities at Rosales, Philippines.

3. Preparation of basic public relations paper by Commanding General, Joint U.S. Military Advisory Group, Philippines.

4. Question of tax exemption for license plates on privately owned automobiles of U.S. military personnel.

Meeting of May 16, 1963

1. Discussion of impact of revised Philippine legislation affecting Philippine armed forces.

2. Discussion of inclusion of Filipino employees of the U.S. in the Philippine social security system.

3. Question of SEATO interference with Philippine radio frequencies.

4. Discussion of substance of a proposed letter to the Philippine Department of Foreign Affairs regarding difficulties encountered in phasing out military scrip.

5. Announcement that "the space vehicle *Mercury* will be over Luzon at 2 p.m. today."

Meeting of July 25, 1963

1. Briefing by Ambassador and his staff on the current political situation in the Philippines.

2. Problems of relinquishment of certain U.S. military installations in the Philippines.

3. Briefing on status of military scrip phase-out.

4. Announcement of JUSMAG reorganization.

5. Announcement of U.S. Seventh Fleet Conference at Camp John Hay in

Baguio, Philippines, in October, to be attended by 60 U.S. flag officers.

6. Announcement of SEATO exercises and weapons demonstration next April in the Philippines.

Military problems, always dominant and predictably similar, intensified after 1964-65 with escalation of the war in Vietnam. Simultaneously, a galloping Filipino nationalism produced mounting pressures for return of "excess" U.S. military base lands to Philippine control, and for diminution of U.S. civil and criminal jurisdiction over U.S. servicemen for unlawful acts committed in the Philippines. The latter problems went beyond the purely military category and eventually became important political issues involving the two countries at the highest levels.

A listing of individuals by category and number who attend country team meetings at the Manila mission reinforces the impression that military personnel dominate country team meetings there. It will also identify the principal actors in an actual large U.S. mission. During the 1960s these included, besides the ambassador and the deputy chief of mission, the heads of the traditional embassy sections—i.e., the political counselor, economic counselor, administrative counselor, and the consul general; the chiefs of section of non-traditional elements of the mission—i.e., the director of AID, the chief of USIS, and the CIA station chief; the ranking representatives of the United States Department of Defense in the Philippines—i.e., the rear admiral in command of the Sangley Point Naval Air Station (since returned to Philippine control), and his legal, supply, and operations officers; the chief of the Joint U.S. Military Advisory Group (a major general); the rear admiral in command of the Subic Bay Naval Base; the commanding general of the Thirteenth Air Force at Clark Air Force Base (a major general), plus his legal and operations officers; and, finally, the secretary of the country team, a middle-rank Foreign Service Officer in the embassy.

In essence, the country team meeting in Manila was a meeting—almost an engagement—between the ambassador and his staff on the one hand and the military hierarchy on the other. With two advocate positions clearly evident, the meetings turned into negotiation sessions between the opposing groups. At times neither the political, economic, legal, nor public relations perceptions of the two groups coalesced to a degree sufficient for meaningful negotiation because of the differing value systems they represented. But the predominant number of military personnel at the meetings, the symbols of their rank, the perquisites enjoyed by flag officers, and the superior material and budgetary resources which they controlled combined to provide them with sufficiently effective political resources to achieve their objectives.

It should be noted that an exceptionally strong military input has characterized the U.S. mission to the Philippines. At one point after World War II,

U.S. military installations in the Philippines numbered in the hundreds, and during the age of alliances in American diplomacy (1945-65) the archipelago was transformed by the United States—with the enthusiastic approval of the Filipinos—into a major permanent defense bastion. Moreover, several times since World War II, and specifically during the period described, the American ambassador there has been a non-career diplomat, capable but not experienced in the resolution of intramission conflict. Variations of the pattern can be found in most of the larger U.S. missions in East Asia, particularly in Cambodia, Thailand, Laos, Japan, Korea, and Vietnam.

Example of DOD Emergence: Cambodia   The problem of competing interests is clearly demonstrated by the field situation that prevailed in Cambodia in 1970-71. In March 1970 the United States and Cambodia reestablished diplomatic relations on a "low profile" basis, reflecting the new Nixon Doctrine for U.S. policy in Asia. Initially the Department of State was the sole agency dealing with the Cambodian government and the mission indeed kept a low profile. "American affairs in Cambodia were run by a *chargé d'affaires*, his assistant, and one secretary from a villa by the side of the Bassic River."[11]

Subsequently, with the overthrow on March 18, 1971, of Prince Sihanouk as chief of state, the United States raised the *level*, but not substantially the size, of its diplomatic representation in Phnom Penh by assigning career diplomat Emory C. Swank as American ambassador. One of his primary chores was to supervise "a small Military Equipment Delivery Team [MEDT] to assess requirements for and audit the delivery of military aid to Cambodia as required by law."[12] The MEDT had been established in the wake of U.S. military action in May 1970. The Department of State emphasized in February 1971 that "we do not intend to have a military assistance advisory group or an AID mission in Cambodia" and that "the MEDT performs no advisory or training functions in Cambodia; it operates under the supervision of the U.S. Ambassador in Phnom Penh and the Saigon military command. Most of its personnel are located in Saigon; the rest are assigned to the U.S. Embassy in Phnom Penh."[13]

But the MEDT, which had commenced operations with sixteen men, comprised twenty-seven individuals by August 1971 and had expanded to fifty persons, including a brigadier general, by November of the same year.[14] By August 1971, 110 people were listed on the embassy staff,[15] although the *Foreign Service List* of October 1971 shows fewer than twenty-five *State Department* personnel, including medical and technical staff, assigned to the mission. Some embassy officers predicted the number would expand even further "under pressure from the Pentagon, the State Department and the

Agency for International Development in Washington."[16]

The threefold pressure reflected advocate interests and the almost desperate, albeit reluctant, effort of the Department of State to retain control within the mission by increasing its own personnel. By mid-1971 the embassy in Phnom Penh had grown from the "villa by the side of the Bassic" to a four-apartment block in the city, and three new buildings were under construction, including a warehouse.

Before the arrival of MEDT, the department sought a "low profile" approach for Americans in Cambodia by combining several jobs in one person, by simplifying procedures, and by deliberately blurring job responsibilities.

Jonathan F. Ladd, counselor for political-military affairs, before formation of the MEDT handled the transfer of millions of dollars of military hardware almost single-handedly. MEDT subsequently performed the same chore, in not much greater volume, with a staff which was reportedly seeking to augment its numbers by "pushing for a 100-member MEDT unit in Phnom Penh."[17]

As a result, "It used to be that a couple of senior American Military men here could transact all their business with the dozen or so officers of the Cambodian high command in a single morning meeting. Now there is a procession of cars from the Embassy to the high command all day long. The Cambodians are reported to be having trouble remembering which Americans are responsible for which part of the military aid program. The program is still running at a modest $200 million annually."[18]

"Swank was outfought," according to one of his supporters. "This was the first time he's had to battle the Pentagon as a mission chief, and he didn't realize how persistent the generals are. His style is low key and concise—which may be fine elsewhere, but not in a policy fight against the Pentagon."[19]

Ambassador Swank *in Cambodia* was faced with emergency conditions which were perceived by the foreign policy system *in Washington* as requiring a vigorous military-oriented input. The Department of Defense thus could justify the proliferation of military personnel in Phnom Penh in spite of the desire of the Department of State to maintain a low profile. In Cambodia the sheer numbers of officers present at the mission eventually overwhelmed the civilian leadership of the mission.

Ambassadorial Control: Vietnam and Laos   Military preeminence within a mission is not inevitable, however. Even in missions where the military presence is overwhelming in numbers, strong ambassadors can and do maintain control of their missions. The publication of *The Pentagon Papers* in

1971 dramatically brought to light one example of an ambassador's success in exerting his authority during a conflict with the military within a U.S. mission. Ambassador Henry Cabot Lodge and the military commander in Vietnam, General Paul D. Harkins, had sharp differences of opinion as the Vietnam War intensified in the early 1960s. According to the Pentagon documents, General Harkins complained that he was excluded from Lodge's inner councils and from participation in the preparation of policy cables.[20]

The source of Lodge's strength was plain. Prominent among the elite of the Republican party, he had been specially chosen by a Democratic president for the ambassadorial post in Vietnam to reinforce and to dramatize the non-partisan quality of American intervention there. As such, he had personal access to the chief executive in Washington and had few scruples about ignoring either the traditional "consensus" which mission country teams are supposed to reflect or the standard communications channels of the bureaucracy.

Another case which suggests that the ambassador can counter the preeminence of the military elements if he is strong enough to do so involved the U.S. mission in Laos. Arthur Dommen, writing in the *Los Angeles Times*, April 1, 1971, stated that Ambassador to Laos G. McMurtrie Godley, "personally directs one of the most private wars being fought on the globe today . . . aside from the usual appendages of American missions overseas, such as the U.S. Information Agency, the Agency for International Development and the Central Intelligence Agency, Godley inherited a staff of 234 military attaches, the nerve center of the American military effort in Laos, both on the ground and in the air."[21] Godley's success in handling the situation drew the ire of Senator Stuart Symington, who said he behaved like a "proconsul," operating as chief of staff in a military sense, as well as chief of mission in the civilian field.[22]

Whether Godley was a "proconsul" is debatable. However, his lengthy history of successful infighting within the Foreign Service bureaucracy, his knowledge of and liking for paramilitary operations, and his bulldog approach provided him with significant political resources which he could employ most effectively, given the political environment in Laos.

Other career Foreign Service ambassadors have employed similar combinations of political resources to maintain their control of missions despite strong military influence. Ambassador Leonard Unger in Thailand (1967-73) successfully managed one of the largest U.S. missions, one which included in 1972-73 a military assistance command comprising 45,000 U.S. troops and hundreds of U.S. war planes.

Ambassador Graham A. Martin in Saigon, a strong anticommunist with a reputation as a martinet, proved to be a greater hawk than the military elements of the mission—and thus was accorded great legitimacy. In 1974 Martin led a struggle to obtain more military aid for the South Vietnamese government, even taking his case to the United States where he persuaded one major newspaper to reverse its editorial stand on such aid.[23]

To summarize, at missions where either a military command or a significant military assistance or advisory group is present, Department of Defense actors may be preeminent or even dominant in the intramission power struggle. The prospect is much less likely, however, if the ambassador is a Foreign Service Officer, experienced in the procedures of bureaucratic conflict, and with political resources within the Department of State, or an experienced operator with sufficient political resources in the White House.

AID Political Resources

The Agency for International Development is a major mission element wherever a U.S. economic assistance program is in operation. As a non-traditional element with a separate budget and administrative staff, it enjoys substantial autonomy. Official tables of organization depict the AID element as outside the chain of mission command to which the traditional elements are subject. AID fiscal and technical expertise is often not shared by traditional embassy sections. When an AID director at a country team meeting draws subtle distinctions among lending practices of the International Bank for Reconstruction and Development, the Asian Development Bank, the International Development Authority, and the United States Export-Import Bank, he is proceeding in areas where his expertise is often superior to that of the other country team members.

At the operational level AID officers are concerned with such specialties as agricultural yields and community development; in consequence, they travel more extensively in the host country than do other mission operatives. Some are permanently stationed in provincial areas and become experts on particular provinces. Such persons are valuable sources of political and economic information needed for reporting purposes by the political and economic sections of the mission. Possession of detailed local knowledge affords a certain political advantage to AID within the mission. Moreover, since AID provides tangible assistance to the host country, the AID operation and its officers are usually well known and often enjoy wide acceptance by host-country officials. (AID role-playing will be fully discussed in Chapters 8 and 9.)

Because they carry out programs which are separately funded and which directly help the host country, AID elements possess significant political resources within the host country and within the mission where they operate.

Political Section: First in Embassy Rank-Order

The maintenance of diplomatic missions is vested by law in the Department of State, which normally appoints only its own career personnel to head traditional embassy sections. The political section is *primus inter pares* because its role is to maintain official political communication with the host country, the primary objective of a diplomatic mission. The chief of the political section is usually senior in rank to chiefs of other mission sections. The primacy of the political section is acknowledged among other elements in the embassy, which affords it a psychological advantage.

Political officers enjoy a number of perquisites which are linked to their roles. Political negotiation is often complex and always requires close cooperation with, and step-by-step concurrence of, the ambassador, with whom political officers, as a result, tend to develop special relationships. Political reporting assesses host country political developments, makes judgments about individual actors in the host country, and predicts consequences, all of which are sensitive matters requiring confidentiality. To maintain confidentiality outgoing "political cables," as well as responses or initiatives from the Department of State, are often categorized as privileged information, and their distribution *within the mission* is limited to the ambassador and the political officers.

Since politics is an all-encompassing concern, political officers are normally assigned coordinating and drafting responsibilities for formulation of mission-wide action and planning studies and reports. The nature of their role-playing is such that political officers are *expected* to possess the best insights into the host-country political environment and the best understanding of how the United States should interact with it. They are *expected* to identify U.S. interests in the host country and to recommend allocation of U.S. resources to further those interests.

The traditional Foreign Service belief is that the door to promotion opens more easily for the officer who can point to political affairs assignments during his career. Political analysis and reporting are thought to be as important for the successful diplomat as troop command for success in the military.* Deputy chiefs of mission are frequently chosen from among chiefs of political sections, and the *chargé d'affaires ad interim*, who is selected to

---

* David Garnham's empirical study in 1973 of Foreign Service Officers substantiates the commonly accepted generalization that FSOs evaluate political and economic functional specializations above administrative and consular ones. Moreover, Garnham states that "there is no relationship between functional specialization and career success; however, economic and political officers do have mean success scores higher than those for administrative and consular officers." David Garnham, "Attitude and Personality Patterns of United States Foreign Service Officers," *American Journal of Political Science*, August 1974, p. 545.

head a mission to which an ambassador has not yet been appointed, is usually a political officer. Therefore, just as Foreign Service Officers in Washington vie for assignment to a regional geographic bureau, at field missions the objective of the Foreign Service Officer is the embassy political section.

Since 1970 the Department of State has stressed to its personnel that other career specialties, i.e., economic, administrative and consular, are equally as desirable as, or even superior to, the political "cone." But it is difficult to project a world of U.S. diplomatic missions, even in an era of rapid change, where administrative expertise, or the "dismal science" of economics, or the processing of visas will constitute as much of an attraction as the opportunity to exercise political judgment. Barring attitudinal changes on the part of Foreign Service Officers, political sections will continue to be first in rank order importance in U.S. embassies, and first in rank-order in career assignments.

Central Intelligence Agency: Low Profile

Central Intelligence Agency personnel within a mission role-play in a special relationship to the ambassador, a relationship founded upon confidentiality, their reputation for accuracy and encyclopedic knowledge, and their undivided loyalty within the mission to the ambassador. Each of these qualities is carefully nurtured by the mission's intelligence community because they are political resources. CIA "station chiefs" and their subordinates are chosen from their colleagues in Washington on the basis of professional competence and ability to carry out low-profile roles, both inside the mission and in the host country. These attributes are the political resources of the mission intelligence unit rather than sheer numbers and plentiful funds, as is the case with the military; or tangible developmental programs, as is the case with AID; or control of libraries and printing presses, as is the case with USIS.

Intelligence collection, the principal CIA role in an embassy, is tedious, never-ending, and not necessarily exciting work. It is mainly concerned with the accumulation of large amounts of raw data about host country individuals, organizations, and political developments.[24] The data are initially evaluated at the mission and become incremental additions to mission and Washington CIA files. The files are similar to those maintained by the political and economic sections of the mission, although CIA files emphasize information about communist activity in the host country.

"Dirty tricks," a phrase once used by Secretary of State Rusk to categorize certain covert political actions to achieve specific objectives, are minimal in most CIA mission operations. Major efforts to bolster or to overthrow national regimes take place in some cases, but were more frequent during the cold war period (1945-65) than currently. Emphasizing that CIA conducts such covert operations only when specifically authorized by the National Security Council, CIA Director William E. Colby was quoted as saying in October 1974 that since national policy has changed following the cold war period "CIA's involvement in covert action has correspondingly changed."[25] When covert actions are disclosed, as was the case in September 1974 concerning previous secret U.S. assistance to anticommunist elements in Chile, the resulting publicity tends to encourage distorted public perceptions of the degree of CIA role-playing devoted to such activities. (Rusk stated flatly that "dirty tricks" comprised no more than five percent of CIA activities worldwide.) Covert political actions by an embassy are most likely to be confined to payment of professional agents in the host country—both American and non-American—who supply information, or to lending financial support to a friendly newspaper, labor union, or educational institution.* This was essentially the CIA action in Chile.

Chiefs of mission value embassy CIA units because they are a dependable resource for factually accurate reports and thoughtful analysis. Intelligence collection also provides a data base for verifying mission political and economic reporting. Since the CIA station chief and his aides operate principally under the cover of the political section, they expect little in terms of recognition or reward. Confidentiality is emphasized and conflict with other sections is held to levels of lowest visibility.

Intelligence collection is basically distinguished from data collection for normal political reporting by its sources, rather than by its content. Important information sources for the CIA station chief include host country police, internal security, military and intelligence agencies. The willingness of these sources to disclose sensitive information is directly linked to the degree of confidentiality which the CIA will assign to both the data and the source, and, not insignificantly, to a *quid pro quo* process whereby the mission intelligence unit makes data available to the host country intelligence agencies. Continuity of the relationship is equally important because data of an intelligence nature is useful only in terms of how up-to-date it is. In other

---

* The Soviet Union's Committee of State Security (KGB) is comprised of an infinitely more formidable intelligence apparatus than the American CIA. According to Gwendolen M. Carter, "It is, at least, a vast intelligence organization employing more than seven hundred thousand men and women in external espionage—dramatically exposed late in 1971 through the defection of KGB spy, Oleg Lyalin to Great Britain—and internal surveillance." Gwendolen M. Carter, *The Government of the Soviet Union* (New York: Harcourt Brace Jovanovich, Inc., 1972), pp. 39-40. John Barron believes that KGB agents, both military and civilian, normally occupy over half of the total positions in Soviet embassies and that the figure is as high as eighty percent in some missions. See John Barron, *KGB: The Secret Work of Secret Soviet Agents* (New York: Reader's Digest Press, 1974).

words, the mission's intelligence unit draws upon privileged sources, those not normally available to other mission elements and which must be protected if the relationships are to survive.

To carry out its role the CIA element must itself be a privileged unit, not visible within the mission on the table of organization. On a rank-order scale within the mission hierarchy, the intelligence unit ranks at least equal with the political section.

United States Information Service

The United States Information Service (USIS), found at almost every mission, has a combined informational and cultural role. USIS officers produce press and other media materials, operate information centers and libraries, sponsor English teaching classes and visits of persons prominent in American life and letters, and administer exchanges of American and host country scholars and students. Programs are highly visible and afford USIS personnel broad opportunities for contacts with host country media, educational, and artistic leaders. As an impresario bringing to the host country U.S. cultural programs, such as the Martha Graham dance troupe, USIS may exercise a major role in host country cultural life, especially in developing countries which otherwise could not attract artists of such high caliber. Contacts in the host country and impact on cultural circles thus become USIS political resources within a mission.

The director of USIS is also counselor of public affairs. His ability to assess probable host country response to U.S. policies and to devise information programs which will achieve public acceptance, or at least understanding, of American foreign policy can also be an important source of influence within the mission. (USIS role-playing will be analyzed in detail in Chapter 7.)

Since USIS is concerned with intangibles—the promotion of ideas and images—success is difficult to document. Favorable host country media treatment of an aspect of U.S. policy may or may not be a consequence of USIS efforts. Although changes in host country attitudes are measured by USIS, it is difficult to establish whether or to what degree USIS influenced the change. The inability of USIS to demonstrate measurable results of its programs adversely affects its status within missions. Moreover, programs which attempt to create images receive less emphasis than "important" mission business—i.e., successful political negotiation, perceptive intelligence evaluation, improvement of host country security forces through military assistance programs, and modernization of host country agriculture through AID programs. On the basis of rank-order influence within the mission, USIS falls below the military, AID, political, and intelligence sections.

Economic/Commercial Section

Skill in interpreting and assessing economic data and trends is the chief political resource of economic/commercial sections in U.S. missions. Economic reporting is a demanding and time-consuming function because the Department of State maintains a complex set of economic indicators which require periodic inputs from missions to keep them current. Quantitative economic data from missions is incorporated into various statistical abstracts used by executive departments throughout the United States government. Accuracy, timeliness, and ability to gauge the significance of data are essential attributes of economic affairs officers in missions. Their stature is directly related to the utility of what they report.

During the decade of the 1960s the economic sections inherited from the Office of International Trade Fairs, Department of Commerce, certain long-term responsibilities for promotion of trade between the United States and host countries. Accordingly, "commercial attachés," whose roles tended to supplant the trade facilitation roles of American consular officers, were increasingly assigned to mission economic sections, especially at posts where trade development is a basic political objective. By 1970 the mission economic section had been redesignated as the economic/commercial section. The worsening U.S. trade balance in the early 1970s, however, prompted the Department of Commerce to challenge the overseas role of the Department of State in economic matters. A bill introduced in Congress shortly thereafter by Senator Warren Magnuson (D.-Wash.) was, according to the Foreign Service Association, "the Commerce Department's attempt to snatch away the [Department of State's] economic and commercial functions."[26] The Magnuson bill was defeated when the Department of State marshaled resources against it and then fortified its rewon legitimacy in 1971-72 by upgrading the chief economic affairs position in the department from deputy under secretary for economic affairs to under secretary status.

The Department of State next set out to bolster economic/commercial functions at missions. In December 1973 Secretary of State Kissinger's directive to all missions emphasized that "we must go much further toward making commercial expertise a trademark of the Department and the Service."[27] The department mobilized and added to its resources in the commercial area by increasing travel funds for commercial attachés, developing commercial libraries and newsletters at missions, and inaugurating telegraphic transmission to and from missions of all trade leads. Marketing research officer positions were added to the economic/commercial section at key commercial posts.

The new resources of the economic/commercial section are changing the rank-order status of the formerly rather prosaic economic sections within missions. Moreover, further upgrading of the trade facilitation role is likely in a world of increasing interdependence.*

Administrative Section

For many foreign service officers the widely used term "post management," referring to the role of the mission's administrative section, evokes the specter of having to comply with internal procedures and decisions over which they have little influence. Post managers allocate funds and physical resources—at larger posts amounting to several million dollars annually—and enforce procedures mandated in the *Foreign Affairs Manual*. Administrators significantly determine who gets what, when, and how within the embassy. When administrators prepare budgets they are also assigning priorities; when they interpret regulations they are also determining procedures. Among administrative section responsibilities are personnel administration, preparation of budgets, post accounting, fiscal planning, management of all post property including real estate, procurement, supply, security, medical services, and, at some posts, operation of a commissary. Every section and individual within the mission is affected by the administrative section. As missions have grown in size and complexity, and as management technology in the computer age has required ever greater expertise, the importance of the administrative section has steadily increased at missions.

The role the administrative section plays regarding other mission sections is roughly analogous, on a mini-scale, to the role of the Office of Budget and Management regarding the executive departments of the federal government. Post managers compute costs charged to the several mission elements for shared services such as office space, the mission's radio communications system, telephone and utilities, motor vehicles, supplies, and the costs of general administration. Estimates and allocations of costs can rarely be disputed successfully by the elements affected because only the administrative section is privy to all relevant data affecting all mission elements.

Mission administrative units maintain close working relationships with elements of the host country government and economy, whose continuing services and goods are essential to embassy physical operations. Certain national employees of the administrative section, i.e., locally employed citizens of the host country, are a unique political resource of the administrative section. These employees are principal links between the embassy and the middle-level bureaucracies of host country tax offices, licensing authorities,

---

* Trade and commercial opportunities are particularly sought in Japan, Brazil, the Federal Republic of Germany, Iran, Austria, Poland, the Soviet Union, South Korea, and Taiwan. *Department of State Newsletter*, February 1974, p. 11.

and managers of sea and airport facilities whose cooperation is essential to mission operation. The permanent national employees of a mission can discharge their responsibilities without much direction from the Americans who nominally supervise them. But the reverse does not apply. American administrators—the "housekeepers" of the mission—cannot operate a mission without effective national employees. The expertise gained by local employees, by reason of their permanence, makes them essential to mission operations. The political leverage inside the mission which such employees afford the administrative section can be significant. In host countries where so-called "exotic languages" prevail, i.e., difficult languages such as Chinese or Arabic, even the relatively few Americans trained in these languages are seldom fluent enough to use them in an extended business relationship; instead it is the bilingual national employee upon whom the mission depends and who becomes the link to host country governmental agencies, business firms, utility companies, transportation authorities, and other mission suppliers.

To summarize, administrative section responsibility for post management, its control over mission physical property, and its links to units of the host country government and to mission suppliers in the country are important political resources within the mission. In a rank-order list the administrative section is exceeded only by the political section and the intelligence unit in terms of influence within the embassy.* Administrative-section influence on substantive policy, on the other hand, is limited.

Consular Section

The traditional role of consular officers is that of agents of one nation physically located in another nation to facilitate commercial and trading relationships of their fellow nationals with the host country, to protect the rights of their fellow nationals, to issue U.S. visas to foreign nationals, and to discharge certain notarial types of duties. The role of the consular section parallels that of the commercial unit when consular officers advise American firms about host country economic regulations and business practices. Consuls are notaries public for recording births, marriages, deaths, and other statistics concerning Americans in the host country. They have certification roles

* The role of "post managers," however, is changing as the Department of State develops regional administrative service centers abroad which centralize certain administrative services for a group of U.S. missions within a geographic region. The Regional Finance Center in Paris is an example. During the coming decade general services roles and personnel services will increasingly be centralized at a few regional posts, especially in Europe. See Thomas M. Tracy, "Automation and the Foreign Service," *Foreign Service Journal*, March 1971, pp. 21-22.

regarding documentation of imports of U.S. products and specific responsibilities relating to protection of the rights of American commercial aircraft and ships, their masters and crews. The consular section interacts with the host country as an advocate for the rights of private American citizens to ensure that American citizens are provided due process under terms of host country law. Conversely, American consuls apprise Americans of host country regulations applicable to foreigners, such as laws pertaining to the use and possession of drugs, residency and property restrictions, and taxation.

The consular section interacts widely with host country nationals in the course of processing applications for visas to travel or emigrate to the United States. The consular section possesses political resources within and without the mission in respect to its judgmental role about the veracity, suitability and legal acceptability of visa applicants.* American consuls are often cultivated by prominent host country nationals who try to influence visa decisions on behalf of applicants who are their "clients." Rather than endeavoring to win the confidence of prominent host country political actors, as do the political, economic, and other mission elements, American consuls frequently find it necessary to discourage intimacy.

The chief of the consular section in some missions is also designated as supervisory consul general and exerts certain directive authority over consulates general and consulates outside the capital city. His directive authority extends only to consular matters at the subsidiary posts. Political and economic reporting at consular posts is supervised by the principal officer at each post—the consul general or consul—who is directly responsible to the chief of mission at headquarters in the capital city.

As a power center within the mission, the consular section follows the administrative section in rank order of importance.

Peace Corps

A philosophical dichotomy has plagued relations between the mercurial Peace Corps and other mission elements since the inception of the program. It is therefore difficult to categorize this foreign policy element and to assess its political impact either within or beyond the confines of the mission.

Established in 1961, the Peace Corps was reluctant during its earlier years to identify itself with the mission establishment, believing this would compromise its credibility. The problem was exacerbated because many of the

* Some 350,000 aliens arrive in the United States annually with immigration visas, each of which must first be approved by an American consul. Consuls must also approve student and visitor visas which may number hundreds of thousands annually. At the U.S. mission in Manila the queue of daily applicants for visas usually extends through the chancery lobby, across an intervening walkway, and fifty yards into the public street.

early Peace Corps country directors were distinguished private citizens from academic and professional life, strongly imbued with a John Kennedy-like idealism. They wanted *to do for* their country without however being *identified with* their country. Moreover, they had been informed that they and their organizations, in whatever countries they operated, were, in effect, free spirits. Thus when they arrived at their field posts accompanied by legions of volunteers, Peace Corps directors proceeded to act according to their own viewpoints. The philosophy and behavior of Dr. Lawrence Fuchs, Peace Corps country director for the Philippines in the mid-1960s and a prominent personality in the academic world, suggest the dilemma that faced many chiefs of mission.

Fuchs directed the activities of some 800 volunteers (mostly college-age young people) throughout the Philippine archipelago. Soon after his arrival he announced to the American ambassador that he would not attend country team meetings because he intended to move his headquarters from Manila to Zamboanga, a small provincial city at the southern tip of the Philippine island chain and some 700 miles distant; he wanted to provide physical evidence of his independence of the mission. The ambassador eventually convinced the director to retain his Manila headquarters so that he could communicate personally with him, but the ambassador had little success in persuading Fuchs to alter his philosophy about his independence from the mission. Nevertheless, Fuchs and his 800 young Americans who, although they were drawing maintenance allowances from the United States government, considered themselves "free spirits," played an important role in shaping Filipino images of the United States.

Confrontations between ambassadors and Peace Corps directors continued, and James W. Gould, a former director of the Peace Corps in Malaysia, writes that during the mid-1960s those confrontations in various countries constituted a "death blow to the Peace Corps" because "now volunteers no longer feel themselves free citizens, but government representatives under scrutiny."[28]

The relatively vague definition of the Peace Corps' role has been another major problem plaguing mission–Peace Corps relations. In earlier years the corps recruited literally thousands of very young and often totally inexperienced volunteers. Neither they, nor their supervisors in many instances, had a clear idea of what they were expected to do or accomplish in the host country. In the Philippines, for example, many volunteers arrived expecting to be accepted as teachers, but were relegated to roles as teachers' aides. This was a concession both to reality, since the volunteers were untrained, and to the demands of Philippine teachers, who took offense at what they considered an effrontery and were also concerned about the loss of their jobs.

Large numbers of volunteers in Latin American and African countries worked diligently at various "community projects" which were seldom continued beyond the end of their tours.

By 1971 when the Peace Corps was absorbed in Washington into a primarily domestic-oriented, multipurpose agency entitled ACTION, the problems of philosophy and role had lessened. The corps had gradually become socialized to role-playing *within* the mission. Program emphasis shifted to providing older, skilled technicians to developing countries which requested them.

Some 50,000 volunteers have served in the Peace Corps.[29] In 1966, the peak year, 15,556 volunteers were sent to requesting nations.[30] By 1973 the number of volunteers had dropped to 7,354,[31] serving in approximately sixty countries.[32]

Volunteers serve physically outside the mission and are not actors in intra-mission conflict; only their supervisors are considered an element of the mission. Until the change in program emphasis and the reduction in Peace Corps autonomy with its absorption into ACTION in 1971, the corps was not of importance as a role-player within U.S. diplomatic missions. The future role of the corps within the mission is unclear. Its new volunteers, far fewer but more skilled and older, may have a greater impact on missions as well as on host country economies. At present the rank-order importance of the Peace Corps in typical missions is well below that of the previously discussed mission elements.

New Embassy Elements

Two additional elements have been added to larger U.S. diplomatic missions since 1970 in response to demands upon the foreign policy system.

A proliferation of United States government scientific and technological activities abroad led to establishment of a section within larger missions to coordinate American scientific and technological programs with those of host nations and to influence the development of such programs in consonance with U.S. policy objectives. The new mission science and technology sections usually represent several United States government agencies. Areas of involvement include defense research, education, physical measurements, and environmental impact studies.

As noted earlier, one consequence of broad concern in the United States over drug abuse was the effort to influence other nations toward effective drug control measures. In mid-1973, with the establishment of a Drug Enforcement Administration (DEA) within the Department of Justice, personnel representing DEA were assigned to the larger missions to interact with

TABLE VII   ACTION

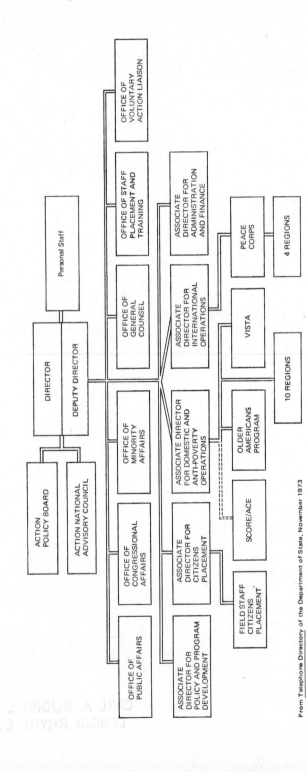

From *Telephone Directory of the Department of State*, November 1973

TABLE VIII   ARMS CONTROL AND DISARMAMENT AGENCY

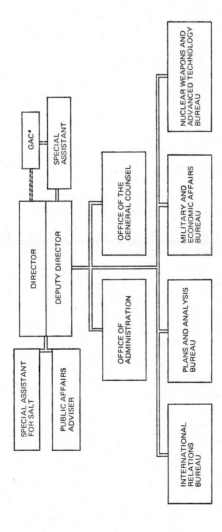

* General Advisory Committee

From _Telephone Directory_ of the Department of State November 1973.

host countries regarding drug law enforcement and to suggest prevention programs. The Drug Enforcement Administration was thus thrust overnight into a delicate diplomatic role, one it shares at many missions with the U.S. Customs Service of the Bureau of Customs, Department of the Treasury.

The impact of these two newest non-traditional mission elements upon mission power structures is as yet unclear, but each of them possesses political resources. Science and technology programs, by reason of their scope and diversity, command attention in host countries and in the foreign policy system at home. Drug enforcement programs enjoy significant political legitimacy at present and they often include monetary resources for inducing host country cooperation, as in Turkey. The section chief in each case reports directly to the ambassador.

RELATED SUBSYSTEMS

Arms Control and Disarmament Agency

The Arms Control and Disarmament Agency (ACDA) was created in 1961 as an autonomous agency, but it is actually a subsystem of the Department of State. Its director reports directly to the secretary of state and its personnel abroad are associated with U.S. diplomatic missions. ACDA conducts research on the formulation of arms control and disarmament policy and participates in U.S. negotiations with other nations on these subjects. ACDA had a significant role in negotiations concerning the limited test-ban treaty (1963), the outer-space treaty (1967), the non-proliferation treaty (1968), and the seabed arms control treaty (1971). The agency played a major role in the strategic arms limitation talks which culminated in the 1972 SALT I agreement with the Soviets, although summit diplomacy bypassed the ACDA in the critical stages of the negotiations.*

---

* The *Los Angeles Times* reports of SALT I that "in the first round, in which Gerard C. Smith [Director of ACDA] was the American negotiator, the delegation was constantly by-passed at key points along the way by 'back channel' dealings directly between President Nixon, Henry A. Kissinger, and the Kremlin." (Don Cook, "2nd Round of SALT Resumes in Geneva," February 20, 1974, p. 18.) United Press International supports this view of the negotiations when it reports that Smith "who had done all of the hard work in negotiating the 1972 SALT I agreement was shunted aside at the last minute by Kissinger who wrapped up a quick final agreement so Nixon could sign it while he was in Moscow." ("Nitze Resignation Clue to State Dept. Unrest," *Pomona Progress-Bulletin*, July 4, 1974, p. A-11.) In June 1974 Kissinger admitted to a Senate subcommittee that the memorandum of interpretation of the SALT I agreement had contained a loophole, since closed, which he had not been aware of. The *Los Angeles Times* commented editorially that "the episode dramatizes the fact that experts serve a

U.S. Diplomatic Missions to International Organizations

The Department of State maintains U.S. diplomatic missions to eleven international organizations in Washington, New York, and a number of European capitals. As missions, these units are fully autonomous overseas elements of the department, headed by an ambassador or a "United States representative" and staffed by Foreign Service personnel. The largest and best known is the United States Mission to the United Nations in New York.

These missions to international organizations differ in organization and role from missions to individual countries. With the exception of the U.S. mission to the United Nations, they interact with numerous other nations in a regional capacity (U.S. mission to the Organization of American States [OAS] or to the North Atlantic Treaty Organization [NATO]), or in a specific field (U.S. Representative to the United Nations Educational and Cultural Organization [UNESCO], or to the Food and Agriculture Organization [FAO]).*

---

purpose in even the most secret diplomacy—and one purpose is to spot loopholes that might not be visible to Presidents and secretaries of state." *Los Angeles Times*, June 26, 1974, Pt. II, p. 6.

* The other six missions to international organizations are: United States Mission to the International Atomic Energy Agency (IAEA), Vienna; United States Mission to the United Nations Industrial Development Organization (UNIDO), Vienna; United States Mission to the International Civil Aviation Organization (ICAO), Montreal; United States Mission to the Organization for Economic Cooperation and Development (USOECD), Paris; United States Mission to the European Office of the United Nations and other International Organizations, Geneva; United States Mission to the European Communities (USEC), Brussels.

CHAPTER 5

USIA:
Its Role in the
Foreign Policy
System

Early in his term of office President Kennedy announced a massive U.S. outer space program which was to culminate in landing men on the moon by 1970. Throughout the 1960s information and cultural programs designed to impress foreign target audiences with the strength and progress of the United States exploited the dramatic space program. At the United States Information Agency (USIA) in Washington programs were conceived and orchestrated to utilize press, publications, radio, TV, exhibits, films, lectures, and even the astronauts themselves to dramatize U.S. space achievements. At U.S. diplomatic missions abroad the U.S. Information Service (USIS) components of the missions exhibited actual space capsules, featured books and reference materials on space activities in USIS-operated libraries, provided motion pictures on U.S. space activities for showings to remote villagers by means of mobile film units, installed television sets in public buildings for video reception of space shots, and at many world capitals were able to introduce the astronauts in person to host country audiences. The U.S. foreign policy goal was to impress upon other nations of the world the preeminence of the

United States in space exploration, with the implication that the United States would be in the forefront of the "giant leap for mankind" in scientific, industrial, and military achievement that it presaged.

The United States Information Agency is the propaganda subsystem of the foreign policy system. "Propaganda" in this sense is "communication aimed at influencing the thinking, emotions, or actions of a group or public."[1] The external informational and cultural programs of the United States are efforts to influence the international political system of which it is a part and within which it competes for power and prestige.

All nation-states engage in some form of propaganda activity. Developing countries in Africa and Asia sponsor national religious festivals which, in their low-key approach and high-key color, reflect concerted efforts to impress outsiders with the glories of the traditional societies to which the new governments are the heirs. In the more technologically advanced political systems the mass media are the principal vehicles utilized to communicate values.

In 1972 the United States government expended $251.8 million, or one percent of its annual budget, for "external information and cultural programs"—the collective category for propaganda activities. In the same year the Arab Republic of Egypt expended almost two percent of its total annual budget, while the Federal Republic of Germany spent an estimated $310 million and France an estimated $430 million, or approximately nine percent of their annual budgets, for external propaganda.[2]

The communications revolution of the last fifty years has literally transformed the techniques of external propaganda. During World War II international radio broadcasting was adopted by all of the combatants as a psychological tool for warfare. A young female disc jockey, "Tokyo Rose," who played records and sweetly suggested that perhaps sweethearts back home were not being faithful, was the creation of the Japanese radio in efforts to destroy the morale of American troops in the Pacific theater. The British Broadcasting Corporation (BBC) and Radio Berlin each attempted in its own way to influence enemy civilian as well as military forces. By the end of the war all the major powers, including the United States, had incorporated international radio communication as a permanent tool to promote their foreign policies.

The electronic age opened many new avenues of propaganda dissemination. Within a generation after World War II, high-speed presses in the American regional production center in Manila could produce billions of leaflets for air drop over Vietnam; French, German, Soviet and U.S. cultural centers around the world could use films, language instruction cassettes, exhibits, cheap and colorful posters and books to communicate national political values to others. Television provided another dimension, and the perfection of relatively inexpensive videotape recordings by the early 1970s vastly expanded the impact of the telecast. The giant stride in communications made by utilizing space satellites now threatens a possible "electronic invasion" of the entire world by whichever nation or nations can dominate access to communications satellites.[3] According to the United States Advisory Commission on Information, "Scientists and engineers now believe that satellites in the near future will be capable of transmitting televised broadcasts from one country directly into home receivers of viewers in neighboring countries or distant countries without the need of intermediary ground stations."[4]

EVOLUTION OF THE PROPAGANDA ROLE

The United States first established an international propaganda agency during World War I when President Woodrow Wilson formed the Committee on Public Information, headed by George Creel. His short-lived propaganda apparatus, which included libraries and offices abroad, was dismantled after the war in 1919.

It was not until 1938, on the eve of another war, that the United States government again ventured into the international propaganda field. The Interdepartmental Committee on Cooperation with the American Republics was established to promote inter-American solidarity against the Nazis. Simultaneously a division for cultural relations with the American republics was created within the Department of State for the same reason. By 1941, when President Roosevelt established the Office of Coordinator of Inter-American Affairs, the cultural component of international propaganda was institutionalized.

When the United States entered World War II at the end of 1941, a coordinator of information had already been established. The coordinator, William J. Donovan, set up a Foreign Information Service, which on February 24, 1942, began international broadcasting under the title, "The Voice of America." An over-all Office of War Information (OWI) emerged in June 1942, combining the twofold role of censor and provider of news for domestic consumption with broadcasting American war aims abroad. At the end of World War II the Office of War Information was dismantled and the informational role assigned to the Department of State, where it was combined with the cultural role already assigned to the department.

The United States Information and Educational Exchange Act of 1948 (Public Law 402) institutionalized within the Department of State a peacetime, worldwide information and cultural exchange program administered abroad under the aegis of the United States Information Service.*

Conflict with Department of State

Linking the informational and cultural programs and locating them within the Department of State created problems. In the first place, the two roles are dissimilar. International informational programs of the United States are overtly propagandistic in nature. They attempt to influence attitudes on a short-term or immediate basis. The cultural programs are a long-range effort to influence people and governments. The core of the cultural program is the academic exchange of individuals, i.e., students and professors, between the United States and other countries. Other aspects include the short-term exchange visits of prominent foreign and American personalities, subsidized tours of American artistic, athletic, or entertainment groups, and operation abroad of American libraries.

Problems of an operational as well as organizational nature soon arose. Foremost was the reluctance of the department, and particularly of the foreign service, to accept the *permanency* of the informational and cultural roles, although they accorded greater legitimacy to the latter than to the former. The information and cultural role-players who were beginning to serve abroad in increasing numbers were specialists, rather than generalists in the foreign service tradition. As a result, the department was unwilling to grant such employees Foreign Service Officer status, designating them as either Foreign Service Staff Officers (FSSOs) or Foreign Service Reserve Officers (FSRs). They were thus deliberately barred from the mainstream of the Foreign Service and were not fully assimilated either in Washington or abroad.[5]

At the same time the methods of operation of the information and cultural officers did not fit the mold of the traditional bureaucracy, which carefully avoided the innovations, dramatics, and "hucksterism" it perceived in the new role-playing. Driving a motion-picture van, complete with its own generator, to an Indian village and showing USIS films ranging in subject matter from how to eradicate hookworm to portraying the good life enjoyed by the American farmer, was not the role-playing expected of traditional diplomacy. Colorful exhibits extolling American political and economic achievements reminded the traditionalists too much of Madison Avenue.

* The name United States Information Service, and particularly the initials USIS, became so well known abroad that the *Agency* has continued to use the term *Service* in its overseas operations. In the ensuing discussion of the United States Information Agency, the term USIA is used in referring to the Washington office, and USIS when referring to its overseas posts or programs.

Moreover, the department had its own domestically oriented news office and press spokesmen, and the confusion and rivalry between the two sets of public informational role players proved dysfunctional to the system.

Creation of USIA

The uneasy relationship persisted through several in-house reorganizations until the appointment of John Foster Dulles as secretary of state in 1953. Dulles conceived of the department as a policy-making subsystem which should confine its role principally to the reporting and analysis of political-economic-military developments. In his view, program activity, i.e., information and cultural programs as well as economic assistance programs, was beyond the scope of the department. All were scheduled for removal from the Department of State; the information and cultural programs were to be transferred to the newly created United States Information Agency.

However, Senator J. William Fulbright (D-Ark.) objected to the State Department's attempt to transfer the educational exchange program bearing his name to the new agency, which he considered to be an overt propaganda organization. Senator Fulbright had sponsored the original exchange-of-persons legislation (Public Law 79-584) in 1946, and the recipients of the grants became known as "Fulbright scholars." They quickly earned the respect of the international academic community because they were free to pursue research, teach, or study without direction from any governmental source, foreign or American. Fulbright feared linkage of the Fulbright program with the United States government informational activities would taint such scholars. Fulbright was halfway successful in his effort to prevent the transfer. The roles of financing and administering in the United States the academic as well as the non-academic exchange programs were retained by the department; their continued administration abroad as the major feature of the USIS cultural program was formally assigned to the new agency.

On June 3, 1953, Presidential Reorganization Plan No. 8 established an independent agency to be known as the United States Information Agency. Executive Order 10477 made the plan effective August 1, 1953. Because USIA did not come into existence by statute, it is technically subject to modification or outright curtailment by future presidential action.[6]

USIA AS A POLITICAL SUBSYSTEM: AN IDEAL MODEL

In setting up the new agency, efforts were made to create an organization which would be as invulnerable to its domestic political environment as possible. Autonomy, it was hoped, would not only afford escape from the "second-class" status to which the organization had been relegated within the Department of State, but would also provide the framework for a greater role in the foreign policy decision-making process. It would allow for innovations which the Department of State could not dampen and would permit a separate identity for the press, publications, radio, motion-picture, and cultural specialists who were among the role-players. USIA thus emerged overnight as a political subsystem in which function and structure were explicit and were reinforced by the formal allocation of authority conferred by Reorganization Plan No. 8.

Unlike other subsystems of the Department of State—i.e., the Arms Control and Disarmament Agency and the Agency for International Development—USIA is not attached organizationally to the department. Although one of the smaller subsystems of the federal government, USIA possesses a unique degree of autonomy within the foreign policy system. The agency prepares its own budget, which, in addition to programs, it is responsible for defending before Congress. It determines its organization both in Washington and abroad, administers programs which it alone designs, and operates its own personnel system. The director of USIA reports directly to the president in the same manner as the secretary of state and heads of other cabinet-level departments.

USIA policies and programs, like those of other political subsystems, emerge as the result of subsystem conversion of various inputs—supports, demands, and expectations. Among inputs to the USIA subsystem is the fundamental one of external support for the concept that governmental propaganda, mounted through media tools, can help achieve foreign policy goals. Specific support inputs arise from the bureaucracy, principally the Department of State, the presidential subsystem, specialized interest groups, and Congress, which appropriates funds for the agency and its programs.

Demands as inputs originate within essentially the same framework. During the cold-war period of American foreign policy, for example, the Departments of State and Defense expressed demands for informational programs to rationalize the American commitment to the "containment of communism." In the wake of the Soviet *sputnik* (earth satellite) of 1957, the American political system—spearheaded by the scientific community—was galvanized into action to "catch up" with the Russians. The larger foreign policy system assigned USIA the role of conveying to the world, through media facilities, American determination and American progress in science and education.

Expectations also comprise an important input. During the Truman years the foreign policy system expected information programs to influence states in the international political system to accept as moral the involvement of the United States in Europe and later in Korea. In the 1950s Congress, American labor, business, and academic groups expected the foreign policy system, and thus USIA, to demonstrate effectively the righteousness of such concepts as "peoples' capitalism" and "collective security through alliance," and American contributions to arts and letters. The promotion of the concept of "peoples' capitalism" was to demonstrate that capital in the United States is broadly held by small investors throughout the American economic system. The expectation was that when the true nature of American capitalism became known, communist claims of "monopoly capitalism" in the United States would be discredited. "Collective security through alliance" referred to the expanding systems of regional and bilateral security agreements between the United States and its allies, initiated largely by Secretary of State Dulles. These were depicted as the "free world" alternative to a non-viable United Nations collective security system which had been paralyzed by Soviet intransigence. The expectation was that the logic and reasonableness of the American security initiatives would be apparent if they were explained within such a rationale.

An emphasis on American achievements in arts and letters was expected to show the peoples of the world that American economic and military might were accompanied by corresponding growth in intellectual and cultural fields. The overriding expectation was that exposure of the free and non-aligned world to American economic and cultural achievements, and to American willingness to guarantee the security of the non-communist world, would make other nation-states more receptive to free world leadership by the United States.

Supports, demands, and expectations regarding information policies and programs also arise outside the national political system. The largest information and cultural programs in USIA's history have been mounted partly in response to input demands and expectations of allies of the United States—for example, Germany, Korea, and Vietnam—to underscore mutual dependence.

USIA constitutes an excellent model for the concept of a political system. Its inputs are easily identifiable and are derived principally from specific actors within the foreign policy system. The USIA subsystem has few constituencies—i.e., groups to which it must report or justify itself—outside of government. Essentially the only groups which make representation to USIA are the Department of State, the presidential subsystem, and to some extent, other bureaucratic elements such as the Department of Defense and a few specialized interest groups—principally the academicians who want expanded exchange programs.

In the process of converting inputs into program outcomes, USIA patterns of behavior are fairly predictable. Despite its autonomy, the agency's informational and cultural policy programmers decide only within a narrow frame of reference the specific content, size, and thrust of its programs. In contrast to the Department of State, the narrow scope of the USIA conversion function—to convert information and cultural policy into programs— reduces the variety of demands upon the subsystem. Presumably, it also reduces the likelihood that the subsystem will be confronted with demands which it cannot convert.

A political subsystem must resolve conflict if it is to survive. The autonomy of USIA has assured that conflict about direction and priorities is confined primarily to the subsystem. However, the agency's mandate to mount both informational and cultural programs within the same subsystem has given rise to system instability from the start.

In other national political systems—e.g., France and Great Britain*—the cultural and informational roles are organizationally separated. Moreover, in USIA, although the two often dichotomous roles are organizationally equal, the actors and elements which specialize in informational programs have tended to dominate. For example, none of the agency's eight directors has been associated with arts and letters. On the contrary, most of them have been professional communications specialists.

Cultural specialists, as opposed to communications specialists, have fewer political resources within the agency to win preferment for their priorities and program thrusts. Specialists in cultural activities, notably those involved in the exchange-of-persons programs which are the core of the cultural thrust, are agency personnel, but funding of the programs they administer resides in the Department of State. Moreover, cultural specialists perceive keenly the philosophical inconsistency of attempting to administer academic exchanges —which they consider to possess a self-generating validity and effectiveness— while operating within a subsystem devoted primarily to deliberately attempting to influence attitudes through mass media communication.

Conflict within the agency about its role in foreign policy decision-making, including what kinds of programs to mount and through what media facilities, and conflict about the foreign service status of its employees have plagued the subsystem. At times failure to resolve these conflicts has threatened system survival. However, divisive factors have been repressed or papered over by successive USIA directors, who, possessing complete administrative autonomy within the foreign policy subsystem, have made the

---

* The Alliance Française, the cultural arm of the French government, is separate from the French informational program, as is the British Council from the British Information Service.

agency mirror their individual philosophies.

For example, the agency's first director, Theodore Streibert (1953-56), a former radio executive, concentrated his efforts on making the Voice of America (VOA) a serious rival to the British Broadcasting Corporation (BBC), at the same time maintaining a heavily anticommunist content in VOA programming to reflect American foreign policy during the coldest of the cold war years. (The endeavor was a logical impossibility since BBC owed the allegiance of its worldwide radio audience to its essentially impartial reporting.) Like Streibert, Frank Shakespeare, agency director from 1969-72, leaned to a heavy anticommunist orientation. He evoked considerable press attention for allegedly being more anticommunist than the Nixon administration[7] and for allegedly failing to obtain clearance from the Department of State for his directives to USIA overseas personnel.[8]

Among other directors who charted a different direction for the agency were the widely known radio commentator Edward R. Murrow (1961-63), and journalist Carl Rowan (1963-65), both of whom strove for an expanded agency role in foreign policy decision-making at the White House level.*

Relationship to Foreign Policy Environment

The kinds of programming and themes used by the USIA subsystem depend in large measure on the nature of interactions between the United States and the international political system. As the patterns of international relationships change, the agency responds to feedback from other national political systems by shifting its programs and emphases. Opportunities for the USIA to play a significant role in the foreign policy system vary considerably, depending on the nature of the changes in international relations.

When the United States embarked upon a strategy to contain communism through the NATO Alliance of 1949, and then extended the same commitment to Asia in the Korean War of 1950, the role of informational programs gained in importance. USIS posts and programs expanded rapidly, especially in Germany, Japan, and Korea. The expanded informational role gave impetus to the pressures for creation of a separate agency in 1953. By the decade of the fifties, economic and military assistance had also become semi-

---

* USIA has had eight directors. The orientation of the other four directors has varied. Law professor Arthur Larson (1956-57), an Eisenhower appointee, resigned after a short tenure without discernible impact on the agency. George Allen (1957-60), career diplomat, and Leonard Marks (1965-68), Lyndon Johnson's lawyer for his radio interests in Texas, focused on restructuring the agency's personnel system, which had been a source of both internal and interagency conflict. James Keogh (1972-   ), a former executive editor of *Time* magazine, has emphasized the USIA role in the larger foreign policy system as a vehicle to promote trade and tourism for the United States.

permanent thrusts of American policy which informational programs were intended to support. Cold-war and aid-support themes of the agency were legitimized by American political attitudes and by the agency's principal constituencies, the presidential, bureaucratic, and congressional subsystems.

However, numerous questions arose concerning role content. Should the agency engage in "black propaganda"—i.e., propaganda actually originating with USIA but attributed to either a controlled source such as the Congress for Cultural Freedom or to a fictitious source—or should such activity be the province of an intelligence agency? Should VOA reflect an obvious anti-communist posture? Should the economic assistance subsystem carry on its own informational programs or should propaganda support for economic assistance be an integral part of the USIA subsystem? The USIA role became diffused, congressional support became more difficult to obtain, and reductions in personnel were ordered by the White House and Congress.

The Soviet Union's globe-circling *sputnik* feat of 1957 served to rejuvenate the USIA role. U.S. response to *sputnik* was quick and aggressive. Congress immediately voted massive financial support to education and technology. USIA was expected to communicate these emphases to other nations and to propagandize the ability of the capitalist system to respond to needs and to excell. A spinoff from this development was creation of more programs to communicate the achievements of American arts and letters.

USIA role-playing in foreign policy remained relatively constant in scope and format for several years. Meanwhile, however, costs of programs and of administering them began to rise. The agency was forced by Congress to cut back on either programs or personnel. Against this threat the subsystem determined internally to retain personnel at the expense of programs. USIA hoped the cutbacks would be temporary and it was easier to contract and expand programs than to fire and rehire personnel. The cutbacks proved permanent, however, and the result was as might be expected. In the early 1960s, for example, the chief of the United States Information Service in Taiwan, after calculating the costs of "keeping the doors open" at the USIS post in Taipei and at the several branch USIS posts in the provinces, concluded that his annual operating budget of approximately $130,000 allowed only some $10,000 for program.

With the escalation of the Vietnam War, the agency was forced to shift priorities again. Major emphasis was placed on coordinating information activities to justify American intervention in Vietnam, a thrust which had an adverse effect upon its programs in other parts of the world. A larger percentage of resources were devoted to the Vietnam operation than to any previous program in agency history, requiring cutbacks elsewhere. The Joint United States Public Affairs Office (JUSPAO) in Saigon became the core of an expensive, massive propaganda effort in that country. At one point in the late 1960s about one-fifth of all overseas USIA personnel were assigned to JUSPAO or to the Civil Operations and Rural Development Support (CORDS) program in Vietnam. The agency had become locked into a one-theme role—the survival of South Vietnam—that diminished rapidly as pressures mounted for American withdrawal from Indochina.

By 1974 the agency was in search of a new worldwide role. Commenting on USIA's twentieth anniversary in 1973, the *Foreign Service Journal* editorialized: "The 20th anniversary is a good time for stock taking, and we urge USIA to use the occasion to take a careful look at its organization, program and policies. USIA was born a child of the Cold War, and its earlier activities would be out of keeping with the changing relationships we are building with the Soviet Union and China."[9] In March 1974 the General Accounting Office, an agent of Congress, asked Congress to consider reorganization of USIA to resolve "continuing controversy" about what information the agency should communicate to other nations.[10]

Insofar as a new role has emerged for USIA, it appears to be mainly in the direction of serving as an overseas communication channel for various actors in the foreign policy system rather than serving abroad as a spokesman for the United States government—the role it had previously enjoyed. In November 1973 the director of USIA told his overseas posts that they must change emphasis "to support, through their information activities, the various trade promotion programs of State and Commerce, and to work with U.S. Travel Service representatives, Commercial Officers at U.S. embassies, and the private sector, in efforts to stimulate U.S. exports and to encourage foreign national visits to the United States."[11]

Role Legitimacy

Information and cultural programs reflect the expectation that the external political environment can be influenced through specialized communications. USIA is the subsystem of the foreign policy system to which the mass informational communications role has been formally assigned. Survival of the USIA subsystem is dependent upon certain prerequisites: (1) consensus within the national political system and the foreign policy system that informational and cultural programs can contribute to foreign policy goals; (2) consensus that USIA is a legitimate subsystem for carrying out a political communications role; and (3) consensus that feedback from the international system verifies that the programs have an impact on the international system which is favorable to the United States.

The differing priorities which the foreign policy system has accorded the information and cultural role at different points in time during the history of USIA can be interpreted as recognition by policy makers that information and cultural programs are only *means* to policy ends, more applicable to advancing some policy ends than others.[1][2] Though the priority accorded the communications role has shifted, the shifts have occurred within a broad continuum of political system support for employing propaganda to help achieve foreign policy goals.

While there is general support for the concept of a communications role, consensus within the foreign policy system about the efficacy of USIA as a subsystem for carrying out this information and cultural role is much weaker. Congress, a principal element of the foreign policy system, has been indifferent, critical, and at times hostile regarding USIA. For example, in 1973 the authorization bill for USIA included a section requiring a fund cutoff if the agency refused to comply with congressional requests for USIA documents. President Nixon vetoed the measure and USIA literally operated in limbo until Congress reluctantly approved a later authorization bill from which the section had been deleted.

Since USIA presents its "product" abroad, Congress has little direct feedback as to the effectiveness of the programs and thus little incentive for supporting them in annual appropriations. In fact, USIA has few advocates with the Congress outside of the presidential subsystem and the bureaucracy, principally the Department of State. For most of its years USIA has achieved only grudging acceptance by Congress in the form of minimal appropriations for its operations.

Individual members of Congress have been constant critics of USIA. As recently as 1970, some legislators urged abandonment of USIA operations in European countries. Congressionally sponsored studies of the agency have questioned its role, organization, and effectiveness. Recommendations of congressmen have variously urged restructuring of the agency, its reabsorption into the Department of State, and its dissolution. Representative John Rooney (D.-N.Y.), the long-time chairman of the House Subcommittee on Appropriations for State, Justice, USIA, and several other agencies, refused for years to accord USIA more than grudging recognition while seeming purposely to confuse its cultural and informational roles, to the detriment of both. Some senators have been particularly critical. Senator Allen J. Ellender (D.-La.) made repeated visits to USIS facilities during the decade of the 1950s. His "inspection" trips were feared by USIS field officers because invariably his perceptions of program effectiveness were negative. Senator John L. McClellan (D.-Ark.), directing his criticism at the exchange-of-persons programs which are funded by the Department of State but administered abroad by USIS, has insisted that nations whose citizens participate in the programs should share costs of the exchanges. He overlooks the fact that the exchange-of-persons program was established within the American foreign policy system as a means of effecting American foreign policy goals. Senator J. William Fulbright initially refused to consider the confirmation of Frank Shakespeare as director of USIA when he appeared before the Senate Foreign Relations Committee in 1969.

Part of Congress's seeming hostility to USIA undoubtedly stems from confusion in the minds of its members as to USIA's role. Some see it as a purveyor of information, others as a vehicle of cultural expression or even cultural "imperialism," and still others as a cold-war warrior. Disappointment in the results produced by the agency are in proportion to USIA's failure in fulfilling the particular role envisioned.

Feedback from the international political system on the impact of USIA is conditioned by the fact that the role of USIS is often confusing to the countries wherein it operates. No other major power combines information and cultural functions in a single department, bureau, or agency. However, at U.S. diplomatic missions the USIS carries out both cultural ("soft-sell") and informational ("hard-sell") activities. As a result, the advantages of the cultural "soft-sell" approach are often dissipated or lost, and the credibility of the cultural attaché is diminished because he is attached to a "hard-sell" propaganda organization.

Moreover, USIS is constantly required to distinguish its role from those of the intelligence community. The agency has consistently refrained from the "black" propaganda, noted earlier, which requires covert action and involves deception. But it has at times indulged in "gray" propaganda, i.e., the placement of informational materials in media channels without identifying their source. USIS must also contend with the fact that many nations use their government information subsystems as intelligence-gathering units—e.g., the Soviet Union and the Republic of China (Taiwan). Translations from English into other languages also create misunderstandings about the role of USIS. For example, the full term in Arabic for USIS is *Maktab Al-Isti'l Amat Al-Amerkiyeh*, which carries a connotation of gathering information as well as disseminating it.

Efforts have been made to gather data within foreign countries about the effectiveness of USIA programs, but the reliability of such data is questionable. In the countries where USIS teams are allowed to conduct direct research, they can measure changes in attitude by opinion surveys but have difficulty linking such changes directly to USIS efforts. In countries such as the Soviet Union and the People's Republic of China—both major VOA targets—direct surveys are manifestly impossible because of the political climate. Indirect means, such as requesting listeners to send postcards to

VOA, can at the most gauge the size of the listening audience, not attitudinal change.

Although Congress has hardly perceived it as such, the "brain drain"—the immigration to the United States of highly qualified persons from other nations—can be considered as positive feedback for USIA, since many of them come to the United States as a result of USIS informational activities and exchange-of-persons programs.

In the final analysis, feedback on efforts to influence opinion is inherently difficult to measure. Understanding is a slow growth and understanding does not necessarily lead to acceptance. As the agency itself has noted, "in an era where communication plays an increasingly crucial role and more and more people are exposed to international communication, it becomes increasingly difficult to relate cause to effect."[13]

IS THERE A FUTURE FOR USIA?

It seems clear that within the American political system, particularly within the foreign policy system, information and cultural programs are generally supported as one means of achieving foreign policy goals. What is not clear is whether or not actors within the American foreign policy system perceive USIA as the appropriate institutional device for playing a major political communications role. The object of long-term congressional criticism, USIA has suffered from meager appropriations which have forced it to sacrifice programs or personnel, or both. Its role is misunderstood both abroad and at home. It has few constituents within the foreign policy system and its principal constituent, the Department of State, has been consistently inconsistent in the degree of support it accords the agency. At best, consensus about the legitimacy of the agency is weak. Why, then, does USIA persist as a viable political subsystem?

If USIA has had few constituents in the foreign policy system, it has also normally been beholden to far fewer claimants and been subject to less domestic political pressure than other subsystems at the national governmental level. One reason is that the agency role is to communicate to an international audience national values, developments, and points of view which have already been essentially agreed to by the American political system. Moreover, since its "product" is marketed abroad, it does not appreciably affect the domestic political system. In consequence, USIA has been a relatively free agent. Even its personnel system, the Foreign Service Information Officer Corps, is statutorily separate from the larger Foreign Service Officer Corps of the Department of State. Congress, in institutionalizing the

FSIO personnel system in 1968 also, in effect, legitimized anew the information role and the Agency. The major constraint upon USIA has traditionally been the annual congressional budget hearing.

By 1973, however, there were growing indications that the official consensus about the legitimacy of USIA as the chief actor in political communications was dissolving. In its *26th Report* issued in January 1973 the United States Advisory Commission on Information complained that, among other things, the agency was not involved in the foreign policy decision-making process at high enough levels, and that Congress was not supporting it with meaningful appropriations.* If neither the president nor the Congress remedied these and other difficulties, the commission recommended either the return of USIA and all of its activities to the Department of State or dismantling it and making a threefold division of its activities. The information role would be returned to the Department of State, the Voice of America would become an independent "group," and a new United States Educational and Cultural Agency or Department would be responsible for educational and cultural activities.[14]

On March 12, 1974, the president of the American Foreign Service Association testified to the Senate Foreign Relations Committee that "among many career professionals in the information and cultural fields and others in the foreign affairs community, there is little sentiment for maintaining the status quo."[15] At the same time a senior USIA officer wrote in the *Foreign Service Journal* that "the USIA mechanism is hopelessly ill-adjusted to its function so long as a majority of its officers are [in Washington] where the job isn't." USIA, he continued, "has lost control [of its role] through downgrading of its status, Congressional parsimony, duplication of functions with State and over-emphasis on bureaucracy."[16]

The future of USIA may well be decided by the Murphy Commission (discussed in Chapter 10), whose two-year study of the foreign policy system will be submitted to Congress in June 1975.

* "Recent studies of the USIA appropriations record for the past two decades show that the annual appropriation has risen from $84 million in FY-54 [fiscal year 1954] to slightly over $200 million for FY-73. However, measured in stable dollars the fiscal level in FY-73 is not much greater than it was in FY-54." United States Advisory Commission on Information, *The 26th Report* (Washington: Government Printing Office, 1973), p. 19.

CHAPTER 6

USIA in Washington:
Organization and Role

With a zeal characteristic of the United States Information Agency, the address of the seventy-year-old building that became its headquarters in Washington was changed from 1778 Pennsylvania Avenue to the far more patriotic *1776*. From this appropriately modified address, USIA embarks on its mission "to tell America's story to the world."

The role of USIA in Washington is to service its posts abroad. A catalogue of role-playing activities abroad by USIA would include, in more or less rank-order: (1) operation of the Voice of America, a global radio network designed to promote American policies and values; (2) operation of libraries and information and cultural centers; (3) administering academic and non-academic exchange-of-persons programs of the Department of State; (4) presenting American cultural and artistic achievements; (5) mounting exhibits depicting facets of American life and achievements; (6) subsidizing production of low-cost, foreign-published editions of representative American literature; (7) publicizing international programs of other U.S. agencies, such as the Agency for International Development and the Department of Commerce; (8) advising U.S. missions on the implications of foreign opinion for U.S. policies; (9) publicizing common interests between other countries and the United States; (10) publicizing achievements of nations allied with the United States; (11) participating in paramilitary programs which support military intervention of the United States in the international system, as in Korea and Vietnam; and (12) production and distribution of general informational materials on American life and institutions. Participation in paramilitary programs engaged a major portion of USIA's talent and energies during the latter stages of the Vietnam War, but with American withdrawal from Southeast Asia this activity has become a lesser element in USIA role-playing.

WASHINGTON HIERARCHIES

Four hierarchical subsystems operate within the USIA system. The senior hierarchical subsystem is responsible for policy and planning. Under the aegis of a deputy director, it is responsible for decisions about the content and application of USIA's overseas programs. Beneath the policy and planning hierarchy are three organizationally coequal hierarchies, headed by assistant directors whose roles are: (1) area hierarchy—to supervise the programs which are administered abroad; (2) media hierarchy—to produce or contract for—and, in the case of radio broadcasting, deliver—media materials for overseas programs; and (3) administrative hierarchy—to engage in administration support activities. In consequence, the USIA table of organization reflects extreme proliferation at the supervisory level. In addition to the director of the agency, his generalist deputy and the deputy director of Policy and Plans, the table of organization shows fifteen assistant directors.

Because it is an independent foreign affairs agency whose principal interactions within the foreign policy system are with the Department of State, USIA from its inception has endeavored to model its organization on that of the Department of State. Parallel organizational hierarchies, USIA reasoned, would afford it access to all levels of the State Department. The title "deputy director of the United States Information Agency" conveys an impression of approximately equal status with that of deputy secretary of state. Similarly, the designation "assistant director (Africa)" in USIA should equate with that of assistant secretary for African Affairs in the Department of State. Moreover, the salary scales within these two foreign policy agencies, as well as within the Agency for International Development, are similar.

Area Principle: Theory and Practice

When USIA was established as a separate entity, it borrowed the geographical

—or, in USIA terminology, area—principle of organization employed by the Department of State. Assistant directors on the Department of State model were created for each region of the world. Just as State's regional assistant secretaries are formally responsible for government-wide interactions with specific regions of the world, USIA area assistant directors originally were assigned responsibility for coordinating all aspects of USIA programs in nations within corresponding geographical areas. Moreover, in its early years USIA restricted use of the title of assistant director to USIA officers who headed area offices. These officers were encouraged to role-play in a manner to suggest their coequality with the Department of State's regional assistant secretaries. Their communication with the Department of State, written and telephonic, was expected by USIA to take place at the assistant secretary level. USIA assistant directors tended to avoid interagency meetings not also attended by State assistant secretaries.

Initially the area assistant directors of USIA had greater impact on the USIA subsystem than did their counterparts at State on the Department of State subsystem. They were less subject to external pressures. Regional assistant secretaries at State have to contend with inputs from an enormous variety of sources within and outside government in their attempt to coordinate all foreign policy of the United States government. USIA area directors, on the other hand, experienced few demands and expectations' from governmental subsystems other than the Department of State, or from domestic interest groups, since USIA outputs were confined to informational and cultural communication of previously decided foreign policy thrusts.

In the mid-1950s the preeminence of the area assistant directors within USIA began to dissipate when the agency's foreign policy role suffered erosion in the foreign policy system with the slackening of the impetus which independent status had given it. Despite their titles and formal responsibilities, the area directors had failed to evoke from the larger foreign policy system the degree of influence and legitimacy which USIA desired. In attempting to remedy the problem, the USIA leadership began to impose guidelines on the area directors through the vehicle of the policy and planning hierarchy. The hypothesis advanced was that conversion of U.S. foreign policy posture into more effective foreign information programs to support it could be achieved by centralizing the responsibilities. Gradually the policy and planning hierarchy acceded to the leadership role. The major tools possessed by the policy and planning hierarchy were the authority to veto or modify individual geographic-area office planning and to allocate Agency resources to support specific themes and programs, regardless of area-office judgments.

The primacy of the geographic areas was also adversely affected by the

TABLE IX   UNITED STATES INFORMATION AGENCY

U.S. ADVISORY COMMISSION ON INFORMATION

EXECUTIVE SECRETARIAT

DIRECTOR
DEPUTY DIRECTOR
DEPUTY DIRECTOR (Policy & Plans)

OFFICE OF POLICY AND PLANS

FOREIGN PRESS CENTERS WASHINGTON-NEW YORK

OFFICE OF THE CHIEF INSPECTOR

OFFICE OF EQUAL EMPLOYMENT OPPORTUNITY

OFFICE OF PUBLIC INFORMATION

OFFICE OF THE GENERAL COUNSEL AND CONGRESSIONAL LIAISON

OFFICE OF SECURITY

OFFICE OF PERSONNEL AND TRAINING

OFFICE OF RESEARCH

OFFICE OF ADMINISTRATION AND MANAGEMENT

MOTION PICTURE AND TELEVISION SERVICE

PRESS AND PUBLICATIONS SERVICE

INFORMATION CENTER SERVICE

BROADCASTING SERVICE

RADIO PROGRAM CENTERS AND RELAY STATIONS

REGIONAL SERVICE CENTERS

OFFICE OF ASSISTANT DIRECTOR (Africa)

OFFICE OF ASSISTANT DIRECTOR (East Asia and Pacific)

OFFICE OF ASSISTANT DIRECTOR (Soviet Union and East Europe)

OFFICE OF ASSISTANT DIRECTOR (Latin America)

OFFICE OF ASSISTANT DIRECTOR (North Africa, Near East, and South Asia)

OFFICE OF ASSISTANT DIRECTOR (West Europe)

PRESS AND CULTURAL SECTIONS

USIS POSTS

USIS POSTS

USIS POSTS

USIS POSTS

agency's perceived need to marshal its resources as effectively as possible in order to maintain its role identity vis-à-vis State. Rather than considering USIA as an autonomous subsystem and interacting with it on the basis of a symmetric relationship, as USIA desired, the department tended to view the agency as simply another among a growing number of subsystems dependent upon the department. Despite USIA's organizational autonomy, the department largely dictated the agency's substantive role in the foreign policy system and almost entirely determined the conditions under which U.S. Information Service posts operated abroad.

A third factor which diluted the influence of geographic area offices was the consequence of the division of the cultural role between the Department of State and USIA. The agency was assigned the cultural role abroad, but a principal tool for mounting effective cultural penetration of other national political systems, namely funding and administering the exchange-of-persons programs in the United States, had been left in the Department of State. Thus limited in its cultural role, the agency turned decisively toward development of its media elements. The most modern technological developments were utilized, and the agency organized a series of media hierarchies, each headed by an assistant director, both to dramatize its information role and to reinforce its legitimacy. A principal result was that by 1974 the number of assistant directors had gradually increased from the original four area directors* to fifteen—including four in media and four in administration. The original concept of allocating complete coordinating authority to area assistant directors had disappeared.

MEDIA ELEMENTS

Media elements came ready-made to USIA upon its separation from the Department of State in 1953. Radio broadcasting by the Voice of America, inaugurated in 1942 during World War II, had been legitimized and institutionalized within the foreign policy system. Consensus had also grown within the foreign policy system for utilization of press materials, publications, libraries and information centers, and motion pictures as foreign policy tools.

Primacy of the Voice of America (VOA)

The Voice of America (VOA) subsystem within USIA constitutes a major

* Six assistant directors supervise USIA programs in the geographical regions of the world; four are responsible for production of media materials; three direct, respectively, administration and management, security, and personnel and training; and two administer the equal opportunity employment programs and the domestic public information programs.

national investment in communications technology. VOA is perhaps more correctly depicted in system terminology as a subsystem *formally attached* to USIA rather than a subsystem integrated within the agency. VOA's role, namely worldwide radio broadcasting, is perceived differently from other USIA elements by foreign policy decision-makers, both inside and outside of government, who have consistently conferred a greater degree of legitimacy upon VOA than upon USIA itself. Congressional authorizations for expenditures within USIA bear this out. During the mid-1950s, a period of rapid expansion for VOA, one-third of the entire annual USIA congressional appropriation of approximately $150 million was authorized for construction of radio transmission facilities in the United States and abroad. In fiscal year 1973 almost one-fourth ($49,978,560) of the total USIA authorization ($210,778,800) was allocated to VOA, even though it had not engaged in a major new technical project since fiscal year 1966. The expenditure for VOA in fiscal year 1973 was five times greater than that for any other media branch, exceeding the total expended for all other USIA media combined.[1]

The executive branch and Congress have continued to perceive the value and potential of international broadcasting as a foreign policy tool, perhaps because this is an era when, as the International Press Institute has concluded, "barely 20%" of member nations of the United Nations do *not* impose some form of censorship or internal control of the mass media.[2] In many countries, therefore, international broadcasting is the only way the United States can communicate with indigenous audiences. Competition among nations in the use of international broadcasting to achieve foreign policy ends has also influenced American foreign policy actors and interest groups to provide support for VOA.

Since the significance of VOA's role seems to be accepted without question, whereas political consensus about the legitimacy of an independent USIA is maintained only with difficulty, VOA may be viewed as the chief legitimizing agent within the Agency. In colloquial terms, the agency "leans on" VOA rather than vice versa. Should VOA be separated from the agency and established as an independent or quasi-independent unit as has been suggested on occasion, it is questionable whether USIA could survive as an independent subsystem.

Despite its demonstrated functionality within the foreign policy system, its visibility, and its legitimizing impact upon USIA, the Voice of America is not immune to problems relating to its continued viability. Almost paradoxically, a major system problem for VOA has been that of defining its goal. A continuing objective of VOA directors has been to achieve the audience acceptance enjoyed by the British Broadcasting Corporation, whose worldwide reputation as an objective source of information has afforded BBC such a high degree of legitimacy.

In an attempt to imitate BBC, VOA has expanded its English language news programs to around-the-clock, worldwide news service, and has developed a staff of VOA correspondents in the United States and abroad whose reportage is included in VOA news broadcasts. But VOA's quest for objectivity is in part defeated because the subsystem, as an element of USIA, must help achieve the agency's mission, which USIA defines as supporting "U.S. national interests by conveying an understanding of what the United States stands for as a nation and as a people . . . [and by] explaining U.S. policies and the reasons for them."[3] Since it operates within this prescribed framework, it is difficult to distinguish VOA's role, except in degree, from that of the openly propagandistic Radio Moscow, Radio Cairo, or broadcasts from the state radio of the People's Republic of China.

The Voice of America subsystem, formally entitled the Broadcasting Service of the United States Information Agency, is headed by an assistant director (broadcasting), also entitled director of VOA. There are two vertical, relatively parallel, hierarchies, one concerned with programming and the other with construction and maintenance of facilities. On an average, VOA broadcasts 856 hours weekly in thirty-six languages via short and medium wave.[4] Ninety-four percent of VOA broadcasts are shortwave.[5] VOA facilities in the United States include forty-one transmitters, ranging in power from 50 to 500 kilowatts. VOA operates seventy-three transmitters abroad, which range in power from 35 to 1000 kilowatts. Relay and transmission facilities are positioned abroad in order to provide a global radio network.[6]

Major technical difficulties had to be surmounted in developing VOA into a global shortwave radio network. Since radio waves are linear, they are affected by the physical terrain and also by the ionosphere. On the wave spectrum, longer radio waves are less expensive to transmit and they "bend" to a degree which permits their reception by radio receivers despite atmospheric and physical impediments such as mountains. But long- and medium-wave broadcasting is sharply limited in terms of the distance the waves can be transmitted.

In the case of shortwave broadcasting, although the linear problem remains, the high-frequency waves may be bounced off the ionosphere and directed to relay transmitters which rebroadcast them to specific areas of the world. The strength, and thus the distance, of their signal is primarily dependent upon the amount of electrical energy expended in their transmission. Thus international radio networks which span seas and continents broadcast almost entirely by shortwave.

Another difficulty is that radio signals deteriorate when they are broadcast from the United States through the northern auroral zone to Eastern Europe and to Asia. The auroral zone deflects radio waves consistently enough to prevent effective broadcasting to many parts of the world from the continental United States.

VOA resolved the problems of the auroral zone, the weakening effect of distance, and the linear quality of waves by making large investments in an integrated network of relay stations located abroad where signals from the United States would be transmitted in straight paths, avoiding the auroral zones. Shortwave relay stations are located in Morocco, Germany, Greece, the Philippines, Okinawa, Sri Lanka (Ceylon), England, and Liberia. These stations rebroadcast the signals with increased power so that they are strong enough to be heard competitively in all areas of the world at peak listening time. Resolution of these technical problems, however, did not provide final answers to effective radio communication with the rest of the world.

The period of greatest VOA physical expansion, from approximately 1955 to 1965, coincided precisely with two other developments which currently may be limiting the impact of VOA shortwave broadcasting. If, in consequence of these two developments, impact is in fact limited, the question should be raised as to whether the expensive VOA worldwide relay station network is worth the investment from a cost-effectiveness standpoint in contrast to other feasible kinds of mass electronics communication. These developments are: (1) the advent of the inexpensive, medium-wave transistor radio, and (2) the rise of national government radio in most nations of the world.

In 1974 VOA estimated that there were about 387 million radio receivers in the world, exclusive of the United States and Canada, neither of which are target areas. Of these only an estimated 130 million are equipped to receive shortwave. Thus, the VOA relay station network, broadcasting 94 percent of its programs over shortwave facilities, is denied access to more than half of all radio receivers worldwide. Moreover, as VOA readily admits, the developing countries are rapidly "increasing their use of shortwave radio to inform their own people and those in adjacent countries of their progress and points of view."[7]

Since both shortwave and medium-wave signals are stronger when nearby, national radio networks are able to compete more effectively for the radio audience in their physical area than even the strongest shortwave transmitter located a long distance away. Moreover, the types of shortwave transistor radios that people can afford in poorer countries (meaning most of the world, including the prime targets, China and the Soviet Union) are not of high enough quality to isolate distant shortwave broadcasts effectively, especially when they compete with closer and stronger shortwave signals originating within the country.

VOA is well aware of the relative advantage of medium-wave broadcasting over shortwave transmission. At relay stations close enough to a target country to bridge the distance, extremely powerful medium-wave transmitters are used. A megawatt medium-wave transmitter on Okinawa broadcasts to the Soviet Far East, Korea, and much of China. In the Philippines another 1000-kilowatt medium-wave transmitter is beamed to China, southeast Asia, and Indonesia. A third superpowered facility is the single megawatt transmitter at Bangkok, Thailand, which provides medium-wave coverage to Bangladesh, southeast Asia, northeastern India, Burma, and western Indonesia. At relay stations adjacent to target countries, medium-wave transmission is invariably utilized. A 300-kilowatt medium-wave transmitter in Munich, Germany, broadcasts to East Germany; a 150-kilowatt transmitter in Kavala, Greece, and a similar one on the island of Rhodes beam medium-wave broadcasts to the Mediterranean area. Hue in South Vietnam is the locus of a 50-kilowatt medium-wave transmitter. A little publicized appendage of VOA is *Rund-Funk im Amerikanischen Sektor*, or Radio in the American Sector (RIAS) in Berlin. RIAS broadcasts in medium- and shortwave via six transmitters in West Berlin and the Federal Republic of Germany. Its programs are avowedly anticommunist in nature.

VOA and its advocates contend that they need to keep pace with the rapid acceleration of competition in international radio by both new countries and those with long histories of international broadcasting. The United States Advisory Commission on Information, for example, states flatly: "The Voice of America is falling seriously behind the rest of the world in its ability to deliver a competitive signal. . . . *While VOA stands still, the rest of the world is building high power shortwave installations at an accelerated rate.* The result will be an outgunned VOA."[8]

This contention, however, appears to disregard the fact that, unlike VOA, most nations do not maintain an expensive worldwide network of relay stations. Neither the Arab Republic of Egypt, the People's Republic of China, nor the Soviet Union—to name three nations which broadcast more shortwave hours per week than does VOA—possesses an extensive externally located relay network even remotely comparable in size and cost to that of the VOA system.

However, international radio broadcasting may have already passed its zenith as a result of the worldwide preoccupation—by governments and viewers alike—with television. As suggested earlier, the advent of the communications satellite for transmitting televised broadcasts will have important consequences. It may, for instance, drastically reduce the impact of international radio broadcasting, no matter who the nations are. What may count for more in the near future is which nations have access to the facilities of the profit-oriented satellite system of INTELSAT.*

Television—especially color television—has a multidimensional appeal which has already proved irresistible. For example, Zanzibar, in the African state of Tanzania, has set up a national color television system and subsidizes citizen purchases of television receivers. The government services the receivers, and homes without electricity are provided batteries, which are recharged every twelve days by a television station van! "Every night," the *Los Angeles Times* reports, "at crowded community centers and in private homes an estimated audience of 120,000 (a third of the island's population) gather around 3,146 sets."[9] It can only be a matter of time until ready-made national television systems on the Zanzibar model are objects, whether one likes it or not, of international satellite television broadcasting.

The Applications Technology Satellite (ATS-6), launched in May 1974, is actually a new special television broadcasting center for an international community. The ATS-6 broadcasts from a station over the Galapagos Islands in the eastern Pacific to isolated areas in the United States, and from a station over Kenya, East Africa, to 5,000 villages and cities in India. Unlike the INTELSAT system which relays its television programs through expensive ground stations, the new ATS-6 system utilizes small low-cost converters on receiving units.[10] The logical next step would be a technological breakthrough which would dispense with the need for even the low-cost converters. Such a development would indeed enable one country to transmit televised broadcasts from its homeland directly into home receivers of viewers in another country regardless of the latter's wishes. Foreseeing a sensitive situation in the future, the United Nations General Assembly has already voted overwhelmingly—102 to 1, with only the United States dissenting—to formulate principles governing use of the INTELSAT satellite.[11] The opposing U.S. position is based on the contention that the free flow of information, regardless of frontiers, is central to the Universal Declaration of Human Rights.

Press and Publications Service (IPS)

Compared with the publications of other governments and similar commercial materials, USIA's Press and Publications Service (IPS) maintains high

---

* The International Telecommunications Satellite Consortium (INTELSAT), formed in 1964, is a global *commercial* communications satellite system in which COMSAT, the Communications Satellite Corporation, a private U.S. corporation, holds a majority interest.

standards of professional journalism. At its inception USIA inherited talented publicists from the Office of War Information and it has consistently recruited qualified personnel, lured from private journalism by attractive government salaries. USIA defines the mission of IPS as that of supplying "the printed word in support of U.S. policy objectives overseas [and providing] USIS posts with materials to help U.S. officials promote a favorable climate of informed opinion in which American interests [can] be advanced."[12]

Program materials are produced and distributed by IPS through a wide variety of means. A worldwide radioteletype system transmits a wireless file to 127 USIS posts five days a week. IPS regularly mails feature stories, by-lined articles, reprints from U.S. publications and photos to overseas posts. The service also produces seven major magazines for wide distribution abroad, plus eight smaller periodicals for specialized audiences.

The wireless file consists of U.S. policy statements and interpretative materials about them which are radioteletyped in five regional transmissions. Average word volume of the file on a daily basis is: Europe, 8,000; East Asia and Pacific, 8,000; Near East and South Asia, 7,500; Africa, 11,200; and Latin America, 8,700 in Spanish and 5,000 in English. Obviously an operation of such magnitude in a subsystem as small as USIA is not only a major consumer of time and personnel but also is very costly.

The wireless file, according to John W. Henderson, a biographer of the agency, "was created as a news service for press and radio abroad but now serves mostly as a rapid means of communicating the official U.S. position on various policy questions."[13] The news service filled a perceived need during the postwar years of European reconstruction and while new and undeveloped nations were appearing on the international scene. This need later diminished sharply as many new nations developed their own national news networks, motivated by the political imperative to provide their own interpretations of *all* news, a hallmark of nationalism!

USIA has attempted to adapt to the changing political environment by emphasizing that wireless-file materials are not only for placement by posts in indigenous *media* but are also "distributed directly to influential contacts" and "circulated within U.S. Missions for information and briefing purposes."[14] However, the "official U.S. position" to which Henderson alludes is also transmitted to U.S. diplomatic missions in *daily Department of State policy cables*. Thus U.S. officials at missions abroad are apprised of policy by the Department of State quite aside from the USIA wireless file. Moreover, the content of policy can be conveyed more dramatically, and probably more effectively, to "influential contacts" by verbally paraphrasing the Department of State cables rather than by distributing the USIA wireless file, which comprises yards of teleprinter copy deliberately keyed to broad public use. In June 1973 U.S. chiefs of mission were mixed in their responses to queries from the director of the agency about the usefulness of the file and the consequences which might ensue if it were discontinued. The agency's decision to maintain the file by modifying it so that it "is limited to those materials of highest priority to overseas missions,"[15] suggests that the decision-makers in USIA believe they can buttress its role legitimacy.

While the value of the wireless file may be questioned, general support is evident for the publications role of the Press and Publications Service. The media products it has succeeded in developing are favorably perceived both by policy-makers in the United States and by target audiences abroad. Technical and editorial quality is consistently superior in comparison with products of other countries. Demand for USIA's colorful and informative magazines is especially high. *America Illustrated,* for example, passes from hand to hand in Poland and the Soviet Union. *Problems of Communism,* a journal with a scholarly orientation, provides in-depth analyses of communist affairs of such quality that it is in demand by American sovietologists as well as by foreign scholars throughout the world. Other major USIA magazines appeal to world regional and language interests. *Topic* is written in French and English for sub-Sahara Africa. *Al-Majal* is written in Arabic to appeal to the Arab world. *Horizon* emphasizes the community of interest between the United States and East and South Asia.

USIA has recognized the worldwide trend toward proliferation of specialized periodicals by producing *Economic Impact* and *Dialogue,* dealing, respectively, with economic and cultural-social issues in terms the literate layman can understand and the specialist appreciate. In all, fifteen magazines in twenty-four languages are published by USIA.

Additional resources of IPS include three printing plants, called Regional Service Centers (RSCs), located in Manila, Beirut, and Mexico City, which produce most of the agency's magazines, pamphlets, and other printed materials. Each center is a major investment in modern plant facilities and equipment, employs hundreds of host-country nationals, and is a model of efficiency. Each USIS post in the area has an "impressions account," i.e., an annual credit for a specified number of single-sheet impressions. Credits may be used at the post's discretion for orders ranging from one-page flyers to full-length books in national languages. Even if USIA were not to survive as an independent agency, the RSCs would continue under some kind of organizational arrangement.

Motion Picture and Television Service (IMV)

USIA conceives the role of its Motion Picture and Television Service to be that of producing or acquiring for presentation to foreign audiences films and videotapes "to develop a positive and lasting image of the U.S., its people and their way of life."[16] IMV distributes about 150 film and television documentaries annually, in addition to some 500 clips for use on foreign television. USIA's worldwide film audience is around 200 million persons, and the agency considers its potential television audience in 100 countries as 500 million persons. The agency uses satellite transmission for a few of its programs abroad.

Despite some spectacular successes, such as the documentary film *Years of Lightning, Day of Drums* on John F. Kennedy's presidency and assassination, the Motion Picture and Television Service is accorded minimal legitimacy. In the view of the U.S. Advisory Commission on Information, IMV's message is too frequently lost on foreign audiences, and the quality of production is unfortunately diluted because of the most-common-denominator effect of trying to produce for worldwide audiences.[17]

During the first four years of the Nixon administration when USIA was directed by Frank Shakespeare, IMV came under commercial media and congressional attack for preoccupation with an anticommunist theme, for an alleged reluctance to portray racial problems in the United States objectively, and for politicizing its output by dramatizing on film the "silent majority" theme of the Nixon White House.[18] The criticism culminated in the sudden resignation in April 1972 of Assistant Director Bruce Herschensohn who headed the service. The assistant directors who have followed him have managed to keep the Motion Picture and Television Service out of the news, but have not improved its product or its rank-order image within the Agency.

"CULTURE": ICS

The Information Center Service (ICS) should be categorized as a cultural as well as a media element. It provides "cultural programming services" and is the principal cultural component of USIA's Washington operations.

ICS develops multimedia programs for presentation abroad at United States information centers; it supports overseas library operations and book presentation programs; it produces exhibitions for international fairs, expositions, and festivals in cooperation with other executive branch agencies such as the Departments of Labor and Commerce. ICS also sponsors English language teaching at its overseas centers and encourages the development of American studies programs abroad. ICS produces smaller exhibitions for use in USIS information centers, provides subsidies to American and foreign book publishers, and is the agency's focal point with U.S. academic institutions for supply of various educational materials, especially in the area of American studies, to foreign universities.

In response to criticism that the Agency does not sufficiently stress cultural programs, USIA has assigned to ICS a broad role in coordinating U.S. participation in international trade fairs and presentation of exhibits abroad, which are arranged under the aegis of cultural exchange agreements between the Department of State and other countries. Recognizing the value of multimedia approaches, ICS has pioneered the use of videotape recording (VTR) equipment and "electronic dialogues" to conduct cultural programs abroad. VTR technique employs a one-half inch videotape which is inexpensive to make and to project, completely portable, and, unlike motion-picture film, can be erased and reused. "Electronic dialogues" involve presentation to a selected audience abroad of a previously filmed exposition by a prominent American on a topical issue. When the film concludes, the American speaker in the United States answers questions of his overseas audience via an amplified telephone connection.

As ICS shifts its emphasis to multimedia programming, it is, nevertheless, confronted by variables over which it has no control. It is the Department of State rather than USIA which concludes cultural exchange agreements with other countries, including agreement about the kind and scope of American participation in international expositions and trade fairs. The Departments of Commerce, Labor, Transportation, and Health, Education and Welfare—any of whom may be exhibitors at a particular international exposition—possess far greater financial resources, and therefore political clout, than ICS, whose activities are confined to those possible under the Agency's shrunken budgets of recent years. When ICS develops programs for information centers abroad which involve the physical presence of a panel of American experts or American performing artists, it is the Department of State's Bureau of Educational and Cultural Affairs rather than ICS which awards travel grants and stipends to the participants.

These problems are principally the result of assigning the cultural role overseas to one agency, while dividing its authority and funding. The problems are dysfunctional to USIA subsystem maintenance and are not likely to be mitigated by the rather simplistic solution proposed by the United States Advisory Commission on Information, namely the appointment of a "distinguished American who is prominent in the cultural field," to head the agency's cultural program. The first difficulty with such a proposal is to define "culture." The second, and very practical one, is that such an appointment would not address the real problem, which involves allocation of roles and resources.

PERSONNEL QUAGMIRE

The inclusion of informational and cultural components of foreign policy within the Department of State after World War II created a number of personnel problems. The Foreign Service of the department had been confined to generalists recruited on the basis of rigorous written and oral examinations. It consisted of an elite corps of diplomats, and the department was reluctant to accord Foreign Service Officer (FSO) status to either the information specialists being transferred from the Office of War Information, or the new cultural specialists being recruited from college campuses and from the arts. To protect the integrity of its elite group, the department appointed the information and cultural employees whom it expected to serve abroad as either Foreign Service Reserve Officers or Foreign Service Staff Officers—two supporting personnel categories authorized by the Foreign Service Act of 1946.

In 1953, when USIA was created as a separate entity, its foreign service personnel were locked into these State Department categories since the Foreign Service Act of 1946 was the sole legislative authority for agency employees serving abroad.

USIA made several efforts to gain inclusion of its foreign service, i.e., Foreign Service Reserve and Foreign Service Staff, personnel in the Foreign Service Officer corps. In 1958 USIA Director George Allen, himself an FSO, devised an in-agency category which he called Foreign Service Career Reserve Officers (FSCR), to which USIA Foreign Service employees could be appointed administratively following written and oral examinations given by the agency. Allen's intention was to create a nucleus of USIA foreign service personnel who would qualify for eventual appointment as FSOs. Allen specifically emphasized the "generalist" qualities of the newly created FSCRs. In response to invitation, USIA officers took written and oral agency-administered examinations in 1960-61 and those who qualified were duly appointed FSCRs. In 1967, however, Congress defeated a bill which would have permitted their blanket appointment to the FSO category. Opposition to the bill was led by Senator Claiborne Pell, a former FSO.

The agency then came full cycle. In 1968 Congress passed USIA-sponsored legislation which created the Foreign Service Information Officer Corps (FSIO). It was based precisely on the assumption that USIA foreign service officer personnel are *specialists* in informational (and, by implication, cultural) roles rather than generalists. The legislation (Public Law 90-494, 1968) makes FSIOs secretaries in the diplomatic service, thus giving them equality with Foreign Service Officers. It stipulates the same conditions for them (but only up to the level of career minister) concerning promotion and selection out as for the traditional Foreign Service Officer. It affords them the greater advantages of the Foreign Service retirement system in place of Civil Service retirement. A new category, Foreign Service Reserve Unlimited (FSRU), was also authorized. In consequence of the 1968 legislation, the USIA personnel system in Washington is an amalgam of Foreign Service Information Officers (922); Foreign Service Reserve Officers Unlimited (745); Foreign Service Reserve Officers Limited (111); Foreign Service Staff (359); Civil Service personnel (1508); and a mixed category of Wage Board and alien employees (544). Overseas foreign service personnel comprise FSIO (618); FSRU (33); FSRL (102); and FSS (206). FSIOs comprise less than one-fourth of the total full-time employees, who number 4189.[19]

Several potentially dysfunctional consequences have emerged from the 1968 personnel legislation. The law created *information* officers but said nothing about *cultural* officers. It confirmed that FSIOs are specialists rather than generalists, which, psychologically at least, diminishes the possibility for officer exchanges with the department's more generalized FSO corps. USIA desires such exchanges because they expose FSIOs to broader diplomatic experiences and thus provide the agency with more leverage for wider participation in the foreign policy process. Although a few FSIOs are utilized by the department, and although the Foreign Service Officer corps itself is increasingly fragmenting into specialist categories, the barriers to officer exchanges—and to USIA officers becoming ambassadors or principal officers in U.S. missions abroad—are real.

Still another problem arises in that USIA, unlike the department, is not a large enough subsystem to absorb *efficiently* the number of FSIOs, FSRLs, FSRUs, and FSSs on Washington assignment at any particular time. In mid-1974, only 959 of the 2144 employees in all Foreign Service categories were assigned abroad, or about 44 percent. Under conditions prevailing in mid-1974, therefore, positions in the Washington hierarchy had to be found for some 1185 employees in the several Foreign Service categories, along with the 1508 Civil Service employees. A consequence is that USIA in Washington, especially in the regional area offices, is seriously overstaffed. Numerous positions are of the make-work variety, adversely affecting morale and efficiency.

POLITICS OF USIA

Interactions within USIA, and between its role players and those of other subsystems of the foreign policy system, reflect patterns of directive authority or political power. An approach which focuses on such interactions can be categorized as a bureaucratic perspective. Morton Halperin, who believes a bureaucratic perspective is particularly applicable to the study of the foreign policy system, suggests that "organizations with missions strive to maintain or improve their (1) essential role, (2) domain, (3) autonomy, and (4) morale. Organizations with high-cost capabilities are also concerned with maintaining or increasing their (5) budgets. These organization [i.e., system] objectives are the source of the stakes and stands of organizational [i.e., system] participants."[20]

The United States Information Agency is an ideal model to study from the standpoint of Halperin's bureaucratic perspective. Its *role* is narrow and well defined in contrast to very large executive agencies and departments whose roles are numerous and diffused. Paradoxically, precisely because its role is narrow and particularistic, the USIA subsystem tends to devote a larger proportion of its resources to safeguarding that role than is the case in subsystems which discharge multiroles. Survival for USIA equates with continuing consensus within the foreign policy system that information and cultural programs to support foreign policy should be performed by USIA (see Chapter 5).

Halperin's remaining four system interests appear to flow from the first objective, that of maintaining and improving the subsystem role. Thus *autonomy* and parameters of *domain* must be maintained to insure differentiation of USIA subsystem role-playing from that of its would-be usurpers and to provide an internal environment free from constraints. *Morale* in USIA is of particular importance because the Agency's legitimacy and the status of its personnel have been uncertain throughout much of its history. Finally, USIA is decidedly a subsystem of *high-cost capabilities* whose budget must be maintained and improved if it is to survive. The Voice of America, USIA's chief legitimizing element, is also its highest-cost program. It claims one-fourth of the USIA budget. It is within this interest framework that "the stakes and stands of organizational participants" should be studied.

USIA Power Structure

Building upon Halperin's analysis, it may be hypothesized that the power of actors and elements within a bureaucracy will depend upon their contribution to system maintenance in terms of Halperin's five objectives. By delineating which actors and elements most clearly contribute to system maintenance, one can identify the actual structure of power within USIA.

At the apex of the USIA power structure is the executive committee, the principal element for review, discussion, and formulation of decisions concerning agency role-playing and allocation of agency resources. Other subsystems of the foreign policy system—Congress, the presidential subsystem, other bureaucracies, and interest groups—evaluate USIA in terms of their perceptions of its success or lack of it. Obviously role-playing success is linked to decisions about how to role-play, in USIA an executive committee prerogative. The executive committee is an ad hoc unit and does not appear on the agency's organizational chart. It normally meets weekly. Membership is informal but includes, in addition to the director of USIA, the generalist deputy director and the deputy director for policy and plans, the agency's general counsel, and the assistant director for administration and management. The titles of these role players included on the executive committee provide clues as to the major loci of authority within the agency.

As in the Department of State, the generalist deputy director role-plays as the alter ego of the director. The deputy director for policy and plans is next in importance because it is at this level that commitment of agency resources to specific programs is made in response to demands and expectations arising within and without USIA. The director and the two deputy directors are the principal channels to the White House and its staff and to other foreign policy subsystems, primarily the Department of State.

The general counsel is included in the top echelon of authority because he is the principal link to Congress, upon whose continuing approval the subsystem depends for survival in a degree equal to its dependence upon the continuing support of the White House. The assistant director for administration and management is included on the executive committee because his office is the focal point within the agency for interactions with the Office of Management and Budget (OMB). OMB is the element of the presidential subsystem which basically determines, in its annual government-wide budget formulation, the priority which will be accorded to USIA in financial terms.

Three other assistant directors are resource members of the executive committee. The assistant director for research provides feedback on current attitudes among the foreign-audience targets to which the agency directs its output. Research findings influence decisions about what programs to mount in which foreign countries. The assistant director for personnel and training is included because decisions about assignment of personnel to USIS posts abroad are periodically recurring imperatives which affect agency operations. Unlike domestic bureaucracies in which personnel assignments are for indefinite periods, all USIA Foreign Service personnel overseas are reassigned or transferred at the end of each two- or three-year tour of duty, depending upon the particular post concerned. The assistant director for personnel and training makes recommendations but usually does not make decisions about assignment of senior personnel. Inclusion of the assistant director for public information on the executive committee is a consequence of increasing concern over the agency's image within the American political system.

The broad objective of each member of the executive committee is identical, namely to marshal, coordinate, and employ USIA resources in ways which will insure the agency's continuing role within the foreign policy system. All other considerations—themes, kinds of programs, employment of media facilities—are secondary to the imperative for survival.

Among the intraoffice hierarchies, the Office of Policy and Plans (IOP) ranks first in terms of influence and, therefore, power. IOP is the principal element engaged in substantive interaction with the Department of State, whose support is essential to USIA's survival. The department's major substantive inputs are information guidelines concerning foreign policy, which IOP uses as the basis for formulating programs and committing agency resources. "Fast" information guidance reflects the department's public posture on daily developments within the international political system—for example, on a Common Market tariff arrangement—as well as how the department believes its position on such developments should be presented abroad. IOP relays the day-to-day "fast guidance" to its two "fast media" elements, the Voice of America and the Press and Publications Service, along with IOP's instructions on how the news should be "played" to foreign audiences—within the department's guidelines—in the radio broadcasts and the nightly wireless file. Without the information on foreign policy and guidance about its use to achieve foreign policy objectives, the United States Information Agency would have no role to play; hence the importance of IOP among the agency's hierarchies.

IOP also receives longer-term thematic guidance from the Department of State, the Agency for International Development, and the Department of Defense, as well as from other bureaucratic subsystems such as the departments of Labor and Commerce for which USIA increasingly plays an information-servicing role. IOP also plans the allocation of agency resources to information programs on the basis of the guidance it has received.

The Office of Policy and Plans is also agency spokesman to the bureaucracies of other foreign policy subsystems. The agency's image within the foreign policy system is shaped by IOP, and the dimension of the agency's foreign policy role depends to a significant extent upon the degree of usefulness or legitimacy accorded to the agency as a result of IOP interactions with other bureaucracies. Only IOP is headed by a deputy director and only IOP addresses itself to worldwide information policy questions.

Over 300 of the approximately 3000 Washington-based employees of USIA are attached to the Office of Administration and Management (IOA). The most important power resource of this hierarchy is preparation of the agency budget in which its priorities are stated in financial terms. In bureaucracies budget officials perform a critical role in their attempt to gauge what amount of funds will appear reasonable to financial decision-makers in the national political system. Beginning with the appropriation for the preceding year, an agency's budget officials calculate within as broad an interpretation of OMB guidelines as feasible what increase in appropriation might be favorably considered by financial decision-makers, given their perceptions of the degree of success of the agency's operations during the preceding year.[21] The crucial nature of judgments made within the Office of Administration and Management provide IOA an influence base second only to the Office of Policy and Plans in USIA's actual power hierarchy.

Since USIA is primarily a subsystem for dissemination of propaganda, its media elements are central to performance of the agency's role. Each of the media elements is concerned with tangible objects—the regional service centers, radio relay stations, books, films, tapes, television and movie equipment, and exhibit materials.

USIA's media facilities are "built-in" to the subsystem. They cannot be utilized one year and abandoned the next, as ideas may be. Moreover, as stressed earlier, the Voice of America is the chief legitimizing agent of USIA, one which is recognized throughout the national political system and about which consensus has been broadest. The USIA media hierarchies, therefore, are essential to USIA structure and are significant power bases within the agency, ranking next in influence to the Office of Administration and Management.

The decline in the coordinating role of USIA's area or regional offices alluded to earlier has seriously reduced their influence within the agency and their interactions with the Department of State. Each assistant area director's office includes a deputy assistant director, a policy officer, a program coordinator, and several "country offices" which USIA formally considers counterparts of the Department of State's regional assistant secretaries and their staffs of country directors and specialists.* Area offices, however, must conform to decisions of the Office of Policy and Plans and are unable, except

---

* Organization of any of the six area offices illustrates Parkinson's law that work expands in proportion to available personnel. Since USIA is obligated to assign foreign service personnel to Washington positions in normal rotation from field posts, area office staffs tend to contract or expand depending upon the number of employees in the "pipeline." The volume of work has little relation to the number of employees assigned. For example, in 1974 the Office of the Assistant Director for North Africa, Near East, and South Asia, included the following officers: assistant director; deputy assistant director, South Asia; deputy assistant director, North Africa and Near East; policy officer; program coordinator; program support officer; assistant program support officer; regional Arabic program adviser; and four desk officers to handle the "affairs" of specific countries in the area.

minimally, to influence operations of the media elements, which are controlled by the executive committee and by IOP.

Thus restricted, area offices serve principally as resource facilities for decision-makers in other agency hierarchies, as transmission belts for messages to and from USIS field posts at overseas missions, and to some degree as contact points with the Department of State's regional offices, and with the Bureau of Educational and Cultural Affairs in regard to exchange-of-persons programs. The rank-order of area offices in the USIA power structure is distinctly below that of the media elements.

Although the offices of Research, Personnel and Training, Security, Public Information, and Equal Employment are each headed by an assistant director, none has major influence on agency decisions. The Office of Research was relieved of a number of its roles in October 1973, although it continues to provide feedback to the agency by conducting foreign public opinion surveys. Resource analysis and evaluation were transferred to Administration and Management, while media reaction and inspection and audit were transferred to Policy and Plans.

The Office of Personnel and Training was instrumental in passage of Public Law 90-494 in 1968, which provided career status for Foreign Service Information Officers of the agency, but the office does not make major personnel decisions and its training programs are sharply curtailed because of the small number of new officers recruited annually.

During the period 1950-54 Senator Joseph R. McCarthy (R.-Wis.) mercilessly exploited widely held anticommunist views in the United States when he repeatedly alleged that the Department of State was a haven for communists and homosexuals, especially among its information and cultural employees. Despite McCarthy's repudiation and his censure by the Senate in 1954, the new USIA's Office of Security inherited the powerful political resource of absolute determination as to whether individual USIA employees were "security risks." Its power persisted into the decade of the 1960s, sustained by frequent congressional innuendos about the character of the agency's personnel. The power of the Office of Security waned, however, first with the decline of cold-war ideology and subsequently in consequence of changing sexual mores in the nation. Thus, although a "full field investigation" of every employee by the Office of Security is still a major political resource of that element, it is not the formidable one of previous years and the influence of the Office of Security has declined sharply.

The Office of Public Information performs a standard service required of all bureaucracies—answering questions within the United States about the agency. The Office of Equal Employment Opportunity, which dates only from 1973, enforces the government's affirmative-action program for hiring women and racial minorities. The internal power resources of the latter two offices are negligible.

Decision-making

The *actual* authority structure within a political subsystem, as distinguished from the *formal* authority structure, evolves over a period of time. USIA's more than two decades of autonomy have produced a structure in which authority is concentrated at the highest levels so that its decision-makers can exert the greatest degree of direction over all elements of the agency. In their perception, USIA must be capable of rapid adjustment to the dynamics of bureaucratic politics to assure itself of a continuing role in the foreign policy system. Highly centralized decision-making is the key to responsive adaptation within USIA. In the main, USIA decision-making has been concerned with assuring the agency's survival.

Decision-making is principally confined, on a descending scale, to the director, the executive committee, the offices of Policy and Plans and Administration and Management, the media elements, and the area offices. USIA's autonomy and the fact that its output is exclusively for foreign consumption have the effect of insulating it from some of the pressures experienced by other executive departments and agencies. Since relatively few external constraints operate against USIA decision-makers, they are freer to develop the patterns of authority within the agency which they consider appropriate. Nor are they subject to constraints on their authority from internal sources to the same degree as decision-makers in the Department of State. Few among State Department personnel doubt its capability for survival; but many USIA employees question the survivability of the agency and they tend to accept centralized authority and to avoid dissent if that will insure their continued employment.

Decision-makers in USIA are as likely to be political appointees as career Civil Service or Foreign Service employees. George Allen, former U.S. ambassador to several capitals, was the only career Foreign Service Officer among the eight directors in USIA's history. Career Foreign Service Information Officers are more likely to be found among the assistant directors of area offices than of other agency elements.

Decisions tend to reflect the partisan political interests of the key USIA actors. Decision-making is also affected by the style and world view of the director and his principal subordinates, who tend to emulate him. Director Frank Shakespeare, for example, was preoccupied with anticommunism and an aggressive nationalism. After his appointment in early 1969, his views found expression throughout the agency in numerous ways. The newly appointed director of Voice of America was quoted as saying he would undertake a "crusade" to "awaken the world to the blessings of the free enterprise system."[22] At one of the director's staff meetings it was announced that, due to difficulties in transmitting the VOA signal into Soviet Europe, the agency had decided to transmit VOA over a radio frequency assigned to a Soviet-bloc country, a deliberate violation of international convention.

The strong anticommunist thrust which Shakespeare revived in agency meetings during 1969 persisted in subsequent years. In 1970 Shakespeare "instructed VOA to assail Soviet 'deception' in its radio commentaries," and in the summer of 1971 he authorized his staff to produce heavily anticommunist motion pictures.[23] One which was never released depicted the Chinese Communist take-over in Tibet, and another, on the 1968 Soviet invasion of Czechoslovakia, won an Academy Award. In 1971 the *Washington Post* reported Shakespeare's decision to staff USIA's "key posts with officials who have served in Communist capitals in an effort to improve its ability to compete with Communist ideology." [24] All this occurred in the years of the Nixon administration's growing détente with Russia and China.

James Keogh, who became director in 1973, has demonstrated an entirely different style and viewpoint, reflecting more accurately American foreign policy consensus. When USSR General Secretary Brezhnev met with President Nixon at a summit conference in June 1973, VOA announced it would broadcast live the address he would be giving to the American people. Jamming of the VOA signal by the Soviets was interrupted during the address. In September of the same year Moscow stopped VOA jamming; VOA responded with more music and fewer news programs to the Soviet Union and subsequently stopped using the disputed radio frequency. Keogh has emphasized to the Senate Foreign Relations Comittee that the agency has embarked upon "new directions" which "affect the substance as well as the tone and style of USIA activities."[25]

Withal, a portion of the style of USIA directors is prescribed for them and a predictable pattern has emerged. First they communicate to other foreign policy subsystems their individual conception of the agency's "mission." Next they express intentions of becoming "involved" in the content of agency programs and in becoming acquainted with agency elements and operations. The latter requires travel to the agency's USIS posts overseas.

After these predictable first steps, USIA directors tend to be drawn to the task of assuring USIA's survival as a subsystem in a political environment that is thoroughly unpredictable. The dynamics of the larger foreign policy system affect the role of the USIA, and its directors search for new ways to organize and deploy the agency's resources to maintain and improve its image with the

White House, Congress, other bureaucracies, interest groups, and its targets in the international system.

As Director George Allen (1957-60) once remarked, USIA is not designed to formulate foreign policy but rather to explain it to others. Even within this framework USIA is subject to the information policy guidelines of the Department of State. Viewed in these terms—which generally have been acknowledged by the agency—the scope of USIA decision-making is limited to formulation and execution of information policy that reflects the emphases, omissions, interpretations, or responses desired by the Department of State.

During the Eisenhower years and for some time thereafter the director of USIA enjoyed a permanent invitation to attend meetings of the National Security Council. USIA directors such as George Allen, Edward Murrow, and Carl Rowan, distinguished personalities in their own right, could gain ready access to the White House. Leonard Marks had been President Johnson's private attorney and as such had access to the president. Rowan and Marks regularly accompanied President Johnson on international trips. These directors presumably made some inputs into at least the informational aspects of the foreign policy process. But recent USIA directors have fared less well. They no longer travel with the president nor attend NSC meetings and usually they are briefed by the secretary of state and his staff in the same manner as the seventh-floor elements in the Department of State.

In 1973 the United States Advisory Commission on Information, acutely aware of these limitations, urged certain reforms. The United States Information Agency's expertise and resources, the commission said, "should be communicated by its Director and his associates at the highest levels of government—the President, the Secretary of State and the President's Assistant for National Security Affairs. USIA should be in on the takeoffs as well as the landings in foreign policy."[26]

The formidable array of constraints on USIA influence in the foreign policy system tends to force agency actors to turn inward, concentrating on issues whose outcomes they can control. Agency decision-makers can with finality decide what kinds of informational and cultural programs they wish to develop abroad. They can allocate to such programs whatever mix of financial and physical resources they desire. They can apportion funds internally within guidelines approved by Congress, and they have nearly complete control over recruitment, training, assignment, retention, and promotion of USIA Foreign Service and Civil Service personnel.

A large proportion of agency decision-making concerns interactions with OMB and Congress about the annual appropriation: What level of appropriation should be requested? What is the most "sellable" rationale for justifying the request to OMB and subsequently to Congress? What should be the agency's fall-back appropriation request if resistance is encountered? What would be the consequences in terms of impact upon agency programs and personnel if the appropriations were cut back?

Agency actors make decisions about these and related questions on an almost nonstop basis since congressional action on appropriation requests increasingly lags behind the budget cycle. Often USIA is forced to operate under the confining terms of a continuing congressional resolution—an interim authorization to continue operations at a specific percentage of the previous year's appropriation—and requiring further decisions about where and how to make reductions.

FUNCTIONAL AND DYSFUNCTIONAL ASPECTS OF USIA: A SUMMARY

Robert Merton distinguishes between functions and dysfunctions in dealing with the diverse consequences of functional analysis, whether confined to a particular system or extended to interactions between a system and its external environment. "Functions are those observed consequences which make for the adaptation or adjustment of the system; and dysfunctions, those observed consequences which lessen the adaptation or adjustment of the system."[27] According to this approach, a particular system may produce multiple consequences and a net balance of an aggregate of consequences.

Aspects of the USIA subsystem which contribute to functionality are several. The agency's autonomy permits it to adapt internally to meet changing demands with minimum interference from other bureaucracies. Its particularized role of influencing foreign audiences by informational and cultural programs mounted through media channels is practically reserved to USIA within the foreign policy system. Its role is clear; its parameters are definable. It "programs" abroad prominent individual Americans who represent various facets of American life and letters and who thus have an interest in USIA's survival. Its resources include the actual physical apparati for communication via mass means, namely, a global array of radio transmitters, printing presses, books, libraries, motion pictures, television videotapes, and exhibits. Moreover, USIA has its own Foreign Service personnel system, sanctioned by general statute, which enables it to control recruitment, retention, and assignment of its employees. All of these resources can be marshaled and used to achieve outcomes which contribute to system maintenance.

Reflecting Merton's model, certain aspects of structure and process which characterize USIA are dysfunctional to maintenance of the USIA subsystem. First, the agency is charged with the dual informational and cultural role, consequently dividing its resources into compartments which tend to be incompatible and which require recruitment of specialists in both fields instead of the interchangeable generalists who comprise the Department of State's Foreign Service. Moreover, while the agency administers abroad the principal component of cultural programs—the exchange of persons between the United States and other countries—it cannot control recruitment of these individuals, nor does it possess funding authority regarding them. As a consequence, aside from its investment in libraries, USIA has tended to focus upon information programs, facilities, and personnel.

Second, the heavy investment in media facilities and media-oriented personnel during its more than two decades of history has gradually adversely affected the capacity of USIA to adapt. The maintenance of physical properties requires a continually larger portion of the shrinking USIA budget; as a result, programs suffer. Moreover, use and maintenance of media facilities can not be discontinued for varying periods of time and then revived when budget allocations are more favorable as can people-oriented programs.

Third, the electronic revolution of the last twenty years means that facilities developed by USIA in the mid-1950s are becoming obsolete. Long-distance shortwave radio transmission must compete with national government short- and medium-wave transmission. Moreover, space satellites may take the place of relay stations in the near future. Television is replacing radio as a communication medium in many parts of the world and in the future whichever nations control the satellites may be able to control national television programming. Another media technique, the wireless file, has been superseded as a news service by national wire services. The wireless file's value within missions is marginal because it often merely duplicates U.S. policy statements transmitted to missions over Department of State communication facilities.

Fourth, USIA in Washington, with its constantly contracting *actual* budget, is too small a bureaucracy to absorb the numbers of personnel who must be rotated regularly from field posts. These officers tend to be specialists who must be fitted into the USIA hierarchies. Washington-based personnel therefore often lack meaningful work tasks, and the result is a decline in employee morale.

Finally, a serious dysfunction results from the basic structure within which the agency attempts to carry out its informational role. John Henderson inadvertently underlines a serious weakness when he comments that "the deputy chief of the IOP guidance staff is present at the spokesman's meeting, which enables him to know shortly in advance what the State Department will be saying or refusing to say on current issues."[28] In other words, USIA ascertains the Department of State's position only minutes before it is provided to the world commercial press at the department's daily noon press briefing. While procedures and timing have been somewhat modified since Henderson described the process in 1969, still remaining is the basic problem inherent in what amounts to an actual division of the information role between State and USIA. The cumbersome, lengthy procedure of briefing relegates USIA to a position only slightly more favorable than that of commercial newsmen. The agency has very little impact upon even the determination of *information policy*.

CHAPTER 7

United States Information Service: Overseas Subsystem of USIA

In 1961 the press in the United Arab Republic "officially" blamed the United States for the abduction and murder of Patrice Lumumba, an African nationalist leader. Statements by President John Kennedy, U.S. Ambassador to the United Nations Adlai Stevenson, and Secretary-General of the United Nations Dag Hammarskjöld denying U.S. complicity were handed to Cairo editors by the United States Information Service (USIS) there. The government-controlled press declined to print them. Faced with an urgent public relations problem, USIS Cairo translated the statements into Arabic and printed them as leaflets on a USIS-owned press, purposely omitting USIS attribution and bypassing the government censors to whom press materials normally were submitted. Stacks of the leaflets were deposited at entrances to Cairo theaters and public buildings. Citing the failure of USIS to identify its material and to clear it with the censors, the U.A.R. government confiscated the leaflets. Confiscation was followed by wide exposure of the USIS activity in all the national papers, including printing the full text of the controversial leaflet! USIS thereby achieved its goal of communicating the American position to the Egyptian public, albeit in this case in an unorthodox fashion.

This incident, although atypical, reflects the energetic resourcefulness which has marked agency operations over the years.

ORGANIZATION AND SCOPE
OF THE USIS SUBSYSTEM

The United States Information Service is the overseas arm of the United States Information Agency. As relations with various countries fluctuate from year to year, depending on the political climate, these changes are reflected in the number of countries where USIS operates from year to year. In 1974, USIA information and cultural programs were carried out in 109 countries. Establishment of diplomatic relations between the United States and new nations usually includes an agreement for the initiation of information and cultural programs. Resumption of diplomatic relations between the United States and another nation—such as Egypt in 1974—normally includes the revival of USIS programs. The information and cultural role is even included in the U.S. approach to countries where trade and diplomatic relationships are evolving. For example, in its fiscal year 1975 budget, USIA requested $641,000 and fifteen positions "to establish a selective information and cultural operation in East Germany" and $64,000 for "additional informational and cultural program support for the United States Liaison Office in Peking."[1]

Major USIS posts are located in host country capitals and are integral elements of the diplomatic missions to those countries. Branch USIS posts are also maintained in a number of the countries. USIS facilities abroad in 1973 included 130 information centers and libraries and 109 bi-national centers for English teaching. Some thirty USIS posts are in communist countries. In 1973 the largest USIS expenditure of funds was in Japan ($4,813,000), followed closely by expenditures in the German Federal Republic ($4,776,000), both, ironically, former enemies of the United States and major trade competitors. Approximately 1000 American Foreign Service employees of the agency were serving abroad in 1973. The largest contingent was in Brazil, with forty-two authorized American positions. India was second with thirty-nine positions; the Republic of Vietnam third with thirty-two.

Organization

A USIS post is an integral element of the U.S. diplomatic mission in a host country. It is headed by a public affairs officer (PAO), who as chief of his section within the embassy has a three-part role. He serves as operational chief of the USIS post and its branch posts, as well as being public affairs adviser to the American ambassador and a member of the mission country team. The standard organizational structure varies in a few cases, such as at the United States mission to the United Nations in New York and the United States mission in Geneva, Switzerland, where a USIS adviser for public affairs is attached to the mission. Advisers are also attached to the headquarters of the United States commander-in-chief, Pacific (CINCPAC), to SEATO, and to NATO.

Every standard USIS post comprises two sections, cultural and informational, both supervised by the public affairs officer. The two sections are headed, respectively, by a cultural affairs officer (CAO) and an information officer (IO). Reporting to these officers, and depending upon the size of the post, are a varying number of subordinates with specific roles. Thus, reporting to the information officer might be a press officer, a publications officer, an exhibits officer, a motion picture-television officer, and occasionally, an additional information officer assigned a particular role, such as publicizing AID activities in the host country. The CAO may supervise an assistant cultural affairs officer, an exchanges officer, a librarian and/or an information center director.

Although the informational-cultural components are standard at USIS posts, their *relative size* reflects the agency's judgment as to the kinds of programs appropriate to the host country. Another determining factor, not infrequently, is the character of the U.S. relationship with the host country. The cultural rather than the informational component is often more acceptable to countries not allied with the United States. In communist countries where American propaganda is not welcomed, the principal, indeed often the sole, USIS representative may be a cultural attaché or counselor for cultural affairs. With initiation or resumption of diplomatic relations between the United States and another country, the cultural component of the USIS program is usually the first to be accepted by the host country.

Large posts may also include a deputy public affairs officer, an executive officer, often a research officer who mounts public opinion surveys throughout the countries of the region, and perhaps other specialists who perform regional duties for the press or broadcasting services in Washington. The regional officers are under the administrative supervision of the PAO. VOA relay stations and the regional service centers (printing establishments) of the press service are supervised by their own managers or directors who report directly to Washington, but accede to the PAO in intramission matters.

National, or so-called "local," staffs at USIS posts consist of employees who are nationals of the host country.* In 1973 they ranged in number from one each in Barbados, Rwanda, and Swaziland to 494 in India.

In most larger countries the principal USIS office in the capital is supple-

* National employees of U.S. missions are eligible, upon completion of fifteen years of continuous service, to emigrate to the United States under eased conditions. USIS is often the largest employer of host-country personnel in a mission, a significant number of whom take advantage of this provision.

TABLE X   UNITED STATES INFORMATION SERVICE POST

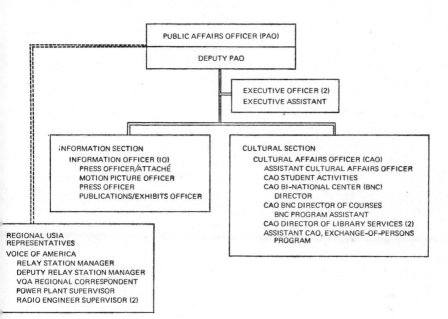

(BANGKOK, THAILAND)
February 1974

PUBLIC AFFAIRS OFFICER (PAO)

DEPUTY PAO

EXECUTIVE OFFICER (2)
EXECUTIVE ASSISTANT

INFORMATION SECTION
   INFORMATION OFFICER (IO)
      PRESS OFFICER/ATTACHÉ
      MOTION PICTURE OFFICER
      PRESS OFFICER
      PUBLICATIONS/EXHIBITS OFFICER

CULTURAL SECTION
   CULTURAL AFFAIRS OFFICER (CAO)
      ASSISTANT CULTURAL AFFAIRS OFFICER
      CAO STUDENT ACTIVITIES
      CAO BI-NATIONAL CENTER (BNC)
         DIRECTOR
      CAO BNC DIRECTOR OF COURSES
         BNC PROGRAM ASSISTANT
      CAO DIRECTOR OF LIBRARY SERVICES (2)
      ASSISTANT CAO, EXCHANGE-OF-PERSONS
         PROGRAM

REGIONAL USIA
REPRESENTATIVES
VOICE OF AMERICA
   RELAY STATION MANAGER
   DEPUTY RELAY STATION MANAGER
   VOA REGIONAL CORRESPONDENT
   POWER PLANT SUPERVISOR
   RADIO ENGINEER SUPERVISOR (2)

mented by branch offices, each headed by a branch public affairs officer (BPAO). In Thailand in 1971, for example, there were nine American-staffed branch offices in addition to an elaborate headquarters in Bangkok. The BPAO is assisted by a small national staff. Branch offices are often, but not necessarily, located in the same city as, and attached to, an American consulate or consulate general.

USIS posts operate libraries or information centers. USIS libraries have long been visible symbols of the United States which enjoy great popularity in many host countries because they have filled perceived needs. Frequently, especially in developing countries, the USIS library is the best reference source on the United States—and, on occasion the best library—in the country. Each library contains a predetermined, balanced book collection to reflect principal aspects of American civilization, a standard reference collection, and a selected variety of American newspapers and periodicals.

An information center is a multipurpose facility having as its core a general library and reference collection, an exhibit and lecture area and often a film theater. English language instruction may be conducted at either the information center or a bi-national center. Information centers, usually staffed by Americans, are often given highly patriotic names such as the "Thomas Jefferson Library" or the "Benjamin Franklin Library." A certain amount of propaganda mileage is obtained by employing themes reflecting favorable aspects of American life. A new theme for information centers stresses American technological prowess. The Tokyo information center, for example, bears the name "Infomat" and is replete with a computerized data bank, psychedelic color schemes, and oversized graphics. Since they attract more than 10.1 million visitors annually, the functionality of libraries and information centers is clear.

Bi-national centers, organized primarily to teach the English language, are autonomous entities headed by a bi-national board of directors and usually managed by an American. The bilingual teachers are usually nationals of the host country and are paid from funds generated by tuition fees. USIA makes an annual grant to each center. In addition to providing English language instruction, bi-national centers promote, and endeavor to synthesize, the cultural values of the United States and the host country. In Germany the binational center is called *Amerika Haus*. The center in Saigon is known as the Vietnamese-American-Association, and in recent years some 10,000 persons annually have received instruction there in English.

Scope of USIS Role

At its overseas USIS posts the primary objective of the United States Information Agency is to help achieve specific U.S. policy goals in host countries by mounting effective information and cultural programs. A second major objective is to employ such programs to help achieve acceptance, or at least understanding, of worldwide U.S. policy.

Thematic goals are set forth in the country plan proposal (CPP), which is formulated by the public affairs officer and his staff. Before the CPP is prepared, each USIS country post submits to the agency an annual assessment report which evaluates the degree of success achieved by earlier programs in fulfilling goals in the host country so that attainable goals may be identified.

The rationale for these goals is derived from a national policy paper for each country which is a product of the Department of State, the U.S. intelligence community, the Department of Defense, and, to a lesser degree, other agencies such as the Agency for International Development. The policy paper states short- and long-term policy objectives and estimates the likelihood of their realization, given the impact of observable social, political, and economic variables. This basic operational document governing all U.S. governmental activity in a country is revised periodically.

After acceptance and often modification of the country plan proposal by the agency in Washington, the PAO links programs to the thematic goals of the approved country plan within the parameters of resources allocated to the post.

An examination of the country plan for the Republic of the Philippines, one of the larger USIS posts, with two branches outside of Manila, affords insights into the scope of the USIS role. Moreover, the author served as counselor for public affairs (PAO) at this post from 1962 through 1965. It is also the location of one of the three USIA regional service centers and one of the largest Voice of America relay stations in the world.

Model: Philippines Although the USIS country plan for the Philippines underwent minor change from year to year during the decade of the 1960s, it reflected a continuing basic framework of perceived goals. The obstacles to those goals, the factors favoring their realization, and the mix and volume of resources available for pursuing them also remained relatively constant. The country plan framework of the 1960s persisted, in fact, until internal political conflict resulted in the proclamation of martial law by Philippine President Marcos in 1972, forcing major reevaluation of goals and techniques for attaining them.

In the mid-1960s the USIS country plan for the Philippines identified four major goals: (1) to encourage socioeconomic reform on the part of the government of the Philippines and the Filipino people in general; (2) to depict the United States as a stable and dependable partner which would meet its responsibilities to that country; (3) to promote continued close cooperation between the Philippines and the United States; and (4) to engender continued usage of the English language in the Philippines. The rationale for each of these goals was derived from the national policy paper for the Philippines.

Once the goals have been clearly defined, the USIS field post is expected to analyze in a separate section of the country plan the hurdles which the PAO perceives need to be overcome, as well as any favorable factors which might be exploited. In the Philippines the unfavorable factors were the consequences of economic frustration and the rising tide of nationalism.

By the mid-1960s the Philippines—the former "showcase of American democracy" in Southeast Asia—was experiencing serious tensions adversely affecting American interests there. As a consequence of the highest birthrate in Southeast Asia, the median age of Filipinos had fallen to seventeen years. Although the country had developed light industry, the economy was incapable of absorbing enough young Filipino job seekers to prevent widespread frustration. Frustration led to attacks against the extremely complex United States foreign economic policy posture in the Philippines, which was viewed as partially responsible for the country's failure to achieve the degree of economic progress observable in such countries as Korea, the Republic of China, and Malaysia. At stake was the future of American investments valued at over one billion dollars.

Meanwhile, Philippine nationalism, which began to approach a virulent stage in the mid-sixties, called for termination of the special investment and trade advantages the United States enjoyed by reason of treaty arrangements. It called for a greater Filipino voice in the operation of the U.S. air and naval bases located there, particularly in jurisdictional matters and personnel policy. In an extreme form it advocated complete elimination of American bases and adoption by the Philippine government of a neutralist foreign policy. Nationalism also took the form of a search for Filipino identity, including establishing a national language to replace English.*

Additional impediments to achieving country plan goals included discontent about unfavorable trade balances and the flight of capital, both of which were blamed for various reasons on the United States.

On the favorable side, many Filipinos, including most of those still in positions of political power, had fought beside the Americans against numerically superior Japanese invaders during World War II and had engaged in guerrilla activities during the Japanese occupation. Goodwill toward Americans was particularly evident in the rural areas, where most of the

---

* The Philippine archipelago has three principal and eight regional native languages used by about eighty percent of the people. Pilipino, the new national language, is a modified Tagalog, which is the language of the Manila area.

education had been in the hands of American teachers. There was even sentiment in some quarters—which USIS did *not* exploit—to make the Philippines
the fifty-first state!

Other factors to be exploited were the favorable modernizing impact of
American business; the defense umbrella supplied by the United States, which
vastly reduced Philippine defense costs; the revenues accruing to the Philippine government and the input into the economy from U.S. military installations; and the continuing prevalence of the English language throughout the
archipelago.

After a thorough analysis of all factors, the final sections of the country
plan dealt with how USIS resources would be employed in specific programs
to achieve goals previously identified. All USIS posts possess basic informational and cultural resources, such as an exchange-of-persons program, press
and publication facilities, radio, motion picture, and television equipment,
libraries of films and TV clips, an exhibits department and a USIS library or
information center and/or bi-national center. Even more importantly, personal contacts in government, labor, education, business, the arts, and the
military can be cultivated by USIS personnel to achieve goals by influencing
decision-makers.

In the Philippines until 1972 the extraordinary number and variety of
media targets for USIS products favored goal realization. In Manila alone in
the 1960s there were seven television channels, thirty to thirty-five radio
stations, six English-language daily newspapers, five Chinese dailies, three
Tagalog dailies, two Spanish dailies, and several nationally circulated weekly
picture-news magazines. The abundance of outlets greatly simplified successful "placement" of USIS materials. For example, USIS Manila achieved
greater placement of the nightly USIA wireless file than any other Asian post.

The themes used by USIS Manila to achieve country plan goals were broad
and the techniques various. One theme was to promote the desirability of
socioeconomic reforms. The presentation included a depiction of the good
life that such reforms would produce; the publicizing of specific examples of
Philippine government reform undertaken with or without American aid—
such as land reform; and the advertising of successful external examples of
reform, such as "Operation Bootstrap," which had transformed Puerto Rico
with American help in earlier years.

A second theme was to stress "partnership" and to erase the Filipino
perception of the "big brother - little brother" relationship of the immediate
postwar years. The theme stressed the idea that political, military, and economic relations between the two countries are undertaken on a basis of
equality, in consequence of free choice, and that the "special relationship"
which pertained as a result of post-independence commitments was mutually

advantageous. Allied with this was the theme that the United States could be relied upon to honor its commitment to the defense of the Philippines. This theme dovetailed with U.S. objectives regarding the war in Vietnam. Continued American commitment in Vietnam was depicted as proof of U.S. dependability as an ally. Techniques utilized included sending Philippine journalists to Vietnam to observe, publicizing American and Philippine binational military exercises and their joint participation in SEATO maneuvers, and emphasizing the importance to both countries of the maintenance of American bases on Philippine soil, as well as the cooperation of the government of the Philippines regarding them. Also stressed was the financial savings to the Philippine government as a result of the American defense umbrella. It was pointed out that since the United States guaranteed Philippine external defense, the country's military expenditures were relatively small. Another theme was to emphasize the contributions of American bases to the Philippine economy.

Still another major theme was to promote the value of continuing English as the *lingua franca*. Former colonial powers have learned that they can communicate more easily with—and thus influence more readily—their former colonies when a common language is the agent of communication. Put coldbloodedly, if English continues to be the language of the Philippine archipelago, development of an effective national language is impeded and the likelihood of the rise of a xenophobic nationalism is reduced. It might be added that France pursues this goal in former French Africa, as does the United Kingdom in former British colonies such as India and Pakistan.

Mission Youth Committee: A Goal-Oriented Program   Increasingly, as USIS posts have become more fully integrated within U.S. mission subsystems, USIS goals are pursued in collaboration with other mission elements. "Package programs" which make use of mission-wide facilities and personnel rather than simply of USIS resources are planned to achieve specific impact. Since they have a beginning and an end, they also lend themselves to evaluation. An examination of the mission's Youth Committee program in Manila will illustrate the broadening scope of propaganda efforts within a U.S. mission.

A mission Youth Committee was formed in Manila in 1965 to identify youth leaders in the Philippines who might be expected to become national leaders and plans were developed to influence them favorably toward the United States. The plans called for specific programs over a period of time aimed at youth groups and youth leaders, to be followed by an evaluation of which groups and individuals had been influenced to the extent that they could be considered responsive to USIS efforts.

To discover youth leaders, the committee identified groups, both organized and informal, within Philippine society, assigning a numerical factor to each group in terms of its perceived importance in the formation of opinion. Individual persons were identified within the groups in terms of their influence. An important informal or non-organized group, for example, might be the patrons of a cafe or coffee house frequented by artists and writers. Formal organizations would include all the governing hierarchies of student unions in the dozens of colleges and universities in the Manila area.

The primary working tool of the committee for carrying out the program was a "youth roster," a file of cards bearing names of target leaders with supportive biographical data and, if possible, information about their political beliefs, attitude toward the United States, behavior patterns, and an estimate of their leadership potential. A basic problem was to define "youth" and eventually the committee's files contained names of persons up to the age of forty!

As each target leader was contacted via invitation or meeting, notations giving the date, circumstances, and result of the contact were made on the individual's card. Careful count was made of the number of invitations extended to the target and his response.

The guiding principle regarding programs was to find new ways and improve old ones for bringing target groups and individuals into association with Americans and American ideas. Programs included forums, seminars, debates, home hospitality, invitations to embassy functions (especially those of a patriotic nature or which emphasized Philippine-American cooperation), offering the USIS library and information center for use by local organizations, book presentations—i.e., providing U.S. publications and books on a gift basis, and, for a selected few, invitations to visit the United States on one of several short-term visitor or educational grants available through USIS—for example, a .Fulbright-Hays grant for study at an American university, an invitation to participate in the *New York Herald Tribune* Youth Forum, or a 4-H Club visit. Youth groups were encouraged to borrow USIS films. Motion-picture projectors were offered on long-term loan and USIS projectionists were made available to screen films at group meetings.

Since USIS in Manila maintained a small radio production unit and studio, it was possible to develop "talk programs" featuring local youth leaders. These were taped and made available to dozens of local radio stations. The press section of USIS produced youth-oriented pamphlets for selective distribution among groups and provided Washington-produced materials concerning young people.

The multifaceted youth program was slow to develop. The Youth Committee had difficulty initially in categorizing names on the youth roster and in assigning priorities to categories and to individuals within them. The problem was eventually resolved by the fact that the names of the same target individuals appeared again and again on the lists supplied by younger officers throughout the mission who had been invited to submit suggestions.

Acting in response to the Youth Committee's name priorities, USIS altered its mailing lists to insure that its printed materials, invitations, and announcements about the availability of facilities would reach the targets. At the same time other mission elements—especially AID, the political section, and the Joint United States Military Advisory Group (JUSMAG)—cooperated by supplying speakers and resource persons for discussion groups organized by USIS and by searching for new ways to expand contacts with Filipino organizations and individuals.

Response was initially gratifying and the range of contacts throughout the mission with younger Filipinos was significantly expanded. Eventually, however, a disproportion began to develop between the degree of mission effort expended and the degree of response achieved from target individuals. Target individuals received invitations and materials to a point of saturation and eventually tended to discount them. In the short run, nevertheless, the program was successful in that a number of potential young leaders in the Filipino national community were exposed to American rationales about why socioeconomic reform is essential to political development and modernization, to illustrations of what has been accomplished elsewhere, and to the desirability of continuing cooperation with the Americans in economic, political, and national security matters to help achieve perceived goals.

Unfortunately, however, events overtook the program. Meaningful socioeconomic reform was not achieved. The nation slid further into economic morass and political consensus dissolved. In 1971 President Marcos suspended the writ of habeas corpus. On September 21, 1972, he placed the Philippines under martial law "to save the Republic and form a new society."[2] Hundreds of "subversives" were arrested, including the leader and the secretary-general of the opposition Liberal party.

But these negative national results do not necessarily invalidate the concept of the youth program. On the contrary, its initiation demonstrated a perception of anticipated trends in the Philippines, trends which antedated the mission's program and which had prompted formation of the mission-USIS goals in the first place. Over the longer run, the ideas and values communicated to Filipinos by the youth program may influence Filipino politics of the future. Indonesia, which in some relevant respects is similar to the Philippines, survived a like era of national crisis from 1959 to 1965. Indonesia's economic reform efforts of the 1970s are directly linked to the ideas of young Indonesian economists (sometimes termed the "Berkeley

Mafia") who were trained in the United States and who maintained contacts with this country despite internal crisis.

USIS INTERACTION WITH THE MISSION

Although the organizational structure and scope of the USIS role are much the same at all posts, the character of the relationship built up through the years between USIS and the mission is highly important in determining how USIS will operate at a given post. If the relationship is good, USIS will usually enjoy greater mission support, including more extensive use of shared facilities such as office space, housing, automobiles, and equipment.

The key relationship is between the ambassador and the public affairs officer. The degree of legitimacy, trust, and intimacy which the ambassador accords the PAO will set the tone for relations between the various other mission staffs and the USIS staff. A PAO who is compatible with his ambassador, who has genuine public relations expertise, and who manages an effective USIS post can enhance USIS functionality, and thus power, within the mission. All mission elements are highly conscious of the quality of the American image in the host capital. A low-key USIS operation which does not aggressively compete for intramission status, an attractive and well-attended library or information center, and USIS officers who make significant community contacts evoke the respect of the mission at large, with corresponding advantages to USIS operations.

On the other hand, a PAO who is more aggressive than his ambassador, who emphasizes USIS compartmentalization vis-a-vis the remainder of the mission, or one who declines to play the game the ambassador has decided to play may find himself isolated within the mission power structure. Diminished administrative support and cooperation will inevitably result.

The intramission role of the PAO is a difficult one. Since USIS from its inception has had to struggle for legitimacy, many PAOs have attempted to impress other mission elements, have been insistent about their prerogatives, and have been inordinately conscious of their status. By its nature, the USIS effort to influence foreign audiences implies overt action toward a goal, an approach markedly different from the relatively passive, reporter-observer role of the traditional diplomat. PAOs, moreover, have been conditioned to be insistent about their prerogatives within the mission because frequently USIS offices have been relegated to the least desirable parts of chanceries or to inferior auxiliary buildings. Occasionally USIS is not provided with office space at all. On occasion posts have found they have been charged for shared administrative services which were not actually received.

Partly as a result of these problems and often for reasons of greater public access, USIA in Washington has increasingly authorized USIS posts to lease offices—sometimes at a considerable distance from the chancery.* The agency also leases housing for its personnel and has accumulated inventories of equipment such as automobiles, office equipment, and furniture, physical assets which it can control and which tend to enhance USIS status within the mission.

PAO: Status and Role-playing

USIS initiative in providing its own physical facilities at specific posts has tended to inhibit integration of the organization within the mission and to perpetuate its compartmentalization vis-à-vis the remainder of the mission. Emphasis on quasi-autonomy has also had an important bearing on the official and personal status of the PAO. In consequence of repeated urging by USIA, the PAO has been accorded steadily higher diplomatic rank by the Department of State over the two decades of the agency's life. Agreement has been reached that at large USIS posts the PAO will be a Class I or II officer and will be assigned counselor rank in the mission hierarchy. The counselor for public affairs is coequal in such cases with the administrative, political, and economic counselors, and occasionally he will outrank them. In any case the PAO at larger missions is likely to be among the half dozen or so highest-ranking mission officers.

Both he and USIA wish him to reflect the visible perquisites of office in the form of ever handsomer offices, official automobiles, and, above all, an imposing residence suitable for representational purposes. Some PAO residences, specifically in a capital such as Tokyo, are more opulent than the accommodations of anyone else on the mission staff except the ambassador. Host country nationals are understandably confused when they compare the affluent housing of the counselor for public affairs with the more modest housing of the counselor for political affairs who, in their perception, discharges a more substantive role.

Publications and exhibits, motion-picture programs, press know-how, and even libraries and information centers can command only a degree of mission-wide interest. Their perceived importance within the mission is usually less than that associated with political negotiation and reporting, economic development, trade problems, or joint national security matters. Most of these substantive categories are the province of the traditional mission

---

* In many countries the mission is not disinclined to have USIS located elsewhere. Demonstrations against the United States are normally directed against USIS offices and libraries, a compliment no doubt to their visibility in the host country environment.

elements whose legitimacy is not in question. The PAO and the USIS staff role-play in areas which are often perceived as peripheral by other mission elements. On the other hand, when the PAO proposes actions by which USIS might influence host country attitudes, or makes judgments about the impact of United States policy in the host country—both of which USIA expects him to do—he must be careful to remain within his public affairs frame of reference. Although the line between public affairs advising and making political judgments is imprecise, the frontiers are zealously guarded by ambassadors and political sections.

A further impediment to PAO role-playing is the tendency of significant numbers of chiefs of mission to consider the exchange-of-persons programs of more value than media programs in attaining United States objectives. A problem arises since (1) most PAOs have been media trained; (2) funding and decision-making concerning the exchange-of-persons programs are controlled by the Department of State; and (3) the exchange programs in the field are usually administered by junior USIS officers. The PAO is thus painfully aware that his own position depends more upon organizational prerogatives hammered out over the years in his favor than it does upon the perceived substance of his role.

However, with his personal diplomatic rank and official status firmly established, with office and residential facilities guaranteed by his agency, with a separate budget, and possessing formal directive responsibilities for the USIS post, the PAO's position and his autonomy approach those enjoyed by his mission colleagues who represent agencies such as AID or CIA. He is free to develop programs within the framework of the country plan approved by USIA, as long as such activities are not unacceptable to the ambassador. Unlike his colleagues, the counselors of political and economic affairs, who interact closely with the ambassador, the PAO role-plays at a psychological, and often at a physical, distance from the chief of mission. Operational memoranda, field reports, and even cables to Washington which exclusively concern the USIS program are normally not seen by the ambassador or the deputy chief of mission (DCM) until after they have been dispatched and carbon copies appear in the daily file of outgoing messages. Normally only when the PAO forwards a joint embassy-USIS message or cable, such as one to the Department of State concerning the exchange-of-persons programs, need he secure message clearance from the ambassador or his deputy. Even in these cases clearance is *pro forma* except for cables—possibly a reflection of the fact that in today's Department of State only cables seem to command attention.

PAO interactions with the ambassador and the DCM mainly concern three general areas. First, most ambassadors display an acute sensitivity about the image of the mission they head and of themselves as depicted in the local media. Accordingly, ambassadors are interested in the press relations of the mission and how the PAO conducts them. Second, ambassadors try to influence prominent national figures of the host country toward a favorable view of the United States. They tend, therefore, to interest themselves in the segment of the exchange-of-persons program which provides grants to such persons for visiting the United States. Finally, but with reservations because ambassadors consider themselves public affairs analysts as well as diplomats, they are interested in the PAO's assessment of local attitudes toward the United States.

In a word, ambassadors want a favorable ambassadorial and mission image, skillful utilization of exchange-of-persons programs for political ends, and a confirmation of their own analysis of host-country attitudes toward the United States. Libraries and information centers, production and distribution of USIS media materials, academic as distinguished from politically inspired exchange-of-persons programs, English teaching, and other USIS-administered programs may interest ambassadors only minimally.

The PAO's influence within the mission is frequently dependent upon his skill in developing meaningful personal contacts within the local community. His direction of information and cultural programs enables him to penetrate the local community in several guises. His information role calls for inter-action with media leaders who influence public opinion; his cultural role permits contacts with literary, educational, religious, and other community leaders. Each of these can be sources for feedback of information via the PAO to the ambassador. The range of contacts open to the PAO is broader than that which a political officer or a specialist in economic affairs can expect. A PAO can wear one hat when talking to an editor and another when talking to an educator. Both contacts can be valuable information sources.

The PAO has a mission-wide role by reason of his membership on the country team, the body which, under the ambassador's supervision, is expected to coordinate all U.S. activities in the host country. The role of the PAO on the country team varies. Some policy thrusts are more suitable to USIS exploitation than others. In a locale such as Vietnam, where psychological and paramilitary programs were major ingredients of USIS actions, the PAO has had a significant country team role. In developing countries where United States economic assistance is a major mission thrust, the PAO's input to the country team may be confined to reporting USIS efforts to publicize economic development programs of AID in pursuance of guidelines adopted by the country team.

Information Officer

Since most USIS facilities and programs are information oriented, the information officer (IO) supervises both American officers and substantial numbers of national employees. At larger posts, press officers, editors, translators, and artists prepare USIS publications, produce and distribute press releases, and maintain extensive files of the local press. Motion picture, radio and exhibits sections of the information office are headed by specialists in each of these fields. The information officer's status within the USIS post and within the mission is enhanced because of his role as supervisor of media elements, which gives him considerable control over physical properties. At larger posts these include photo-offset presses, photographic laboratories, duplicating machines, drafting and design equipment, wireless file reception facilities, and radio and television studios.

It is precisely the IO's information "empire," however, which gives rise to certain frustrations. Traditionally, USIS information officers have been individuals with fairly extensive backgrounds in press reporting, radio and television production, or general writing. Although the profile of IOs is changing as USIA grows older and as young officers who have had little outside experience rise through the ranks, the overseas staffs continue largely to be comprised of persons of some professional background. The problem is one of giving full expression to their talents. Neither the pace nor the volume of USIS press operations approaches those of most private media operations. In a sense, USIS officers possess both personal and physical capabilities to perform at levels far greater than their jobs permit. Writing a mission press release, the content of which might constitute only a minor story in a daily newspaper, becomes a major event in the day's operation. Editing film scripts, radio broadcasts, or USIS publications, none of which are deadline matters, comprise the major "work" of USIS information officers. Much of their expertise and professional judgment is unused. The problem of unused talent also characterizes the work of radio officers, publications officers, exhibits specialists, and press attachés of USIS who are supervised by the IO. Aside from performing minimal professional tasks, their roles are principally to develop and maintain contacts with host-country media actors, that is, editors, writers, motion-picture and television producers, and publishers. In USIS terms these are representational activities.

Cultural Affairs Officer

The cultural affairs officer (CAO) and assistant CAOs perform broad, diffused roles because "cultural affairs" are open ended. When the CAO is a professional person in his or her own right—recruited from the academic or artistic world as some have been—the officer can usually anticipate wide acceptance among host country intellectual groups. An outgoing personality and established professional status contribute heavily to success. While personal qualifications and diplomatic rank (CAOs are cultural attachés and occasionally even counselors of embassy) will assure some response from universities and cultural groups, frequently the CAO finds that ability to influence organizations and, more importantly, key individuals within them, entails doing something personally meaningful for them. Usually this comes down to facilitating a visit to the United States. In most developing countries a visit to the States for study or observation is the consuming interest of the intelligentsia. The CAO's resources to provide it are limited. Even though the CAO administers the exchange-of-persons program, the grants are normally awarded by a committee within the mission, and he must compete with other mission officers, including the ambassador, for the few grants the embassy has at its disposal annually.

A major difference between the activities of the CAO and the IO is that the former is more concerned with personal contact, the latter with contact via the printed word or media image. Of the two basic divisions, the CAO over the long run may be expected to be more closely attuned to the minds and interests of more *kinds* of national leaders. Moreover, the cultural component is usually more acceptable to host-country leaders. As Director Shakespeare reported on his return from an orientation trip in 1969, in Africa educational and cultural exchange activities comprise the only elements of USIS programs which *both* the host-countries and the USIS staffs wished to expand.

USIS IMPACT IN HOST COUNTRIES

USIA's annual appropriation of some $240 million enables the agency to mount sophisticated information and cultural programs abroad which are designed to influence foreign audiences toward acceptance of American policy and culture.* As USIA readily admits, meaningful feedback to the foreign policy system on the impact of USIS programs in host countries is difficult to measure. Favorable changes in foreign attitudes toward the United States may or may not have been influenced by USIS programs. Experience and evidence suggest, however, the relevance of several hypotheses concerning the impact of USIS programs on host countries.

---

* The authorized appropriation for fiscal year 1975 was $239.5 million, signed into law by President Gerald Ford on October 28, 1974.

Hypothesis I The impact of USIS on host country audiences is lessened because informational and cultural programs are combined in one agency, rather than managed separately as is the case with other nations.

Host country actors are often confused by the dual role-playing. Egyptians, for example, are perplexed when they learn that the counselor for public affairs is the focal point for contacts for *both* the Ministry of National Culture and the Ministry of Information. In many nations, especially developing ones such as Egypt, strong nationalism dictates institutionalization of the cultural heritage, a role habitually conferred upon a bureau or department staffed by national poets, musicians, artists, literary figures, or educators. They and their governments tend to distinguish culture from politics and perceive the former as far removed from the overt propaganda role associated with ministries of information. Informational programs are equated with short-term "hard-sell" propaganda; cultural programs are perceived as long-term in their influence, or "soft-sell." The difficulty is compounded because often nations utilize their information personnel in other countries as intelligence agents.

Evidence suggests that when the high-key informational role is combined with the low-key cultural one, consequences can be dysfunctional for both. Time after time USIS *libraries* have been attacked by rioters, sometimes with host-country governmental approval, in retaliation against unpopular American policies. Purely cultural facilities of other nations, such as the Alliance Française, have seldom been targets of vengeance, nor, normally, have the bi-national centers which are supported by USIS but which are not an integral part of it.

Hypothesis II USIS programming is more likely to be successful when it emphasizes positive rather than negative themes.

The anticommunist approach mounted during the first half of the 1950s did little to persuade third-world countries to eschew neutralism or to turn away from communist blandishments. The more positive themes of the latter half of the decade and the 1960s—such as "people's capitalism," emphasis on American assistance, and U.S. recognition of third-world aspirations and values—were certainly more acceptable to host country sensibilities. USIS media products which featured space exploration, scientific development, agriculture and environmental progress found wide acceptance, even in the communist world. The Voice of America's "Jazz USA" programs prompted heavy listener response from Soviet-dominated countries during the coldest years of the cold war.

In defense of USIA, it should be recalled that the negative cold war propaganda of the 1950s reflected the facts of international life as perceived by the

American foreign policy system. The positive propaganda of the early 1960s, which stressed U.S. cooperation with the "free" and "third" worlds, reflected perceived changes in the international system. The war in Vietnam and consequent American intervention failed to produce a fundamental reversal. Even in Vietnam USIS emphasized positive themes, i.e., the value of free choice, community development, massive English teaching through the Vietnamese-American cultural center, national modernization, and an "open arms" program to welcome defectors from the Viet Cong. Although the government of South Vietnam depended heavily on an anticommunist ideology, the USIS propaganda effort was positive, supporting the legitimacy of the government rather than stressing anticommunism.

When Director Frank Shakespeare (1969-72) revived cold war themes in USIS programs, USIS promptly lost ground. Shakespeare found "communists all along the Nile," he insisted that important USIS posts should be headed only by agency officers who had already served in communist countries, and he urged production of heavily anticommunist media materials. Although the Shakespearean tragedy was, happily, a short-lived aberration, USIA may have been permanently damaged in the United States foreign policy system. In June 1974 the American Foreign Service Association called for "proposals to significantly change the government's information and cultural activities." AFSA said the agency had been weakened "by an emphasis on tactical expedience in response to cold war and domestic political concerns as opposed to longer-range considerations, and by the need to be responsive to policies which were formed without consideration of public diplomacy implications in judging policy options."[3]

Hypothesis III Cultural programs are more effective than informational programs.

The exchange-of-persons programs which USIS (and in some countries AID) administers abroad are the core of the cultural programs. Foreign grantees who come to the United States under the programs for study or observation, and American grantees who go abroad to study or to present aspects of American life and letters, are genuinely acceptable. The greatest public successes of USIS have occurred with the presentation to foreign audiences of outstanding artists, athletes, public figures, and scholars. A Martha Graham or an Earl Warren can influence audiences directly and immediately. The impact of persons of this caliber is evident from the fact that USIS posts in every region of the world are requested repeatedly to assure their return.

Foreign professors, researchers, students, and rising political figures who visit the United States under the auspices of the exchange-of-persons programs frequently achieve national importance after returning to their native lands. (At one point during the decade of the 1960s a majority of the French cabinet had visited the United States under such programs.) Experiences of foreign grantees in the United States generally influence them favorably toward this nation, as suggested by the fact that numerous governmental leaders of nations most friendly to this country have been educated here.

Cultural programs, moreover, are easier for USIS posts to "sell." Few nations discourage attendance of their nationals at USIS libraries and few universities refuse access to an American cultural attaché. U.S. progress in the arts and humanities over the past several decades has been extraordinary and is so recognized in most of the world. Individual cultural affairs officers have significantly penetrated the intelligentsia of foreign countries. Skillful CAOs and those who already enjoy some distinction in American cultural life are limited only by their energy. In some countries the CAO enjoys as much prestige as the American ambassador.

CHAPTER 8

AID:
Evolution of
Foreign Assistance
Programs

Foreign aid as one of the instruments of U.S. foreign policy has enjoyed a reasonably long if troubled existence. Limited aid to Latin America during World War II was the forerunner of formal programs that gained momentum during the postwar years. The programs of the immediate postwar years filled an obvious need for the reconstruction of war-ravaged Europe and then, in the 1950s, became a major weapon against communism. The growing involvement of the United States in Southeast Asia was a major factor in increased foreign aid commitments during the early 1960s, but before that decade was half over the programs were beginning to meet resistance in Congress. Although aid legislation continued to be passed, often by very close votes, there were many major cuts in fund appropriations. Nevertheless, until the decade ended, a combination of White House pressure, voices from the program's limited constituency, and congressional fear of being charged with "losing another piece of the free world" always managed to rescue aid legislation.

The axe finally fell on October 29, 1971, when the Senate by a vote of 41 to 27 defeated an authorization to continue the foreign assistance program.

The Agency for International Development (AID)* legislation had moved by fits and starts through Congress the preceding fiscal year. UN agencies and the international banks, as well as bilateral assistance** programs, were seriously affected by lack of congressional funding.

The mood in Congress in the fall of 1971 was the result of complex factors, and was not merely an isolated case of willful irresponsibility on the part of a few neo-isolationists. In a sense the foreign aid crisis of 1971 was another casualty of the war in Southeast Asia, part of the fatigue resulting from extensive involvement with international problems since World War II. (Ironically the Nixon administration was counting on economic and military aid to help get the troops home from Vietnam and to prevent similar entanglements by helping U.S. allies in their efforts to build their own defenses, i.e., the Nixon Doctrine.[1]) Certainly the support for aid had declined as U.S. involvement in the Pacific, Caribbean, and Middle East created strong antiwar movements at home. New concern for the cities, the poor, and other flaws in the fabric of American society also had understandable influence in drawing attention away from problems in distant parts of the globe.

The strong combination of export-minded farmers, industrialists, and labor leaders, who earlier had seen benefits to the U.S. economy in the Marshall Plan, were now less dependent on U.S. government spending abroad. The AFL-CIO continued to support the program out of habit and satisfaction gained from its anticommunist role. The humanitarian lobby of private agencies was troubled by the Southeast Asian war but also continued its support. But it took a brave or reckless congressman to stand up and be counted as a defender or proponent of the program. The agency, with its very mixed record of performance, was perhaps even harder to defend than the programs it administered. Adverse audit reports, financial scandals, and alleged lack of success in transforming recipient nations into prosperous, friendly, and democratic states gave ammunition to the program's professional opponents. There were few supporters or apologists, but enough adherents to administration guidelines to keep foreign aid programs, both bilateral and multilateral, operating into the mid-1970s. The ability to keep

* *AID* stands for both the Act for International Development and the Agency for International Development, created by that legislation in 1961. The accent was on *development*, replacing such terms as Security, Mutual Assistance, Operation, Cooperation, and other jargon of the foreign affairs establishment.

** "Bilateral," i.e., country to country, as opposed to "multilateral," where the United States is a donor to a UN program, development bank, or private agency, which in turn provides assistance to the recipient. Assistance can take the form of a grant-in-aid of goods or services or a loan on "concessional terms" (low, usually subsidized interest rates).

operating lay in part in the tendency of bureaucratic organizations to resist dismantling.[2] Moreover, no one had really proposed alternative ways to support security and political policies while at the same time salving the American conscience about the discrepancies between U.S. wealth and that of less developed countries.

A new rationale for foreign aid emerged with the withdrawal of American forces from Vietnam and the Yom Kippur War in the Middle East—a rationale which in essence was very close to the early cold war-period approach of using money as an instrument of power. The Nixon "Search for Peace" program of 1973-74 marked a reversion to the massive use of funds and material—for both arms and civilian needs—to achieve and enhance two major foreign policy goals of the 1970s: peace in Southeast Asia without the commitment of U.S. forces, and peace in the Middle East without a sellout of Israel or deprivation to the United States of Arab oil. This program has continued to enjoy the support of President Ford, backed by the same secretary of state, Henry Kissinger. Because the proposals called for investment of massive resources in immediate and tangible programs, they were inclined to command congressional support, especially from the hard-liners who had supported AID in the past for reasons of security or political stability. Members of Congress, however, repeatedly reported low or negative interest in foreign aid on the part of their constituents.

THE U.S. CONGRESS AND
FOREIGN AID

Long before the conflict erupted between the White House and Senator William Fulbright, chairman of the Senate Foreign Relations Committee, over the power of Congress vis-a-vis the Vietnam War, foreign aid had given Congress a role in the making of foreign policy not envisaged when the Constitution was drafted. Prior to the post-World War II era, the Senate Foreign Relations Committee and House Foreign Affairs Committee played a relatively limited role in the details of foreign policy-making; their input was concerned primarily with minor agreements, ambassadorial appointments (in the case of the Senate), and attendance at Interparliamentary Union conferences in the spas of Europe. During the postwar years, however, with the urgent need to provide aid for the reconstruction of war-torn Europe, the congressional committees were catapulted into roles they were unaccustomed to filling.

In June 1947 Secretary of State George Marshall urged U.S. economic aid to European countries; two years later in his 1949 inaugural address President

Truman proposed the "Point Four" program* to provide technical assistance abroad. Arthur Vandenberg, Michigan Republican and chairman of the Senate Foreign Relations Committee from 1946 to 1948, retreated from his erstwhile isolationist position to assume an internationalist stance as spokesman for the administration in the bipartisan atmosphere that prevailed in the field of foreign affairs during the postwar years. On the House of Representatives side, Christian Herter, chairman of a special committee on foreign aid (and later secretary of state), was admirably suited to lead skeptical colleagues into a hawkish internationalist viewpoint which still prevails.

The explanation for the importance of Congress in the aid field may be summed up in one word—money. With presidential concurrence, the Department of Defense can dispatch troops to foreign lands and the Department of State can negotiate treaties, but no loans or grants can be made without appropriations by Congress. Before appropriations are made, they must win approval from a variety of congressional committees: first the House and Senate committees on foreign relations, then the other authorizing committees, and finally the committees controlling annual funding levels. The annual obstacle course of six committee hearings and two conference committee sessions has gradually resulted in much of the aid program being gutted. In the early postwar years, however, all these hearings provided a useful forum for educating the Congress and the public at large about U.S. cold war objectives and the economic needs of less developed countries.

The Marshall Plan began with a four-year mandate and a $16 billion appropriation to embark upon the task of rehabilitating Europe and thereby blunting communist expansion. Later requests for an unlimited extension of time—and consequently unlimited funding—to assist in the development of South Asia, Latin America, and Africa were less warmly received. A mixed record of administrative management and the unending nature of the task itself resulted in disillusionment.

The growing unwillingness of Congress to give any administration long-term assurance of funds also stemmed from the unique opportunity which aid legislation gave Congress to look into the conduct of foreign affairs. The House Appropriations Committee, particularly the Subcommittee on Foreign Operations, now consistently scrutinized every project and proposal, ruling on its suitability; the authorizing committees were using the annual presentation of new aid programs as an opportunity to review all U.S. foreign policy.

* So called from the fourth point of President Truman's inaugural address, January 20, 1949: "Fourth, we must embark on a bold new program for making the benefits of our scientific advances and industrial progress available for the improvement and growth of underdeveloped areas." The term "Point Four" was generally not an official program or organization term. The organization established as the result of this enunciated policy was called the Technical Cooperation Agency.

Secretaries of State and Defense were regularly subject to cross-examination on past failures and future plans with regard to their entire portfolios of policies, strategies, and programs.

The legislative enactment process also offered the opportunity for special interests to influence foreign policy by amending aid legislation so as to prevent aid to specific countries—for example, to communist states, nationalizers of industry, and military governments—or to earmark funds for favored countries. Thanks to the latter development, Greece, Spain, Taiwan, and Israel were assigned special protected "floors" for aid. Amendments were also introduced, and sometimes passed, to benefit a particular sector of the U.S. economy, such as the shipping industry or the wheat producers.

Over the years, aid programs have become increasingly unpopular, making it ever more difficult to get legislation passed. Constant legislative scrutiny, review, limitation, and qualification have combined to inhibit the legislative process, so that securing an annual appropriation has come to be regarded as a nearly miraculous achievement. In the view of many AID administrators, it is today a fear-hate balancing act which keeps the programs alive but crippled: despite congressional distaste for expending vast sums of money on foreign aid, in the final analysis members of the House and Senate are unwilling to lose an opportunity to serve the cause of peace—or to face the charge of weakening the nation's position in the world.

THE PURPOSES OF FOREIGN AID

The formal U.S. foreign aid program had its origins in the coffee republics and mineral- or oil-rich countries of Latin America during World War II. The United States needed their vital raw materials and took modest steps to prevent the fascist powers from subverting U.S. allies to the south. What began during the last days of the Hoover administration and the era of Cordell Hull (secretary of state for President Roosevelt, 1933–44) as the Good Neighbor Policy, with only amorphous political purposes, assumed greater cogency when the United States went to war with Germany and Japan. The original objective was primarily expanded trade and investment, but political objectives took precedence with the outbreak of the war. Diplomacy, backed with direct-aid programs, sought to increase the flow of war needs—rubber, oil, sisal, copper, etc.—as well as to influence the political orientation of Latin American leadership. This initial effort provides a good example of the "hard use" of foreign assistance to help achieve a short-term strategic or political objective, combined with a "soft use," which aims at longer-term humanitarian and developmental objectives. The dual payoff is measured in terms of the direct contribution to the war effort and the twenty-five to thirty years of postwar good relations between the Americas.

From the beginning, the aid objective has varied in place and time as well as in degree of clarity of purpose. Only a few possibly naïve purists have justified foreign aid exclusively on humanitarian or moral grounds. "Because it is right," a phrase used by President Kennedy,[3] has attracted well-meaning supporters, but he and other presidents have found it expedient to promote at the same time the rationale of American self-interest in order to appeal to wary taxpayers and their elected representatives. Administrations have been most successful, both in securing appropriations for the program and in satisfying the dignity of the recipients, when a good balance of the "hard" and "soft" purposes of aid is proposed.[4]

Aid objectives can be divided roughly into *four* categories: security, political stability, economic development, and humanitarianism.

Security

Aid in this category is explicitly aimed at helping assure the physical security not only of recipient nations but of the United States. World Wars I and II were waged in part by supplying arms and equipment to U.S. allies. Supplying the Soviet Union via the Persian Gulf and developing an air shuttle over the Burma "hump" to China were spectacular examples of logistical support in World War II. At the end of hostilities the United States bequeathed an enormous stock of surplus war goods to its European and Asian (e.g., Philippine) allies. After postwar confrontations with the Soviet Union, further supplies were forthcoming as a result of the implementation of the Truman Doctrine and the establishment of the North Atlantic Treaty Organization (NATO). In addition to actual arms supply, the economic support of military establishments became a straightforward means of pursuing U.S. security objectives overseas. This support ranged all the way from paying overtly for base rights in the Philippines (or covertly in other instances) to shipping cloth to Turkish quartermasters.

In Eastern Europe and Southeast Asia, *security aid* meant not only uniforms, raw materials, and food for the armies but, in some cases, salaries for the troops. *Military assistance* is usually defined as war material from the U.S. armed forces supplied directly to the recipient's forces. This is administered by the Department of Defense, with important interest articulation by the Department of State and the White House. Military and security assistance were and remain the most direct use of assistance to attain U.S. military and political objectives. Taiwan, Korea, Greece, Turkey, and the Western European powers were major recipients of such aid until the late 1950s; now

TABLE XI   U.S. CONGRESSIONAL APPROPRIATIONS FOR FOREIGN ECONOMIC AID / 1948-74

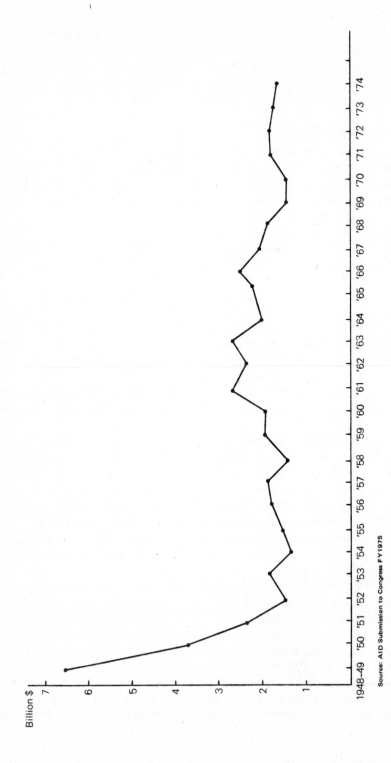

Source: AID Submission to Congress FY1975

Israel, Vietnam, and other Southeast Asian countries are principal cases in point.

Political Stability

Economic aid is used to support U.S. strategic interests when military and related defense-supporting types of aid are inappropriate. In the case of countries that are strategically located, in terms of U.S. political interests, and might be vulnerable to adversary take-over, economic aid has often been used to strengthen the stability of the existing system or to avert its outright collapse. The highly successful U.S. effort in rebuilding Western Europe via the Marshall Plan falls partly into this category. Iran, after nationalization of U.S.-British oil properties, was a case in point during the early 1950s. Jordan, an economically nonviable entity dependent on British support from its inception, faced disintegration when the British could no longer afford its upkeep, and here again, U.S. assistance was a major factor in preventing disintegration. In each case background concern for U.S. security was present, but the essential objective in providing assistance was political and short-term in nature. Economic stability could be bought with aid on the assumption that such an investment might help to assure a more politically stable government (and one sympathetic to U.S. policies).

The aid agencies have usually classified this type of economic aid under security, although its justification has been made on different grounds when the security rationale was unclear or could not be openly admitted. For example, in the 1950s economic aid was extensively used to help secure or maintain air bases in such countries as Spain, Morocco, and Libya, but neither donor nor recipient liked to have the arrangement described publicly as a quid pro quo. The aid was therefore cloaked in the respectable guise of economic development. In the case of Libya, discovery of petroleum led to termination of aid and the American use of the base.

Development

Many Americans conceptualize aid as a transfer of technical skills and capital to foster economic and social development. The Point Four program of the late 1940s was the formal beginning of an effort to work at the long-run task of helping less developed countries modernize and improve standards of living. It is in the development sphere that the greatest number of recipients have obtained aid. In particular, the United States and other development donors have extended massive assistance, both directly and through channels such as the World Bank, regional banks, or the United Nations agencies, in attempting to increase food production, exports, and industrialization, and conversely, to reduce poverty, disease, and population growth.

India and Pakistan are classic cases. Both are strategically important and both have received military help as well, but the main U.S. goal has been to invigorate these countries by contributing to macro and per capita growth. The Alliance for Progress in Latin America was an area-wide program dedicated to similar ends. However, development aid, particularly of the bilateral capital variety, has become as difficult to justify today as arms aid because the desired results—overall economic and social growth, equitably distributed—are hard to evaluate, in many countries seem unattainable, and moreover are not provably related to U.S. political interests.

Humanitarianism

Skeptics doubt that any nation would "give away" even food and medical supplies without some anticipated benefit to the donor. Nevertheless, despite any *Realpolitik* aspect, the traditional American response to humanitarian needs is separable from other purposes which serve clearly identified U.S. interests. The United States can point to a long history of voluntary assistance in the wake of foreign national disasters, whether natural or political. Annual food surpluses, ample means for their delivery, and the abundance of private U.S. agencies for management of relief programs have made a political impact, to be sure, but nevertheless a humanitarian purpose has obviously been a major factor. Despite the Nixon administration's "tilt toward Pakistan" during the Indo-Pakistan War of 1971, the record shows a U.S. contribution of $286 million for relief to Bangladesh in 1972, much of it before the United States had even extended recognition to the new state. This category of assistance will likely continue in the future.

FOUR COUNTRY CASES

Distinctions among the four categories of foreign assistance, it should be quickly noted, are subject to considerable qualification since aid is seldom extended to a given country for only one purpose. The varying mix of objectives and programs will be illustrated by examining aid programs in four countries—India, Tunisia, Costa Rica, and Thailand—each of which has received several types of U.S. aid, usually at the same time. U.S. objectives have shifted as the political environment has changed. Yet in each case a primary objective—security, political stability, or development—is discernible over a long period.

India

Gaining independence from Great Britain in 1947, India became overnight the largest democracy in the world. The maintenance of Indian independence and its democratic system of government have been major political objectives of the United States and the United Kingdom ever since. Indian leaders have consistently shared that objective since independence, although their emphasis on neutralism or non-alignment has often disappointed U.S. policy makers. Determined to avoid dependence on U.S. wheat and foreign exchanges, as well as on European, World Bank, and Japanese technical and capital assistance, the Indians have also turned to the Soviet Union for such assistance. In the wake of a 1962 U.S.-Pakistan defense pact, they broadened their requests to the Soviet Union for military hardware.

As the cold war heated up in the early 1950s, it became a U.S. aim to prove that a democratic India could develop as well as, or better than, a communist China. Although China has perhaps made the greater strides in development, if at great cost to individual freedom, it is undeniable that U.S. economic assistance has been significant in relieving starvation and in providing a base for Indian economic development.

In 1951 President Truman signed the India Emergency Food Act, which authorized a $190 million wheat loan. The Point Four program provided technical assistance, which eventually brought 300 Americans to work in New Delhi and the major states of India. Through 1971, over $10 billion in grant and loan aid was extended, making India by far the largest recipient of international aid. The U.S. share of the amount was almost equaled by the World Bank, Germany, the Soviet Union, Canada, Japan, and others. More than half of the U.S. share was in the form of grains and other agricultural products provided under Public Law 480 (see p. 193), legislation ingeniously designed to help the American farmer at home even as it helped the Indian consumer achieve his minimum caloric intake. Meanwhile, ambitious Indian leadership struggled to industrialize and generally to modernize an almost hopelessly inadequate economy.

During the twenty-year aid period food production more than doubled in India, thanks in part to the "Green Revolution" (see Research), which offset much of the requirements burden caused by a population increase from 300 to 500 million during that period. Today, increasing amounts of industrial products are manufactured in India and a larger proportion of savings go to capital development. Exports are up, and family planning is slowly gaining acceptance. Through it all, despite bad harvests and tensions resulting twice in war against Pakistan, the Indians have preserved democratic values as well as some degree of political independence, belying allegations that economic assistance makes the recipient the political captive of the donor.

U.S. economic assistance has been moderately successful in strengthening Indian independence and promoting development and modernization. However, it has not been successful in encouraging Indian support for U.S. foreign policy, nor was it successful in terms of the former and now obsolete U.S. cold war political objective of fully "containing communism."

Tunisia

Tunisia achieved independence from France in 1956. Political independence and rising nationalism produced pressures for withdrawal of French nationals (numbering 100,000 in 1956), as well as French capital, technology, production subsidies, trade, and military protection. The United States was eager to influence the course of an independent Tunisia because of strategic and political interests. The naval port of Bizerte on the Mediterranean was a NATO base, still flying the French flag until the early 1960s. From a U.S. political standpoint it was judged important that the new state, underdeveloped and with few resources, but with a burgeoning population, should develop strong and stable institutions friendly to the West. Clearly indicated was an economic assistance program to Tunisia which would also serve as an indication that the United States was predisposed to support other emerging nations.

A full-dress aid program began in 1957, with American food grants supplementing technical capital and aid. In a country led by Habib Bourguiba, who was seen as a model of new state leadership, the aid operation had a better chance of success than those mounted in countries less dynamic, less politically unified, and less dedicated to modernization. U.S. economic aid to Tunisia in the form of loans and grants totaled over $350 million from 1956 to 1974, with another $400 million worth of food in the same period. An innovative work relief program beginning in the late 1950s used U.S. food to pay for labor employed to restore forests, expand irrigation and drainage systems, and perform tasks essential to making the land productive and ending dependence on food imports. Nevertheless, periods of economic crisis continued after the French ended their support, and a chronic foreign exchange shortage prevails even today. Family planning has finally become a government objective but the annual population growth rate is still over three percent. Overly ambitious plans to modernize the small farmer have failed.

U.S. aid has now dropped to a level of around $10 million a year and most of the U.S. experts have gone home. AID considers Tunisia a showcase of development. Whether the program has been a triumph of benign foreign intervention or is the result of the dedication and competence of the Tunisians themselves is open to question. But Tunisia remains independent, reasonably stable politically, and favorably disposed to the United States and its allies. Disappointing in some ways, and much more expensive than originally anticipated, the U.S. aid program nonetheless achieved the objectives of the 1950s. The Tunisian program was a creature of the times; it would scarcely be repeated today.

Costa Rica

Whereas U.S. concerns for the course of Indian and Tunisian independence tended to replace those of European colonial powers, aid to Costa Rica simply extended officially, with government resources, a series of private relationships with a country independent since the early 1800s. The U.S. fruit companies had preceded the flag, developing close ties which trade and settlement made into a generally productive relationship.

Foreign aid from the United States began in the early days of World War II in an effort to develop alternate sources of natural rubber and hemp (for naval hawsers), the normal sources having been cut off by Japanese domination of the Pacific after Pearl Harbor. Technical assistance projects to start new plantations included improvement of public health conditions for Americans and nationals assigned to work in the tropical jungles. The crops, incidentally, came into production too late to assist the war effort, but the presence of army and public health service officers may have helped to accomplish the political objective of keeping the country in the Allied camp.

Following the war, health programs, agricultural research, road building, and similar projects, all on a small scale, continued independently until they were absorbed by a formal program of integrated assistance administered by a congressionally authorized organization called the Institute of Inter-American Affairs.* Through "Servicios" (joint associations of host-country and American technicians), projects were initiated in Costa Rica in the fields of education, agriculture, and public health. No longer concerned with expanding the production of goods for the Allied war machine, the two nations now embarked on a mutual endeavor to achieve modernization and thereby to reinforce what was expected to continue as a mutually beneficial relationship.

Direct U.S. aid to Costa Rica amounted to about $100 million under the successive foreign assistance programs of the 1950s and 1960s. But this was only a portion of the monetary flow from Washington. Loans from the Inter-American Bank, World Bank, Export-Import Bank, and Central American Bank have run in recent years from $25 to $50 million annually.

---

* A semi-autonomous government agency, 1949-53, which carried out the Point Four activity in Latin America. The IIAA continued under that name, but as part of the Foreign Operations Administration or International Cooperation Administration until the late 1950s.

Technical assistance has also been provided by international and private organizations. The Act of Bogotá* spawned the concept of the Alliance for Progress, a regional arrangement involving twenty-one nations of North and South America whose political, social, and economic objectives are similar to those of the United States.

Hardly a major construction or institution exists today in Costa Rica which is not the result of one or another U.S. or multilateral aid program. U.S. assistance has promoted political stability, expanded democratic processes, and promoted a favorable climate for foreign investment. The Costa Rican success story is important within the framework of the Alliance for Progress since, among the twenty-one members of the Alliance, Costa Rica especially reflects U.S. value systems. As U.S. bilateral aid has declined, international organizations as well as private industry have provided capital and technology.

Thailand

The U.S. aid program to Thailand began in 1950 as part of an extension of Point Four and the Marshall Plan to Asia, following the communist take-over in China. In the early years, aid consisted of a relatively simple technical assistance operation amounting to some $7 million annually. From this modest beginning the U.S. economic aid program had mushroomed to about $40 million a year by 1955, reflecting U.S. concern over the deteriorating security situation in Southeast Asia and the consolidation of Communist Chinese power. Military aid at that time amounted to approximately $35 million a year.

French withdrawal from Vietnam reinforced U.S. fears about the security of non-communist countries in the area. As a consequence, the U.S. program was augmented by major capital inputs for development of Thai electric power, dams, roads, and irrigation schemes. In 1959 a development loan program was initiated. Thailand's economic growth rates became among the highest in the world, and in the light of a generally satisfactory development

---

* The Act of Bogotá was a response to Fidel Castro and to Soviet influence in Cuba.

"In 1960 the United States had joined with other nations of the hemisphere in the Act of Bogotá, based on a proposal by former President Juscelino Kubitschek of Brazil, pledging a mutual effort to promote social justice and economic progress. President Kennedy then proclaimed the Alliance for Progress and in 1961 the nations of the hemisphere signed the Charter of Punta del Este, committing the United States to specific economic and social goals. The American government undertook to provide 'a major part' of the $20,000,000 needed for the Alliance, including more than $1,000,000,000 the first year."

Robert H. Ferrell, *American Diplomacy: A History* (New York: W. W. Norton & Company, Inc., 1969), p. 847.

record, the United States discontinued budget-supporting aid in 1963. However, two years later, the communists formed a Thai National Liberation Front and increased insurgency operations in the Northeast. At the same time the war in Vietnam accelerated. In 1966 the United States raised the aid level for Thailand to $43 million, where it remained for several years. U.S. air bases also benefited the economy. In return, Thai forces helped in Vietnam.

The content of the U.S. aid program in Thailand has reflected both nations' concerns with security. The Thai government contributed three to five dollars for every one provided by AID in joint U.S.-Thai efforts. The major programs were aimed at building stronger police forces and stimulating agricultural development as a bulwark against the communists through a specially created Office for Accelerated Rural Development. Other supportive programs were mounted in health, family planning, education, public administration, and special training. Almost 10,000 Thai participants have been trained abroad since 1951.

In recent years aid has dropped to lower levels, due more to an increasingly rigorous budgetary approach to the question of economic assistance rather than to diminishing U.S. concern about the importance of Thailand to its security interests. U.S. programs have increasingly addressed the need to help Thailand deal with internal and external security threats on a national basis, supporting Thai leadership in regional cooperation efforts in Southeast Asia.

Since overall Thai growth rates have been impressive, the need for continued heavy U.S. aid is constantly questioned. On the other hand, recent years have been marked by serious economic problems—a poor rice harvest in 1967-68, depressed world markets for Thai exports, phase-down of U.S. military investment in Thailand—all contributing to a loss of foreign-exchange income. Moreover, the ominous military situation in Indochina has impelled the Thais to increase their own military expenditures at the expense of economic development.

As the U.S. involvement in the war in Southeast Asia wound down in the early 1970s and President Nixon made overtures of friendship to Communist China, Thai leadership began to seek independence from U.S. support. Whether the traditional Thai self-reliance and flexibility of policy which have kept the kingdom free for 400 years can continue to accommodate U.S. interests in a changing regional political environment will be a test of the validity of the AID programs from a security-assistance point of view.

ORGANIZATIONAL HISTORY

When the late Paul Hoffman, the first head of the Marshall Plan, retired at the age of eighty from a subsequent position as head of the United Nations Development Program, he announced that he would devote the rest of his career to eradicating the term "foreign aid." In reality the aid program or the agency administering it has never been formally called by that name. Rather, the drafters of titles have tried over the years to describe the process of development as a cooperative or mutual enterprise. While they could never quite banish the expression "foreign aid," it has been de-emphasized by successive reorganization and retitling of the program.

The bewildering array of successive administrative units—Institute for Inter-American Assistance, Technical Cooperation Administration, Economic Cooperation Administration, and Foreign Operations Administration—finally became in 1961 the Agency for International Development. The chart on page 183 shows the lineage of the past and current (1974) headquarters organization.

Detailed analysis of the organizational history of the aid business is a special subject in itself.[5] Two aspects are worth exploring here. The first is apparent from the configuration of the accompanying chart. The early parallel but separate aid institutions were followed by consolidation in 1953 under the Foreign Operations Administration. In 1970 a decentralization began which would have been carried to the ultimate degree of dispersion under Nixon administration proposals. Perhaps this phenomenon simply illustrates the tendency of bureaucracies to proliferate to a degree where consolidation is needed to permit coordination, which is then followed by a swing of the pendulum toward decentralization in response to new inputs, changing institutions, and special purposes. The dynamics of the hourglass-shaped organizational family tree, coupled with frequent agency name changes, have subjected foreign aid personnel to many jests, making it difficult to maintain a solid career staff. The question being asked today is whether the next round of reorganization will result in such extreme atomization that foreign aid agencies will disappear entirely from the United States government's table of organization.

The second important feature of aid organizational history, not apparent from the chart, is the changing relationship of economic aid agencies to the White House and to subsystems of the Departments of State and Defense. Both the Marshall Plan and Point Four were conceived by the Department of State policy planning staff in the days when the State Department had few competitors in foreign policy formulation. The Technical Cooperation Administration was set up within the State Department, although its first chiefs, Henry Bennett and Stanley Andrews, exercised considerable independence. The Economic Cooperation Administration (ECA), however, was given fully separate status under the initial leadership of Paul G. Hoffman. Auton-

TABLE XII   FAMILY TREE OF U.S. FOREIGN AID AGENCIES

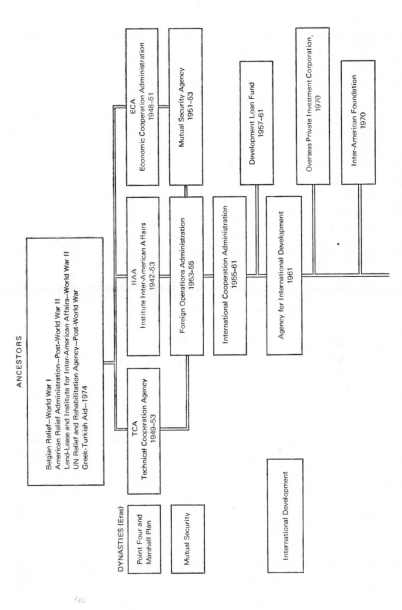

ANCESTORS

Belgian Relief—World War I
American Relief Administration—Post-World War II
Lend-Lease and Institute for Inter-American Affairs—World War II
UN Relief and Rehabilitation Agency—Post-World War
Greek-Turkish Aid—1974

DYNASTIES (Eras)

Point Four and Marshall Plan

Mutual Security

International Development

TCA
Technical Cooperation Agency
1949–53

IIAA
Institute Inter-American Affairs
1942–53

ECA
Economic Cooperation Administration
1948–51

Mutual Security Agency
1951–53

Foreign Operations Administration
1953–55

International Cooperation Administration
1955–61

Agency for International Development
1961

Development Loan Fund
1957–61

Overseas Private Investment Corporation,
1970

Inter-American Foundation
1970

R. B. Black
June 1974

omy provided the agency an opportunity to devise new techniques and organizations which rapidly moved men, money, and goods to Europe. ECA became a model short-term agency (successful perhaps because it was short-term with a specific, relatively clear-cut objective), attracting some of the best talent from Wall Street, university campuses, and specialized government agencies. This team of experts saw in their new roles a happy meshing of American international and domestic interests.

However, the bypassing of traditional diplomatic channels by ECA personnel abroad inevitably led to conflict with old-line Foreign Service Officers. Eventually Congress sought better coordination by creating a super coordinator in the White House, W. Averell Harriman, who had helped set up ECA in his position as secretary of commerce. Harriman headed a small White House office as director of the Mutual Security Agency and had the ear of President Truman. More troublesome than the Department of State–ECA coordination problem, however, was that of coordination between ECA and the Department of Defense, since by 1951 the Military Assistance Program had become a major instrument of U.S. policy in NATO Europe and in Asia. Harriman, assisted by able analysts and administrators such as John H. Ohly, Lincoln Gordon, Richard Bissell, Thomas Schelling, John Murphy, and Norman Paul, successfully maintained independence from the Joint Chiefs of Staff and a reasonable peace among the competitive branches of the armed services (army, navy, and air force).

The Eisenhower administration, however, moved the coordinating role in stages to the Department of State after appointing Harold Stassen (former governor of Minnesota) as director of the newly consolidated Foreign Operations Administration (FOA). Most of the economic aid agencies have continued to reside in the Department of State, but the coordination of economic and military aid is accomplished within the White House by security affairs advisers. While both economic and military aid later declined to a relatively low priority level, an orderly but elaborate programming and coordinating mechanism has evolved under aegis of the National Security Council to resolve the often opposing interests of State, USIA, CIA, the Departments of Defense, Treasury, Commerce, and other agencies with claims on the economic and military aid policy-making process.[6]

PROGRAMMING FOREIGN ECONOMIC AID

Foreign aid is planned or programmed in one of two ways. In the case of war-devastated Europe, an earthquake in Chile, or the sudden departure of a colonial power, as, for example, from the Congo, immediately determinable *requirements* become evident for food, transportation, steel, or policemen to keep order. The donor's job in such instances is only to identify these needs in specific terms and either procure and ship directly or, as is the usual case, establish credits for the recipient to procure the necessary goods or services.

When the European recovery program was launched, the Europeans were asked to form a committee to determine their requirements. ECA, with the aid of its field missions, a central office in Paris, and experts in Washington, screened these needs, determined priorities, and established credits for European governments to procure from the United States (or sometimes from other sources) the raw materials or finished goods they required. In the case of a national disaster such as a Chilean earthquake, teams of experts are dispatched to help the victims estimate their requirements and to draw up specifications for the reconstruction or resupply of disrupted food sources, the restoration of housing, and the meeting of medical and other needs. In the case of the economic and political turmoil in the former Belgian Congo, the problem was more complex, but the essential fact is that a gap existed which could be filled from the outside.

The second way of programming, which is much more difficult, is utilized where the need is *created* as a result of setting targets for growth. Stagnant economies of less developed countries or rudimentary military forces in a country which joins the United States in a mutual defense pact reflect situations where targets for growth must be set. In these cases the programming task is first to establish a model of a growing economy or an effectively equipped and trained security force, then to identify requirements, and finally to assist the country achieve the goal. This may involve procurement, installation, and operation of factories; training, equipping, and supplying armed forces; or developing economic institutions. Point Four philosophy began with the assumption by its administrators that a typical developing country needed anything and everything which could be offered to hasten constructive change.

Initially, agricultural, public health, and educational technicians *sought* targets of opportunity to exploit with their expertise. Neither the United States nor the recipient governments knew how or where to begin. Since the late 1940s, much knowledge has been gained about how to speed economic development, but in the beginning that knowledge was gained principally by trial and error, with an emphasis on error. Food was supplied because the human need was obvious and the assistance permitted the recipient to use scarce foreign exchange or internal resources for building schools, roads, and industrialization rather than for purchasing food. But it soon became apparent that stubborn and recurring food deficits were leading many developing countries to an extremely unhealthy dependence on the United States.

In the mid-1950s the study of economic development acquired a degree of scientific stature with the evolution of more sophisticated analytical techniques. Leaders in this study were economists at Yale, Harvard, and the Massachusetts Institute of Technology, notably Max F. Millikin and W. W. Rostow at M.I.T., whose work resulted in changes in the aid program.[7] Today most universities in the United States, as well as foreign universities, are engaged in further research and study on how to effect economic change. There are enough success stories—Korea, Taiwan, Israel, Brazil—to give them field data to work with.

Programming for a less developed country involves a combination of economic analysis and model-making, designed to determine requirements within the objectives and priorities agreed to by donor and recipient. The aim is to increase recipient capabilities and build indigenous institutions to carry on development programs, as exemplified in this typical simplified case:

a) The United States interest is usually defined as helping Country X be politically independent and economically stable. Stability is expected to become synonymous with economic and social strength.

b) One basic prerequisite to stability and growth is self-sufficiency in cereal production.

c) A strong and effective agricultural research program is required in order to adopt and/or adapt new cereal varieties to local conditions as a sub-goal in the broader agricultural sector.

d) One project to achieve this sub-goal is invariably a research station in the cereal-growing region.

e) The inputs needed to make such a station productive must be identified: x number of senior agronomists, among other talent; a germ bank of laboratory material together with necessary equipment; an operating budget of x units of local currency per annum.

In such a case a program is devised with the host country, which usually requires that the host country supply funds for operating budgets. The United Nations Food and Agricultural Organization may agree to train agronomists and to supply technicians on a short-term basis while the local staff is in training. AID may supply equipment and germ plasma for the laboratory. The programmed project with a dollar aid requirement is the basis for requesting funds from the United States Congress. AID also prepares a plan to make the research station operational and a means for evaluating progress.

The crucial questions then are whether Congress will appropriate the necessary U.S. financial input, whether the United Nations Food and Agricultural Organization will deliver its part of the project, and whether the host government will appropriate the necessary local currency. If Congress approves and if the planning has been basically mutual—and barring revolution or natural disaster in the recipient country, cutback of UN resources, or sudden transfer of the responsible American technician (all of these things and more can and do happen)—the project may become viable and thus contribute to the stated goal and ultimately to meeting a U.S. foreign policy objective, i.e. helping secure a strong, independent country.

RESEARCH

As noted earlier, the mid-1950s witnessed increased research and study relating to development programs. Beginning in 1962 after a decade of trial and error by the aid agencies, the United States faced the realization that the development *decade* might be turning into a development *century*. As a result, AID established a modest applied research program to study some of the bottlenecks of the development process, supplementing research activity already under way under the auspices of the Rockefeller, Ford, and other private foundations. American science was put to work to hasten adaptation of U.S. technology to problems of less developed countries. At the same time, efforts were made to build institutional capacities in these countries by creating international research networks.[8]

The most spectacular result of the utilization of applied science has been the "Green Revolution." This revolution was made possible by international agricultural research centers in Mexico, where Dr. Norman Borlaug's work on wheat varieties won him the Nobel Prize in 1970, and in the Philippines at the International Rice Research Institute, where "miracle rice" was developed. Research discoveries at these centers have transformed rice and wheat production in nations which heretofore had never attained production self-sufficiency, or had lost it due to economic dislocation resulting from war, population increases, natural disasters, land exhaustion, or simply perennial reliance on poor seed and low-yield methods of farming. For example, the Green Revolution enabled India to attain self-sufficiency in cereals for the first time since World War II, and enabled Thailand and Vietnam by the early 1970s to regain their status as rice-exporting nations. In fact, by 1970 the problem in Vietnam had shifted from production to that of moving the new rice surpluses to market.[9] These international research centers, and similar newer ones focusing on tropical agriculture and livestock production, were begun with Rockefeller Foundation funds. AID now shares about twenty-five percent of the cost. It is hoped that these will be models for future breakthroughs.

AID research funds have also been invested in social science research for study of the social/political dynamics of the development process—income distribution, land tenure systems, urban migration, and employment programs. Where little United States government capability in these very complex fields is available, grants are sometimes made to universities to develop staff, research techniques, and leadership to help solve problems. Developing countries, other donors, and, of course, the United States itself, benefit in the long run.

THE POPULATION PROBLEM

No development can be more easily and dramatically summed up than the burgeoning population growth of the developing countries. As early as the 1950s, planners saw their best plans and efforts to increase per capita growth in India and elsewhere thwarted by a two to four percent annual population growth rate. Indian leaders, although aware of this threat to survival, took little action. The United States at first approached the problem with restraint. Both President Eisenhower, a Protestant, and President Kennedy, a Catholic, considered the problem too delicate and inappropriate for intervention. During President Johnson's administration, AID administrator William Gaud, supported by the Rockefeller family, General William Draper, and other concerned citizens, involved the agency in the problem, late but with ample resources. The awakened public concern for the threat of worldwide population growth is attributable to the remarkable efforts of a few effective educator-lobbyists armed with facts and analyses supplied by such professional organizations as the Population Council, Ford Foundation, and Population Reference Bureau, who have been able to convince the U.S. Congress that development could not be accomplished without reductions in world fertility.

As a result of these initiatives, AID legislation beginning in 1967 called on recipient nations to deal with population planning. The legislation includes minimum levels of AID expenditure for population research, delivery systems, training, staffing, communications systems, and even contraceptives. AID's population program is now its single largest technical sector, opening new frontiers in technology and administration. Through more than a hundred channels, AID is financing in almost all developing countries American or international private and public agencies which encourage family planning and population awareness. Constraints are numerous, particularly in the Latin and African areas where underpopulation is the concern of some political leaders and where overinvolvement by the United States may prove counter-productive. However, the program is gaining acceptance. New and promising developments in contraceptive technology may be beginning to affect fertility rates where a desire to reduce family size already exists. Unlike some aspects of development, measurement of progress in the population field is precise. What it shows is that actual reductions in fertility are still distant, and it appears certain that world population will keep growing into the next millennium.[10]

FOREIGN AID: A "GIVEAWAY"?

Endeavoring to meet human needs and national crises constitutes a broad challenge of a very special nature, but the foreign-aid business is basically a process of logistics, hiring, training, contracting, auditing, and reporting. In this it resembles a business enterprise. One major difference, of,course, is that instead of earning money, foreign aid programs are giving it away (albeit with a hoped-for intangible political return).

"Giveaway" is a term much favored by Congress and the news media to express unfavorable reactions to foreign aid. Actually the term is inappropriate in two respects. First, it is not a sack of dollar bills, as portrayed in editorial cartoons, which is involved in the transfer of resources. Rather, AID provides a purchasing authority, or letter of credit, to another party, usually another government, to procure goods or services in the United States.* In most cases, the recipient is paid by such means for the costs of a construction project, delivery of machinery, or any other transaction authorized under a project of program agreement between the two governments. Dollars, as such, seldom leave the United States. Real resources such as tractors or expertise are purchased with dollars and are transferred overseas. If commodities such as wheat are to be sold on the commercial market of the recipient country, the recipient receives first a letter of credit to buy the wheat in the United States. The local currency counterpart of the dollar value of the sold commodity is programmed for use within the country for mutually agreed purposes, such as paying for new schools or maintenance of troops. It is the transfer of the dollar-valued goods to another country which constitutes the assistance from external (i.e., foreign) sources.

---

* The "untying" of aid, whereby donor credits can be used for procurement in countries other than the donor's, is a perennial subject of debate. Some progress has been made in the Development Assistance Committee (DAC) of the Organization for Economic Cooperation (OECD) in getting Japan, Germany, and other industrial powers to permit their aid currencies to be spent where prices are cheaper or procurement sources more suitable to the recipient.

The second inappropriate aspect of the term "giveaway" is that most aid, and all *capital* aid (except in the "hard," i.e., short-term security cases), is provided on a repayable basis. This reform was initiated by Congress when the research studies of Millikin and Rostow resulted in creation of the Development Loan Fund. Some Marshall Plan aid to Europe was on a dollar loan basis and repayments of these loans are now augmenting dollar earnings to help U.S. balance of payments. Later loans were extended on long-term (forty years in some cases) rates of one to two percent, repayable in local currencies. Now, and in fact since about 1961, the loans are dollar denominated, with rates having gone up to three percent in most cases. Loan burdens are a problem for the large borrowers, especially if they have indulged in extensive borrowing on the commercial market or from other borrowers who do not subsidize rates. But generally few defaults occur, a fact which impels many congressmen to prefer loan programs over grant programs. It is thought that loans produce better projects and elicit greater local support. Repayments and interest now total over $350 million annually and offset new loans by that amount. They more than offset the overseas expenses of the AID economic program, resulting in a net favorable effect on the U.S. balance of payments of an estimated $56 million in 1973.*

A second kind of aid transaction is the training of foreign personnel. "Give a man a fish and he will eat once; teach him how to fish and he will feed himself the rest of his life" is the underlying Confucian principle. Training is a major activity, although the costs worldwide are less than the capital loan program for a large recipient such as India. Much technical and administrative training now takes place in the developing countries, often in universities or specialized schools established with U.S. assistance. Nevertheless, a large number of "participants," as AID calls them, continue to come to the United States. These include baccalaureate-level or postgraduate specialists who cannot secure advanced training at home. Moreover, short-term visits to study specific operations are numerous. For example, a team interested in developing a marketing center comes to observe at first hand how fruits and vegetables are processed, sold, and shipped. The impact of this kind of training on European productivity in the early 1950s was probably signifi-

---

* *Foreign Assistance Act of 1971. Report of the Committee on Foreign Affairs on H.R. 9910.* July 26, 1971. (Washington: Government Printing Office, 1971), p. 10. "The balance of payments and gold outflow problems of the United States result primarily from our large defense expenditures, U.S. investments abroad, and tourist spending overseas — not from the foreign assistance program. It is not generally realized that there is currently a dollar inflow from the program as a result of an excess of payments of principal and interest on prior-year loans over the comparatively small dollar outflow caused primarily by occasional off shore procurement and purchases of local currencies." Note: there were net inflows in 1971 and 1973 and a net outflow in 1972; in general, foreign assistance does not have a significant effect on the U.S. balance of payments.

cant. AID maintains a centralized training office which can either place a trainee in one of hundreds of schools in the United States or construct an ad hoc training program to meet a special need. At its peak, over 13,000 trainees were processed by AID each year. Over 150,000 men and women received out-of-country training in this way. An even larger training program is operated in recipient countries, often with UN and other assistance.

A third element of aid to developing countries—after commodities or construction contracts and training—is provision of technical assistance personnel. In a large program, such as those in India, Nigeria, Korea, and Brazil, 200 to 300 U.S. experts work in fields as varied as tax collecting, upstream irrigation techniques, weather forecasting, well drilling, and dozens of others. Gradually the directly hired technicians, that is, those actually working for the AID mission, have been replaced by contract teams or, currently more often, by UN or third-country experts. The principal task of the expert is to help design a development project, implement it with the help of the local experts, and then try to work himself out of a job—in that project in that country—by training one or more counterparts. A technically competent expert with a sense of the local culture and ability to speak the national language can have a lasting effect on the competence and capacity of the counterparts with whom he works. Notable examples of success, and unfortunately many failures, have been recorded.[11]

PERSONNEL: PROBLEMS AND SOLUTIONS

The AID personnel system which supplies these experts and technicians has had a checkered history. As noted above, ECA recruited a first-rate group of businessmen, lawyers, economists, and administrators to assist in the reconstruction of war-torn Europe. Many of these people went back to "civilian" life when the European job was completed. A few joined the Foreign Service and pursued careers in the Department of State or other government agencies. Most AID personnel currently overseas are in Foreign Service Reserve Officer status and move from post to post, or back to Washington "on rotation," as long as they can retain their commissions. At headquarters a basic cadre of administrators, controllers, and general civil service employees akin to other United States government civil servants, are employed.

AID and predecessor agencies have suffered for lack of a genuine career service that offers opportunities and retirement prospects equal to those of the Foreign Service of the State Department, the military services, or the Public Health Service.* Nevertheless, aid agencies have built up a nucleus of

* In 1973 AID overseas personnel finally acquired retirement rights equal to those of State and USIA staff.

high-caliber development economists who have substantially improved AID programming. Technicians in specialized fields exhibit typical strengths and weaknesses. Too many have been "do-gooders" with missionary drive but little capacity to transmit knowledge or experience. Many others have lacked full qualifications for what are very difficult assignments. Another more institutional problem is that AID personnel identify with aid as provided by their agency. They tend to overlook (or ignore completely) the inputs of the United Nations and the international banks, as well as the actually more significant roles in the development process of international trade, private investment, and monetary flows. Despite these problems, the foreign assistance business has attracted dedicated people, and their persistence in the face of agency reorganizations and turmoil is remarkable.

The Use of Intermediaries

Many technical services are provided by contractors, particularly universities in the United States, which have demonstrated an increasing commitment to development. For example, in 1973 AID had 1,226 contracts with 132 universities, in addition to several hundred contracts with other private groups working in sixty-eight countries. The dollar value of these contracts amounted to $751 million.[12]

Many commercial firms have become skilled at performing economic development jobs as agents of host countries or as agents of AID, the World Bank, and other donor institutions. Partnership with the private sector allows greater flexibility than the earlier AID practice of directly employing a pool of experts in some 150 or more professional specialties. It is also sometimes easier to establish a relationship between the expert and the host-country ministry if the local embassy/aid mission is not involved except as a financier in the background.

In recent years AID has broadened this approach by making grants to organizations in the United States which develop and implement programs of their own, augmenting their private funds with those of the United States government. Examples include the International Service Corps, which in 1970 provided more than 500 executive volunteers for short-term assistance to local businesses in thirty or more countries; the Asia Foundation, which has assisted institutions and individuals in Asian countries through training programs and institution building; American cooperative organizations such as the Cooperative League of the U.S.A., the National Rural Cooperative Association, and others which work directly with cooperative movements in developing countries; and labor-training institutes initiated by the AFL-CIO, partially financed from union dues, which work directly with the non-communist labor movements of Latin America, Asia, and Africa.

Eighty-two American church and other volunteer agencies administer relief and technical assistance throughout the world and are often first on the scene when earthquakes, floods, and other disasters strike. AID reimburses these agencies for much of the freight cost of shipping privately donated food, clothing, medicines, and tools, as well as for distribution of surplus U.S. agricultural commodities provided under Public Law 480.

PUBLIC LAW 480

Enacted in 1954 and re-enacted several times since, Public Law 480 is "An Act to Increase Consumption of U.S. Agricultural Commodities in Foreign Countries. . . ." This legislation came about in response to two related problems that faced the executive branch of the United States government in the early 1950s: Congress was increasingly reluctant to raise appropriation levels to meet increasing needs for foreign aid and, simultaneously, rising stockpiles of surplus U.S. agricultural crops were arousing public concern and causing embarrassment to presidential administrations. In an attempt to meet the needs of poorer nations, under P.L. 480 the United States has "sold" or given away over $20 billion worth of flour, corn, dried milk, and other products of the booming American agriculture. The arrangement benefited both the American farmer and the foreign recipient. American farmers sold their crops to the United States government, which in turn sold the products to foreign countries below the market price. The surpluses are a valuable supplement to appropriated dollars since the commodities themselves fill a need, and the local currency proceeds accrue to the United States government for spending in other categories. The uses of P.L. 480 are complex and not restricted to aid agencies.[13] USIS draws on funds accruing under this act for book translation programs, establishment of professorships in host-country universities, and, under the exchange-of-persons program, the Department of State uses funds for travel and maintenance of grantees. U.S. diplomatic missions use the funds for many in-country needs arising from embassy operations. All P. L. 480 funds, however, must be specifically appropriated by Congress annually, and the U.S. agricultural shortages of 1973–74 may result in their sharp curtailment.

P.L. 480's dispersal of agricultural surpluses to India provided a striking example of how the act can benefit both the United States and the foreign recipient. Not only were India's critical food shortages temporarily alleviated, but the United States acquired a politically useful humanitarian image.

Moreover, the stability of the Indian government was enhanced and its response to the United States became more positive. On the negative side, the surplus commodities had the effect of delaying India's progress toward agricultural self-sufficiency. Her developmental planners instead gave priority to enforced industrialization, an error in the view of many economists. This cannot detract, however, from the fact that the almost $5 billion of commodities distributed by the Indian government and volunteer agencies from 1953 to 1974 have, by and large, met a real human need.

ENCOURAGING U.S. PRIVATE INVESTMENT

Private investment to promote trade has always been a handmaiden to official aid. A program of government investment insurance was initiated in 1948. On June 30, 1974, over $4.2 billion dollars of insurance coverage was in force in more than ninety countries to protect U.S. investors against expropriation, currency inconvertibility, revaluation, war, or insurrection.* Other aid to privately funded programs includes guaranties of loans or equity investments against default, investment surveys, some direct loans, and information services to American investors.

A new government agency, the Overseas Private Investment Corporation (OPIC), was created in 1970 to manage these incentive programs. Entirely separate from AID, it is designed to be financially self-sustaining and to apply the principles of risk management to its large insurance program. Authorized by the Moss Amendment to the Foreign Assistance Act of 1969, OPIC also administers an interesting experimental small loan guaranty program through private lending institutions in several Latin countries. This activity is quite different from the regular OPIC portfolio in that it is aimed at the really small borrower ($100 to $2,000) who cannot provide collateral but who has maintained a near perfect record of repayments, a characteristic of some prototype foundation lending activities such as the Centavo Foundation in Guatemala.**

* Nationalization of some American investments in Chile under the Allende regime threatened the solvency of the insurance program, causing some concern in Congress that insurance protection might invite expropriation. The program is being *curtailed* somewhat in spite of strong support from the business community.

** Started by retired New York merchant Sam Greene, who lived in Guatemala. He noted that the Indians in his neighborhood lived without access to bank or even street-corner grocer credit. Greene guaranteed small loans through a foundation from a commercial bank to these small borrowers, and almost never had to redeem them. The foundation flourishes today, in part with the help of AID supplementary capital.

AID also continues to administer a $700 million housing investment guaranty program. The aim is to duplicate, if possible, the success of the savings and loan associations and other private extensions of the U.S. capital market for housing, which flourished in consequence of guaranties provided by the United States government through agencies such as the Federal Housing Agency.

TITLE IX: A NEW APPROACH
TO SOCIAL AND CIVIC DEVELOPMENT

In the view of many congressmen, foreign assistance has been overly dominated by economists and economic considerations. In an effort to encourage wider participation of developing country *populations* in the process and fruits of development, the United States Congress in 1966 added to AID legislation a Title IX section to achieve this result. Congressional concern centered on the notion that perceived non-participation by the broad mass of citizens in the modernization and development process threatened to defeat the political and humanitarian objectives of foreign economic assistance.

Critics of aid had noted that the beneficiaries often appeared to be the governing elites, entrenched oligarchies, or already modernized elements of society. The underprivileged masses, such as the Alti-Plano Indians of the Andes and the urban poor in Bolivia, benefited little from overall growth of their country's gross national product. Evidence suggests that the handful of congressmen—Donald Fraser (D.-Minn.), Bradford Morse (R.-Mass.), and others—who took the lead in the Title IX development were correct. In Brazil, the top five percent of the population own an increasing portion of the national wealth. In Taiwan a reasonable distribution of economic gain was counteracted by a closed political system which denied peasant participation in government.

Although "Title Niners" appeared to be strongly dedicated to a wide spectrum of American national political and economic values, their sole mandate was a congressional direction to AID to seek new approaches for improving the quality of life in the developing countries and to develop in such countries an awareness of the social and political benefits of the development process. As a result, some training of U.S. personnel along these lines, as well as some modest research, was initiated.[14] The object was to develop a wider concern about the beneficiary factor, i.e., "who gets what," in development loans and institutional development. Robert McNamara,

president of the World Bank, has emphasized this concern.* But the donor
community remains somewhat uncertain about procedures for defining and
pursuing the participatory potential of development.

Meanwhile, some of the congressmen responsible for Title IX, led by
Congressman Dante Fascell (D.-Fla.), of the House Foreign Affairs Inter-
American Subcommittee, approached the participatory problem from
another direction. Acknowledging that the United States government is
perhaps not designed (nor inclined?) to promote social revolution through
official channels, these congressmen secured an amendment to the Foreign
Assistance Act of 1969 which created a new agency, the Inter-American
Social Development Institute, later renamed the Inter-American Foundation.
A semi-autonomous corporation with a board of directors dominated by
private citizens, the new entity aims its programs and its initial multi-year
budget of $60 million toward private-sector Latin American institutions
dedicated to social change. Initially approved projects include support for a
Peruvian fishing cooperative, small loan foundations in Mexico and El
Salvador, vocational training institutes in Brazil, and a tiny private rag-picking
enterprise in Colombia, initiated by small entrepreneurs. The foundation
reflects a fascinating and promising experiment in a sensitive and untried area
of development.[15]

The Title IX idea, as a separately identifiable subobjective of AID, has
since 1972 become a major component of all U.S. developmental aid. The
mini-projects which AID first asked political scientists to help design and the
first efforts of the Inter-American Foundation could at best affect only a
small segment of recipient country development programs. More important is
the way aid is channeled and how the target beneficiaries are identified. AID
leadership, along with that of the World Bank, is struggling with the problem
of redesigning aid to reach a wider segment of the population of the less
developed countries while still producing an observable effect on the structure and long-term growth of the economies in which the poor will live.[16]

* "We know, in effect, that there is no rational alternative to moving towards policies of
greater social equity.

"When the highly privileged are few and the desperately poor are many—and the gap
between them is worsening rather than improving—it is only a question of time before a
decisive choice must be made between the political costs of reform and the political risks
of rebellion.

"That is why policies specifically designed to reduce the deprivation among the
poorest 40% in developing countries are prescriptions not only of principle but of
prudence. Social justice is not merely a moral imperative. It is a political imperative as
well."

Robert S. McNamara, president World Bank Group, *Address to the Board of
Governors,* Washington, D.C., September 25, 1972.

MILITARY AID AND ASSISTANCE

Military assistance is the prerogative of the Department of Defense, but it is often closely related to economic assistance. During the early years of military assistance programs the Pentagon, strongly supported by the Department of State, set out boldly, for example, to train the Pakistani air force and the Turkish infantry into copies of U.S. fighting units. The purpose was to prepare for a possible war against a common enemy, the Soviet Union and, later, the People's Republic of China. A more sophisticated approach is now characteristic of the Joint Chiefs' planning staffs. Military hardware requirements of NATO members and of South Korea, recognized bastions against Soviet and Chinese land divisions, continue to be met annually by Congress unless a special political problem intervenes.* Weapons for Vietnam, Laos, Cambodia, and Israel are special cases tied to current threats and strategies. But the case for the piecemeal supply of hardware, ammunition, or training programs for the other forty-five recipients under military assistance programs (MAPs) is more difficult for Congress and the public to comprehend. In these circumstances the Pentagon has shifted its rationale to one which emphasizes internal security needs. Defense enjoys the support of the Department of State for military assistance programs on grounds that the United States needs a means of influencing the military (even democratizing them) because of their importance in the political framework. Moreover, the argument runs, the United States needs sales programs to permit its arms industry to compete with the British, French, and Swiss.

The clearest and most blatant case for military assistance traditionally has been as a quid pro quo for military facilities—air bases in Spain during the 1950s, for example, and landing rights around the world for ships and planes. The Department of State plays a major role in determining the program "requirements" in these cases. With declining budgets for both economic and military assistance, the outlay for bases must perforce decline as well, and so, perhaps, will the perceived military need for the facilities.

American aid, whether economic or military, both affects and is affected by world developments. The traditional concept of military *grant* assistance as a resource for achieving foreign policy objectives may be in the process of being replaced by an arms *sales* program in consequence of the world economic realities of the mid-1970s. Instability in the Middle East has

* As in late 1974, when the Turkish use of MAP-supplied armor in the dispute over Cyprus with Greece almost killed the military program forever and threatened the continuation of economic aid as well. Members of Congress favoring the Greek position held up several appropriation bills and enacted restrictive amendments which crippled the State Department's negotiating flexibility. On other occasions, political actions of Greece, Portugal, or Spain caused displeasure in Congress.

intensified an arms race in that region. Simultaneously, American grain surpluses have shrunk drastically, and what reserves remain are likely to be granted to poor nations. In the wake of quadrupled petroleum prices imposed by the oil producing states, the poor nations cannot afford the petrochemical-derived fertilizers and herbicides to maintain necessary levels of agricultural production. Controlled American arms sales—whether to oil producing nations which want them and can afford them or to Israel which needs them—are bargaining chips to influence political decisions that may also have critical economic consequences.

Clearly, the level and balance of U.S. arms flow to Israel, Iran, Saudi Arabia, and other actors in the Middle East will affect political decisions in those countries. In turn, these political decisions will determine whether oil dollars will be recycled in ways that avoid further disruption of the international balance of payments system, and whether oil producing nations will provide economic assistance to developing nations.

CHAPTER 9

The Politics
of Economic
Assistance

USAID ROLE-PLAYING

As historians study the overriding determinants which have shaped the character of twentieth-century life, they must assess the societal impact of the Russian and Chinese revolutions, the transformations wrought by technology, and the growing demands of diverse peoples and cultures for national identity and for economic and political independence. The drive toward national modernization has been the hallmark of new nation states throughout the world since World War II. The worldwide field missions of the Agency for International Development, which interact with other elements of U.S. diplomatic missions, host country authorities, and international financial and developmental organizations, are the American response to demands by developing countries for assistance in modernization. Host country goals regarding urbanization, literacy, per capita income, social mobility, industrialization, mass communication, and popular participation in the political process are dimensions of national life to which the AID field mission addresses itself. In so doing, the mission becomes a highly important political tool by which the United States can influence the international geopolitical environment and thus press toward U.S. foreign policy ends.

199

A United States AID mission (USAID) is literally a mission within a mission, a self-contained entity with its own administrative, programming, procurement, financial-control, and auditing facilities. The mission director is vested with wide authority delegated from Washington to negotiate agreements and to commit funds, although he maintains an executive-line relationship with the AID administrator in Washington. The mission director has his own controller and often his own legal staff. Acting for AID, he enters into international agreements with the host country government and local contractors. He is responsible for managing monies raised from U.S. taxpayers and appropriated by Congress, and if charges of mismanagement arise, the mission director is responsible, rather than the ambassador, who is the director's policy superior in the field.

The mission director is a functional member of the country team, which consists of the chiefs of the principal United States government agencies at the diplomatic mission and is under the direction of the ambassador. The degree of autonomy within the embassy which the AID mission can command, and its status vis-à-vis other embassy elements, varies widely from post to post, depending heavily on the importance of the aid program in the country, the personalities of the ambassador and his several chiefs of section —political, economic, intelligence, military, information—and the skill of the AID mission director. Delicate problems of role-playing often arise.

The primacy of the ambassador, as the personal representative of the president of the United States, was emphasized by the Kennedy administration in 1961 in a letter from the White House assuring each ambassador that he was in charge.[1] This policy has been reaffirmed by subsequent presidents. Control over aid in the field is complicated by the fact that assistance programs are financed from appropriations provided to AID rather than to the Department of State. However, since the actual programs are designed to be a tool of U.S. foreign policy, the ambassador and his staff have a major role in setting their objectives, timing, style, and, to a lesser extent, their content and magnitude.

Country aid programs originate with an annual country team assessment of the local political environment and selection of a strategy for optimum employment of AID resources to help reach U.S. goals. Diplomatic missions in Latin America have for several years employed the country analysis and strategy paper (CASP) in efforts to approach these tasks systematically. The CASP system is the application of Pentagon systems analysis techniques to the planning and allocation of foreign affairs resources. Previously, it was assumed that weapons could perhaps be quantified and submitted to cost-accounting analysis, but that foreign policy was too delicate and spongy to be systematized. Now it has been found that some elements of modern management can be used successfully by the Department of State. Recommendations of the country team are reviewed in Washington by the Senior Review Group, chaired by the Department of State as the senior foreign affairs agency, and frequently involve reevaluation by the National Security Council and the White House. Funding levels, even for subprograms and individual projects, may be involved in the lengthy review and selection process. Funding, however, is completely dependent on congressional appropriations. In recent years appropriations invariably have been lower than the levels requested by the foreign affairs agencies, necessitating further reviews and assignment of priorities by the president's Office of Management and Budget, the NSC system, and AID administration, as well as consultation with Department of State regional bureaus and others.

Competition within U.S. embassies over the uses of economic assistance as a tool of foreign policy can be severe. Some ambassadors view aid as a means of buying friendship in a country, as a quid pro quo for short-term actions such as a vote in the United Nations[2], or as the price for trade, military assistance, or other concessions. AID mission staff, on the other hand, have been trained to regard long-term economic development as the primary purpose of foreign aid. The give-and-take of trade-offs can engender a state of tension between AID and the rest of the country team. A skillful AID mission director will avoid such pitfalls by constantly emphasizing the primary purpose of the program, but making concessions on short-term issues from time to time. The worst circumstance is when the host country plays off one U.S. agency against another, which can result in a net erosion of the U.S. position. If personality clashes or violent differences of opinion occur between an AID director and an ambassador, the issues are referred to Washington for resolution. This may result in the removal of the AID director, but almost never of an ambassador.

Mission staffs of 200 to 300 Americans and 500 to 1,000 local employees were not unusual in the heyday of technical assistance in the late 1950s. Even in a small African or Latin American post, USAID was often larger than the sum total of the traditional embassy elements, and often larger at some posts than the combined strength of all other U.S. agencies—with the exception of the military. (Currently Peace Corps volunteers often outnumber other Americans, but sometimes prefer not to be included in the official mission community.) The AID mission was, and in most posts still is, located in a building separate from the embassy. Funded from a separate appropriation, AID personnel enjoyed use of their own vehicle pool, hired separate local staffs, and maintained working hours attuned to schedules of local government ministries where many AID technicians worked.

In earlier years the greatest proportion of manpower was devoted to the

202

TABLE XIII   AID OVERSEAS OPERATIONS MISSION AS PART OF COUNTRY TEAM

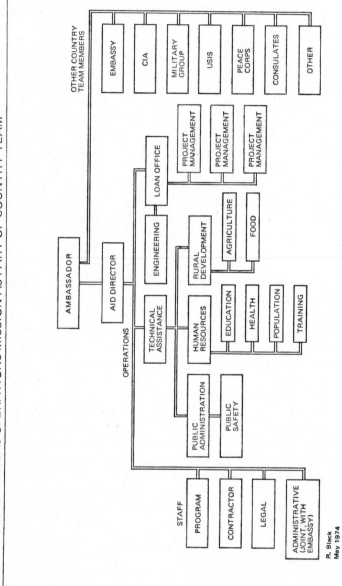

R. Black
May 1974

technical assistance part of the program. A chief of agricultural programs might have twenty-five to fifty experts advising the Ministry of Agriculture in field research, extension programs, or development projects. Currently in areas where the United States is extensively involved with the transfer of technical skills, the experts are more likely to be on contract, paid by AID but in effect seconded to the host government.

Capital grants were replaced by loans in 1958 when the Development Loan Fund was established by Congress to operate as a semi-autonomous bank-like agency. The fund tried to operate without its own field staff, using short-term visits of engineers and loan officers as a substitute for a permanent staff at the host country capital. In consequence, loan applications received from countries desiring capital investment were frequently imprecise in justifying projects and in proposing ways of implementing them.* USAIDs later assumed responsibility for Development Loan Fund operations in the field. Presently most missions have loan officers, engineers, and technical staffs to develop and carry out programs of commodity imports or capital projects and the new sectoral loans, which comprehensively cover an interrelated set of capital and institution-building requirements in agriculture, education, and other fields.

Missions also include small offices charged with promotion of private investment, although when U.S. investors are involved, this is now largely the responsibility of the embassy commercial attaché, backstopped by the Department of Commerce. Several AID officers may handle Public Law 480 programs, especially when they need to be coordinated with school or other child-feeding programs administered by CARE or church organizations, or when there is a massive food-for-work project.

Only large aid missions today have their own administrative support staff. Otherwise the embassy's supply, disbursing, and personnel offices provide these services to USAID as well as to other country team units. Accounting and auditing normally remain separate AID functions because of the separate funding of the AID administration. The keystone of this system is the controller, who, along with his audit staff, will usually remain at the mission long after other AID operations have been phased out.

The era of the large American AID presence abroad has probably ended. In keeping with both reduced budgets and policy dictates, missions are declining

---

* This method of operating at long range has since been pursued more successfully by the International Bank, which maintains a $7 billion portfolio without, or with only very small, field staffs. Overseas staffs, however, are presently being established or strengthened to ensure better program analysis and subsequent project applications which can be approved and implemented.

in size. The AID overseas staff of Americans is presently down to about 2700* from a high of almost 7000. The number of local or national staff has also declined sharply. To some extent, reductions in the number of directly employed Americans are offset by contract, grantee, or other personnel financed by AID money. Also, the number of multilateral agency personnel has grown. In consequence, the host government or institution has a large voice in selection of personnel, who are thus more apt to be both adaptive and competent. U.S. nationals who possess technical capacities will continue to be needed in the developing countries, but in the future their utilization will be a function of the job market and their affinity with a particular national style of living, rather than as a corollary of United States government munificence. The new stress on partnership places U.S. staffs in a different and numerically smaller role.

Relation to Other U.S. Organizations

The AID operation is supported by, and is supportive of, other elements of the country team. The AID economic section, for example, can contribute extensive information on the state of the local economy for embassy economic reporting requirements. AID can often finance a short-term orientation trip to the United States for members of the national legislature who are judged to be politically useful to the embassy. The embassy may not be able to justify this kind of diplomatic "junket" under the Fulbright-Hays exchange-of-persons program, but it may be possible for AID to fit such a trip into its public administration training program. Moreover, AID education officers working at the national university can provide incidental reports on student opinion or unrest which are of interest to the intelligence community.

More formal, and more normal, interrelationships are those with the military or information service and with the Peace Corps. In the case of the military, a special category of economic aid called security assistance helps to alleviate the costs to the local economy of equipping and supporting national security forces. AID may bring in aviation gasoline to fuel jet airplanes supplied by the military assistance program. Joint programming with the military mission is a complicated imperative, especially in cases where national military forces are used to build roads or to deliver emergency relief supplies, because of the duality of category. The AID input to the military

---

* December 31, 1974. This breaks down as: direct hire—1650; contract—900; other staff —150. In addition, there were over 6400 foreign nationals overseas employed at that time, and over 3000 Americans at headquarters in Washington. (Data from Summary Report of Worldwide Direct and Non-Direct Hire Personnel, AID, Washington, monthly.)

may also support a basically civilian and AID purpose. An example is so-called civic action, considered a peaceful use of military forces both to improve the action capability of the armed forces and to make a contribution to the civilian sector of a country. The Turkish forces, among others, have been extensively used between training maneuvers to build roads, teach school, harvest crops, and for other useful tasks which have increased their popularity in the countryside.[3] Joint AID-Department of Defense programs were so closely integrated in Southeast Asia during the Kennedy and Johnson administrations that field operations were carried out by joint teams, as in the Vietnam Civil Operations Revolutionary Development Support (CORDS) program, where AID staff worked under military commands.

The United States Information Service (USIS) provides information to the local media about AID in-country activity. Films, booklets, lectures, and posters are some of the means used to call attention to the work of the development program. The formal dedication of engineering works, the signing of loan agreements, and the delivery of food shipments are heavily publicized. These practices give satisfaction to American congressmen, but often create a counterreaction in the host country. USIS judgment on the desirability or extent of publicity of this kind is essential, and most public affairs officers are skilled at assessing the need for "selling America" and the best means for going about it.

The Peace Corps* is a people-to-people program. Often, however, the volunteers cannot be effective without some visible program such as a demonstration, construction, or training project requiring AID resources. AID cooperates with the Peace Corps to equip some programs or provide financing for an institution with which the volunteers work. In return, volunteers often identify problems in rural areas which AID can help solve. Some of the best U.S. rural development projects are joint Peace Corps–USAID activities.

Finally, other U.S. government personnel from such agencies as Agriculture (hoof-and-mouth disease control), Treasury (monetary matters), the Export-Import Bank (loans to U.S. suppliers), and Commerce (trade and investment) are engaged in activities related to AID. Under participating agency agreements financed by AID, representatives of the Interior and Transportation departments, as well as other Washington-based agencies, carry out functional duties. Usually there is good interagency collaboration and an extensive exchange of information takes place. The new Drug Enforcement Administration and AID's public safety (police training and equipping) program both had roles in helping local forces resolve drug and crime problems during the early 1970s.

* See Table VIII, page 102.

COORDINATION BETWEEN AID
AND OTHER DONORS

The United States was virtually the sole donor nation when large-scale foreign assistance began with the Marshall Plan—although the United Kingdom and France, of course, continued to support their former colonies which had become independent nations. The International Bank for Reconstruction and Development (IBRD), which became a lender only in the mid-1950s, is now the biggest capital supplier. Regional banks, beginning with the Inter-American Development Bank in 1959 (organized as a result of U.S. initiative), now operate for Africa, Asia, the Caribbean, and Central America. Meanwhile, specialized agencies of the United Nations—Food and Agriculture Organization (FAO), World Health Organization (WHO), United Nations International Development Organization (UNIDO), United Nations Educational, Scientific and Cultural Organization (UNESCO), and others—and later the United Nations Development Program (UNDP) expanded their technical assistance, research, and reporting facilities in the development area. UNDP provides a programming system which permits coordination of UN activities, first in the field and then at headquarters in New York, with other donor programs. AID, for example, has an opportunity to influence the content and conduct of the many UN activities. Minimally, AID missions are informed through documentation of what their "friendly" competitors are doing or plan to do.

International aid has become a multifaceted, pluralistic phenomenon during the past decade. Planning or finance ministries of developing countries can look to a number of sources for help. It is quite feasible to bargain for the best deal, playing off AID, with its cheaper money, against the IBRD, which charges higher interest and asks hard questions but permits wider non-communist world procurement ("untied" aid).

During the late 1960s this multiplicity of agencies sometimes gave rise to competition on the part of the benefactors. For example, in Central America during that period there were more lending agencies than good projects to finance. The loan for a road network, for instance, might be made successfully by the agency with the greatest urgency to commit its funds, often by AID, the agency with the most people on the spot in the field. With funding availability now reduced, that kind of competition is less common.

A borrowing country may also obtain commercial credits from private banks and suppliers, often with subsidized or guaranteed credit provided by European governments or by Japan. The United States offers such conditions through the Export-Import Bank. Often the developing country borrows to the hilt, especially in the wake of a natural disaster or a political demagogue's domestic expansion splurge. When the borrower's credit is exhausted an internal monetary and foreign exchange crisis may ensue. With the prospect that loan repayments cannot be met, the lending agencies may then get together, often under leadership of the International Monetary Fund, to work out a scheme of debt moratorium (or loan "roll-over") coupled with a program of fiscal and monetary constraint on the part of the borrower.

Good coordination among donors is essential to the joint interests of the extenders of credit as well as to the borrowers. The International Monetary Fund (IMF) is the watchdog of the monetary world. It is often called upon to develop a stabilization program in cooperation with its sister organization, the IBRD, as well as with the International Development Authority (IDA)—the "soft-loan" agency—and with AID or other bilateral donors. In efforts to alleviate the all-too-frequent financial crises in developing countries, the donors cooperate among themselves as well as operating through such devices as the Development Assistance Committee (DAC)*, which reviews annual programs of donors, and the IBRD, which conducts meetings of consortia or consultative groups of donors.[4] Although the borrowing country may be wary of collaboration among the lenders, may indeed consider such collaboration to be almost dictatorial, rigorous policies openly arrived at are essential and, in most cases, strengthen the borrower in planning aid and addressing financial crises.

MOVEMENTS FOR CHANGE
IN FOREIGN AID PROGRAMS

By the 1960s the United States was no longer the sole donor country providing aid. A host of other countries, international agencies, and private organizations had entered the field, their commitments ranging from technical and military assistance to extending commercial credit and initiating social welfare programs. Concurrently, the 1960s also witnessed increasing disillusionment within the United States about American international involvement, especially in Southeast Asia as the financial burdens imposed by participation in the Vietnam War began to be felt. Moreover, pressing domestic problems within the United States raised the demand for decreasing the U.S. commitment abroad in order to improve the quality of life in the United States. Charity, many congressmen and their constituents were saying, should begin at home. These factors helped to generate a new appraisal of U.S. foreign aid programs. A major question was how foreign aid could be fashioned to support a goal of non-involvement while helping to protect

* The Inter-American Committee on the Alliance for Progress (CIAP) is another forum for Latin American countries, which operates as part of the OAS system.

perceived U.S. interests. During most of the decade of the 1960s, the foreign aid program was allowed to drift without serious efforts to seek an answer to this question.

When the Nixon administration assumed power in 1969, its leaders were determined to reshape U.S. foreign policy in a number of ways, including reducing the degree of U.S. commitment abroad. In his message to Congress in May 1969, President Nixon promised to call for a study of the long-term future of foreign aid. The administration commissioned Rudolph A. Peterson, then president of the Bank of America and later head of the United Nations Development Program (UNDP)*, to head a task force to meet the legislative mandate and develop a rationale for foreign aid in the context of the new foreign policy.

Peterson Report

Peterson and his colleagues prepared a report[5], which is one of a long series of rejustifications for the continuance of aid. Every study would find some need for change, but generally they would confirm the commitment of the United States to support continuing aid for the purpose of promoting international peace and development. The Peterson Report took account of changes in the world since the United States had assumed the aid burden following the close of World War II. The study provides a useful summary of recent aid developments:

1) Other developed countries, restored to economic viability and challenging U.S. technical and industrial supremacy, were now extending significant aid. While AID's funds declined, loans and grants from Germany, Japan, Canada, and other nations more than replaced the solitary U.S. effort.

2) The World Bank, under the presidency of Robert McNamara, with the support of regional banks in Asia, Africa, and Latin America, had more than doubled its annual loan outlays (over $3.2 billion in 1970) to levels four times that of AID's funding.

3) The United Nations Development Program and its specialized affiliates had increased their projects for technical assistance to a level almost equal to that of the United States.

4) New aid mechanisms, international and regional, had sprung up to help plan, funnel, and coordinate development programs. While the United

* The United Nations Development Program administers $200 million in technical assistance programs through specialized agencies in health, agriculture, aviation, and related fields. Peterson replaced Paul Hoffman, who had headed the Economic Cooperation Administration, the Marshall Plan agency.

States continued to play a leading role in these groups, it had become but one of a number of important participants.

5) The less developed countries, with an awakened sense of dignity, discovered in themselves the capacity and experience to establish their own goals, programs, and priorities, even finding their own capital and know-how. On the average, growth of the gross national product (GNP) in these countries has exceeded five percent, resulting in some notable graduates from the recipient to the donor group of nations.* Certain developing nations could now rely on internal or commercially available technology and capital.

6) Priorities for assistance had changed or narrowed. In the 1940s and 1950s a wide variety of aid was offered to almost any developing country willing to accept it. Now external donors could concentrate on selective problems and issues, such as overpopulation and chronic fund shortages.

7) The result of all these factors had been a shift in aid circumstances. Needs and problems of the developing nations were now different. Some of the problems, such as mounting unemployment, growing inequities of trade opportunity, and the mammoth debt burden, were more serious than in the early days of foreign assistance.**

The Peterson Report led to President Nixon's proposals for AID reorganization. Nixon proposed abolishing the Agency for International Development and substituting three new agencies: an International Development Corporation for loans, an International Technical Institute for technical assistance, and an Overseas Private Investment Corporation to promote U.S. investment in developing countries.[6] Except for the last point, i.e., the OPIC recommendation, Nixon's proposals for new legislation did not, however, receive favorable congressional attention. Subsequent internal AID modifications to the program, based on the same fact sheet of changes taking place in the world, called for a different but not necessarily lesser foreign aid effort.

* Brazil, Mexico, Taiwan, India, Israel, Spain, Kuwait, Saudi Arabia, and other Arab oil states. In addition, these and other developing countries make annual contributions to various United Nations programs and in some cases buy IBRD bonds to provide capital for development lending. Note that countries such as Brazil and India are still major recipients as well as small donors. Israel is once again a major recipient.

** "The state of development in most of the developing world today is unacceptable—and growing more so. . . . It is unacceptable, not because there hasn't been progress in the past 20 years—and particularly in the decade of the '60s—but because development programs have been directed largely at gross economic goals, and have failed to ensure that all nations, and all groups within nations, have shared equitably in the economic advance." Robert S. McNamara, president of the World Bank, address to the Board of Governors, September 1971.

This time, however, instead of seriously addressing itself to the proposals, Congress voted overwhelmingly in November 1971 to discontinue the foreign assistance program completely, including appropriations to the United Nations. This negative vote was prompted in large measure by congressional pique when the United Nations voted in October 1971 to unseat the Nationalist Chinese government in Taiwan (which had always enjoyed U.S. support) in favor of seating the Communist Chinese government in Peking. The rationale for the congressional move was that many of the nations receiving assistance had voted against the U.S. position in the United Nations dispute over the two Chinas.

Congress later reconsidered its vote. Within a few weeks the Senate reversed itself and began to process an authorization bill, which finally in mid-March of 1972 (and with only three and a half months left in the fiscal year) culminated in another year of appropriations for the embattled AID. The funding levels were only a bit less than the $3 billion of the previous year, but a full billion under the president's request. Although inured to threats of extinction, the beneficiaries of the program both in the aid agency and in the recipient countries were relieved, albeit temporarily, as they were soon to face new challenges to survival. "Normal" levels of funding continued for 1973 and 1974, but wars, drought, and an energy-resources crunch became far more important than aid flows to the developing world.

A new U.S. approach to foreign economic assistance is needed because conditions have changed both in the United States and in developing countries, and with them the attitudes of the American people. The aid programs proposed by the Johnson administration had not reflected the new conditions; and Congress, which exercises through its legitimizing role more leverage over the aid subsystem than other elements of the foreign policy complex because of the large appropriations involved, did not institute major reforms on its own. The result: reduced funds and uncertainty in the next administration as to how to use those funds still available in pursuit of new strategies and policies.

The direction and amount of change is not yet clear. The fact that the foreign aid program has outgrown its "work clothes" does not necessarily invalidate the original premises of U.S. foreign aid nor the remarkable development effort which has spent over $50 billion of U.S. taxpayers' funds.

Future Trends

In historical context the American aid-giving era, which until recently seemed to be drawing to a close, can be viewed as a consequence and cost of World War II. The reconstruction of Europe, the breakup of colonial empires, and the advent of the cold war provided impetus for the principal aid efforts of the period 1947-69. Why continue into the 1970s and beyond? The American Congress and people are still in search of a rationale.

Other donor countries and the international aid institutions have also recognized a need to take a new look at aid and its purposes. With staff support from the IBRD, a group of prominent experts on the economics and politics of development met in 1968 under the chairmanship of Lester Pearson, a former Canadian foreign minister and a great leader in the UN. The report of the Pearson Commission in fact preceded the Peterson Report.[7] It emphasized the widening gap between developing and developed countries and underlined major requirements for aid for the "second decade of development" (1970-80). But in the view of American decision makers, neither this study nor its American sequel provided a convincing self-interest argument for U.S. outlay of more billions of resources. The Nixon administration envisaged a substantial reduction in the volume of traditional development foreign assistance, to be achieved gradually, and less direct expenditure. In 1972 President Nixon called attention to

... the growth among the American people of the conviction that the time has come for other nations to share a greater portion of the burden of world leadership; and its corollary that the assured continuity of our long term involvement requires a responsible, but more restrained American role.[8]

The period ahead will almost certainly see at least these four new points of emphasis: (1) more multilateralism, (2) greater stress on the *quality* of growth rather than growth itself, (3) reform of the U.S. bilateral aid system and organization, and finally (4) benefits from new technology and different loci of the world's workshops and markets.

Multilateralism

When congressional appropriations for bilateral aid began to falter in the late 1950s, the United States asked its recently recovered European and Japanese partners to share the burden of development. As evidenced by aid flows to India, this strategy has succeeded. Even the United Kingdom, which gave up colonial rule in India in 1947, is heavily involved. So, too, are the communist countries, who reacted to the U.S. bid for the loyalty of the third world with massive, but highly selective (India, United Arab Republic, Cuba, Indonesia, Algeria, etc.) aid programs. The World Bank has expanded loan efforts, raising much of its capital on the U.S. money market to be sure, but much on the European markets as well. Inter-American, African, and Asian banks are now in existence and have begun to compete constructively with the IBRD and the U.S. loan fund. Pressure on the United Nations from developing countries for a large grant program has been diverted in part by the bank programs, and by the expansion of technical assistance and other grant aid through the United Nations Development Program, which as of 1972 had an annual program of over $200 million and aims for $500 million by the end of the decade.

Within the past several years the multilateral-aid programs have begun to surpass U.S. bilateral aid, approaching the bilateral aid total of all other Development Assistance Committee (DAC) members.* As early as 1960, U.S. assistance levels began to slow. By 1967 the U.S. expenditure approximately matched the combined efforts of its DAC partners, a victory for advocates of cost sharing but perhaps not for the developing countries. By 1973 U.S. expenditures for assistance had dropped from first to fourteenth place in terms of percentage of GNP devoted to development aid among DAC members.

The pros and cons of multilateralism have continued to evoke considerable attention in Congress and the executive branch. The Senate and the Nixon administration preferred the multilateral approach because of the decreased possibilities of confrontation with other governments, thus perhaps lessening the likelihood of intervention (and war). Otto E. Passman, chairman of the House Subcommittee on Foreign Operations, and Thomas E. Morgan, chairman of the House Appropriations Committee, feared that the United States would lose political control and that financial accountability would be impossible if U.S. assistance were to be channeled through multilateral organizations. But the fact is that multilateral aid has arrived for the development sector. The 1972 U.S. aid authorization legislation for the first time provided greater amounts of funds for the United Nations and international banks than for AID.

The Quality of Growth

In both absolute and per capita terms growth rates have been disappointing in Latin America (Brazil is an exception), Africa (per capita GNP is still below $100), and South Asia. Moreover, while growth has occurred, it is fair to ask who has benefited from it. Has poverty diminished? Are the rural forty to seventy percent of the populations of most developing countries party to the industrial progress of the overall economy?

* The bookkeeping for aid that flows directly to developing countries is very complex. The 1974 DAC chairman's report indicates the following for 1973: Bilateral Official Development Assistance, U.S.—$2.3 billion; Bilateral Official Development Assistance, other DAC countries—$4.8 billion; Disbursements by multilateral agencies, gross—$3.8 billion.

TABLE XIV   U.S. CONTRIBUTIONS TO TOTAL DAC AID, 1967–73*

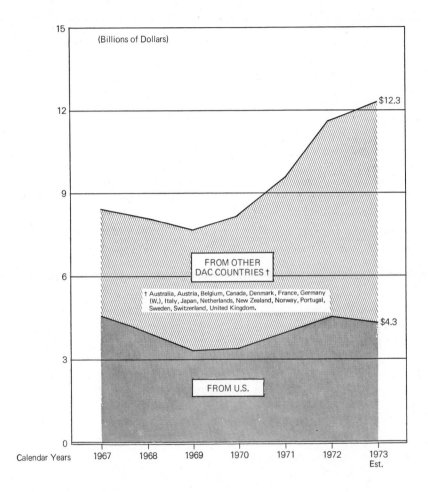

* Commitments to less developed countries and multilateral agencies based on the DAC definition of Official Development Assistance (ODA), which includes, for the United States, all economic assistance programs (A.I.D., P.L. 480, Peace Corps, and contributions to multilateral institutions), but excludes such other resource transfers as Export-Import Bank Loans. Data for other DAC countries are on a comparable basis.

Source: Statistics & Report Division, Agency for International Development, Washington, D.C., April 1974. (AID measured by the Development Assistance Committee of the OECD.)

Mahbub ul Haj, a Pakistani economist at the World Bank, presents evidence that preoccupation with GNP growth has blinded donors to the issue of growth *distribution*.[9] For example, a continuous GNP growth in Pakistan of six percent has resulted in increasing unemployment, particularly in East Pakistan, or Bangladesh, as it is now known (and a correlation can be made between the independence movement and the distributable share of growth, west and east). As a further illustration, Brazil's northeast region has felt little of the impact of the fantastic expansion of Sao Paulo and the southern regions, with political consequences that suggest a Brazilian Bangladesh may be taking shape.

The 1970s are witness to a new concern for problems of unemployment, poverty, and income distribution among political leaders of the non-communist donor group. President Robert McNamara of the World Bank has made this complex of problems a major focus of concern for the bank. Belatedly, the United States government, and particularly AID, are addressing the same problems, but the United States and its agencies remain as uncertain as the other donors and developing countries about how to redirect programs of aid and internal investment to achieve desired results. Communist China may offer some ideas for adaptation by developing countries in the non-communist world.

A second aspect of the quality of growth is increasing concern about the environmental impact of industrialization, urbanization, and modernization. On this question no consensus obtains among donors and developing countries. The latter feel that pollution and destruction of air, land, and water resources are problems for the industrial nations. Let us develop first and then worry about the consequences, they say with some emotion. The World Bank, and to a lesser extent AID, is beginning to add environment to the priority list of development problems to be addressed in the second development decade.

Foreign aid was not high on the list of priorities of the first Nixon administration. As noted earlier, proposals for new directions, style, and organizational changes were frustrated by the House Foreign Affairs Committee in 1971. The aid legislation for that year was not passed until well into the third quarter of the fiscal year and contained only a few of the features recommended by the Peterson Commission and the president's messages to Congress. The new formulation did not contain as much emphasis on multilateralism as Senator Fulbright, chairman of the Senate Foreign Relations Committee, had hoped for, and he refused to support the bill on the Senate floor. (But then the senator's strong anti-bilateralism had not often been shared by his colleagues, especially in the House.) However, the principle of distinguishing between security on the one hand and developmental and humanitarian purposes on the other was contained in the legislative framework.

In 1971 AID administrator John Hannah reorganized the agency within the limits of the congressional mandate. Operational responsibilities were consolidated. Past emphasis on country programming was reduced in favor of functional or sectoral attacks on a few selected problems of worldwide development—food production, population, education, and the transfer of technology. The size of overseas staffs was reviewed and gradually reduced, as was agency personnel in Washington.

AID, like all large bureaucracies, has a built-in resistance to reform which makes radical change difficult. Nevertheless, new emphasis on a partnership relationship with the developing countries, greater reliance on private intermediaries, and coordination with multilateral programs are policy features which have begun to affect operational style.

One change of the Nixon-Kissinger-Ford era, however, has been a reversion to the bilateral aid instrument as a major bargaining element in the administration's "Search for Peace" program of 1973-75. The objective has been to achieve economic and military balance between the Arab states and Israel in the wake of war ravages. In this area, then, political stability has become the principal purpose of foreign aid. It is questionable whether Congress, pressured by the pro-Israeli lobby on the one side and oil interests on the other, will always go along with the use of foreign aid for this purpose, but American politicians can at least understand the reasons for it. And the payoffs in terms of potential peace in the Mideast may be great.

Another important future avenue for the aid program is linked to a settlement of the wars in Southeast Asia. As an inducement to end the fighting there, President Nixon offered a massive $5 billion in assistance to rebuild South Vietnam and another $2.5 billion to help rebuild the north. Certainly some continued peaceful involvement, with economic assistance, is likely. Multilateral aid, or means other than direct participation may be employed to carry out such programs. The new China policy and the potential evolution of new relations with Cuba also suggest a continued role for foreign aid in the 1970s.

In summary, the likelihood is remote for a repetition of the aid experience of the 1947-70 period. Nevertheless, the need of developing countries for external resources is certain to continue for the remainder of this century.

CHAPTER 10

The System in Search of Reform

Efforts to effect operational and organizational reforms within the Department of State, in the interest of greater responsiveness and efficiency, have been an ongoing concern since the years immediately following the close of World War II. Basic to all of these reorganizational studies and changes has been the issue of system maintenance. As a political subsystem, the department must perform functions which assure its continuing viability; in other words, it must fulfill system maintenance functions if it is to survive. While system maintenance functions preserve the *system*, particular attitudes, behavior patterns, and hierarchies within the system are dispensable in order to meet the demands and expectations of the external political environment. The more responsive and adaptive the system, the more likely its survival. The stage is set for change when support for and agreement about change becomes significant, either within or outside of the system.

REORGANIZATION FOR SYSTEM MAINTENANCE

Since 1947, four major governmental recommendatory studies* have been undertaken, each a consequence of new demands and expectations which the existing foreign policy system could not fully satisfy. While these studies have each had a permanent impact on the department, they have also been blunted in some degree by resistance from within the department as well as from other sources.

The Hoover Commission Report of 1949 (chaired by former President Herbert Hoover) recommended substantial changes to make the department more responsive to the expanded post-World War II role of the United States in international politics. In 1954 the Public Committee on Personnel (chaired by Henry M. Wriston, president of Brown University) made crucial recommendations about classification and utilization of foreign affairs personnel. The "Herter Committee" of 1962 (chaired by former Secretary of State Christian A. Herter) concluded that the department was still not responsive to the demands of a complex foreign policy and recommended personnel and organizational changes. Finally, the department's internally initiated reforms of 1970 emphasized the need for modern management and additional changes in personnel administration. Three of the four studies—the Hoover Commission report, the Herter report, and *Diplomacy for the 70's*—focused on almost identical and continuing problems: (1) the necessity for better definition of objectives; (2) the question of chain of command; (3) personnel policy; and (4) the need to blend new and old skills in diplomacy.

Definition of Objectives

The Commission on Organization of the Executive Branch of the Government (the Hoover Commission), which was established by unanimous congressional action in 1947, recommended as a priority matter in 1949 that the definition of U.S. objectives in foreign affairs be made by the Department of State. However, since foreign affairs could no longer be clearly separated from domestic affairs, the commission proposed that other agencies also participate in the inauguration of policies to achieve those objectives. According to the commission, the problem in defining objectives stemmed from the failure of

* A Brookings Institution study of 1960 also called for a reorganized foreign affairs system. Its recommendation for creation of a super secretary of state to oversee secretaries in charge of departments of Political Affairs, Economic Affairs, and combined Information, Educational and Cultural Affairs was not implemented, but the concept has persisted in literature about reform of the foreign policy system. See H. Field Haviland, Jr., et al., *The Formulation and Administration of United States Foreign Policy*, A Report for the Committee on Foreign Relations of the United States Senate (Washington, D.C.: Brookings, 1960).

the department to plan far enough in advance: it lived from day to day, making only short-range decisions.

Thirteen years later the Committee on Foreign Affairs Personnel (the Herter Committee) stressed the same idea in its first recommendation. The Department of State, it said, needed to be strengthened because of the president's dependence on it for "formulation of foreign policy, the development and coordination of foreign affairs programs, and the planning and marshalling of resources needed for their implementation."[1]

In January 1970 the Department of State completed its own reorganization study and published its recommendations in *Diplomacy for the 70's.* The result of this study was a "management reform" inaugurated at the beginning of 1971 by Deputy Under Secretary for Administration William B. Macomber, Jr. Macomber's reforms stressed the need to define foreign policy objectives and then establish priorities and distribute resources to achieve such objectives. A new management evaluation group headed by the department's inspector general was established to evaluate the effectiveness of existing policy and programs. The Planning and Coordination Staff (now called the Policy Planning Staff) was expanded to provide support to the seventh-floor principals in linking policy analysis to resource allocation (PARA). In the department's words, "The process should seek to insure that the resource allocation process is not undertaken independently of policy requirements but is governed by them."[2] Management centers had already been developed at the regional level by 1970.

The policy analysis and resource allocation process called for a basic country paper from each field post. The country analysis and strategy paper (CASP) inaugurated in the Bureau of Inter-American Affairs in 1966 was suggested in the reform proposal as a model for the other regional bureaus. This country paper, as reviewed, amended, coordinated, and approved at the highest interdepartmental levels of government, was to constitute official U.S. policy respecting the country in question. The process would significantly expand the role of the department's policy planning staff, insuring inputs from the seventh-floor management team. Within a year some forty-three PARA/CASP documents and special studies had been reviewed by seventh-floor principals.[3]

Chain of Command

The Hoover Commission determined that the secretary of state should be in command of the Department of State and that the Foreign Service beneath him should constitute a chain of command which would be "clear and unencumbered." Accordingly the commission made specific recommendations about the organization of the department. The recommendations, which essentially were adopted, recommended strengthening the secretary of state's authority by providing him with a generalist under secretary and two deputy under secretaries to whom regional and functional assistant secretaries would report. Planning, operations, executive secretariat, and intelligence roles were expanded and institutionalized, and a partial amalgamation of the foreign and domestic services was effected in order to achieve greater coherence. The department reflected the imprint of the Hoover Commission in its hierarchical organization for the next several decades.

In 1962 the Herter Committee drew attention to what it perceived to be a problem: overgeneralized policy statements on the one hand and faulty program coordination on the other. The solution, according to the committee, was to create an entirely new office, that of executive under secretary, ranking immediately below the under secretary of state. The task of the executive under secretary would be to provide to the secretary the degree of support he needed to conduct foreign affairs by transforming words and policies into action. Responsibility for the "leadership, coordination, supervision and follow up . . . of policy formulation, program development and administration in foreign affairs should be taken by the proposed Executive Under Secretary. . . ."[4] An executive secretary of the department was in fact subsequently created. But while the position is central to department operations and the occupant normally enjoys considerable prestige and authority in his role as head of the executive secretariat, the executive secretary is essentially a staff officer rather than a command official as envisaged by the Herter Committee.

Diplomacy for the 70's is the basis for the 1970-71 reorganization of the Department of State. In a sharp departure from previous study recommendations on the subject of chain of command, the internal departmental study urged that "the Department's leadership make a concerted effort to loosen the chain of command through greater use of *ad hoc* task forces staffed by personnel of all ranks, not only in the missions abroad but in the Department as well."[5]

Emphasizing the need to modernize, *Diplomacy for the 70's* called for the two decision-making levels in the department—the office of the secretary and those of the assistant secretaries—to be reorganized into "management centers" to "bring responsibility for policy analysis and decision-making, on the one hand, and resource allocation, on the other, under unified control, thus ending the present separation between policy formulation and resource management."[6] The uncertain position of the country director in the hierarchy prompted the task forces which devised *Diplomacy for the 70's* to recommend that these officers "have more direct contact with the Assistant

Secretaries" and called for "increased participation by the country director in the work of the National Security Council System."[7]

Accordingly, some six months later on July 6, 1971, the secretary announced "a reorganization of the Department's top echelon—the 'Seventh Floor'—involving changes in the responsibilities of the Under Secretary and other key officials."[8] Simultaneously the secretary "announced the introduction of a new management system on the Seventh Floor and at the level of the Assistant Secretaries which makes use of 'Policy Analysis and Resource Allocation.' "[9]

The secretary subsequently recommended to Congress that the under secretary's title be changed to deputy secretary "to reflect not only his position as the Secretary's ranking deputy for the management of the Department, but also that of principal coordinator in behalf of the Secretary of the overseas activities of all U.S. Government Agencies."[10] Under terms of the reorganization, the under secretary for political affairs retained his position as third-ranking officer in the department. But Congress was requested to upgrade the deputy under secretary for economic affairs to under secretary for economic affairs "for coordinating economic affairs within the Department and for representing the Department in major interagency bodies dealing with development and economic policy."[11] Emphasis on management change was underlined by redesignating the deputy under secretary for administration as deputy under secretary for management, and Congress was requested to authorize a new position, termed at the time of announcement as coordinator for security assistance.

Each of these personnel changes was subsequently achieved. The deputy secretary predictably became the alter ego of the secretary; the title of under secretary for economic affairs became a reality and the new status of his position may have helped the department successfully stave off an effort in 1972 by the Department of Commerce to preempt the Department of State's primary role in foreign economic policy. Macomber, the actual initiator of the reorganization, became a "manager" rather than an "administrator." It was intended that the title of his position would be upgraded from deputy under secretary to under secretary for management after his departure, but as of early 1975 that change had not taken place.

The recommended position of coordinator for security assistance actually emerged on April 11, 1972, as under secretary for security assistance. A White House announcement said the role of the new under secretary would be to supervise military grant-in-aid programs and sales of military equipment and to supervise economic supporting assistance. Until 1972 these roles had been the province exclusively of the Department of Defense and the Agency for International Development.[12]

Macomber's management reform seemed to be a masterful political move in 1971. Macomber, a Republican appointee and a former ambassador to Jordan (although not a career Foreign Service Officer), had apparently resolved internal demands for reform by the "Young Turks" in the American Foreign Service Association,* and had responded to the patent need of the department to reassert its role primacy in the foreign affairs subsystem.

Personnel

No aspect of the three foreign affairs agencies is more important in terms of system maintenance than personnel policy, and no aspect has garnered more attention in the reorganization studies. Recommendations about recruitment, training, and utilization of Foreign Service personnel are to be found in all of these studies. Amalgamation of Foreign Service employees within a single, unified foreign service personnel system is practically a standard recommendation. Criteria and procedures for promotion and "selection out" (i.e., enforced retirement on the basis of time or rank-order in grade) are subject to constant scrutiny and have been under frequent attack, especially since 1969. Controversy over personnel management has been intensified because the Foreign Service Act of 1946, with its extensive amendments, has proved to be ill designed for the kinds of role-playing required for contemporary foreign affairs management. Yet this patchwork quilt remains the basic legislation governing all Foreign Service employees of the three foreign affairs agencies.

Foreign Service Act of 1946   The Foreign Service Act of 1946 was the only major legislative reorganization of the foreign affairs system between the Rogers Act of 1924, which combined diplomatic and consular roles in a single career service, and the supplementary USIA Foreign Service legislation of 1968. The 1946 act set up separate but related categories of personnel to manage foreign affairs in the wake of increased American commitments abroad following the end of World War II. At the heart of the system is the career Foreign Service Officer (FSO) Corps. Subsidiary categories specified in the 1946 act provide for Foreign Service Reserve Officers (FSR) and a Foreign Service Staff Officer (FSSO) Corps. At various times Foreign Service Staff Officers have been downgraded from officer status to "employee" designation in consequence of administrative response to recommendations or other pressures. Foreign Service Reserve Officers under the 1946 act receive the same salary as FSOs but do not enjoy career status since their appointments are limited to not more than five years. The Foreign Service Staff

* The American Foreign Service Association is a nonprofit organization devoted to the interests of professionals in foreign affairs serving overseas or in Washington.

Officer Corps salary schedule is lower than that of the Foreign Service Officer Corps.* FSSOs function under a separate promotion procedure and originally were not included in the Foreign Service retirement system.

It was intended by the 1946 act to accommodate in either or both of the subsidiary categories personnel involved in informational, cultural, intelligence and other functional activities, as well as in temporary programs associated with economic assistance to postwar Europe. Actually, the Foreign Service Staff category quickly became a catchall throughout overseas missions for rapidly expanding technical, specialist, and administrative support personnel, especially at the lower levels.

Serious problems plagued the entire system after passage of the act, most of them arising from the impossible task of managing disparate categories of personnel, charged with carrying out varying roles abroad and in the department, under different personnel policies, yet under authority of the same act of Congress. Thus the issues of amalgamation of the existing Foreign Service categories and integration of the Foreign Service and department-based Civil Service personnel** continue to rank as top priority in reorganization efforts.

Movement Toward Amalgamation of Foreign Service and Civil Service **As** early as the Hoover Commission Report of 1949, a single foreign affairs service was recommended for Civil Service and Foreign Service personnel within the Department of State. All members of the combined service would be "obligated to serve at home and overseas and constituting a safeguarded career group separate from the general Civil Service."[13] The proposal bore fruit five years later when Henry Wriston's Public Committee on Personnel recommended in 1954 the "integration of the personnel of the Department of State and of the Foreign Service, when their official functions converge, into a single administrative system."[14]

The recommendation was adopted and carried out *administratively* under the previously little used *lateral entry* provision of the 1946 act. Hundreds of Civil Service employees occupying "foreign service designated" positions in the Department of State were faced with accepting lateral entry or losing their jobs. Most accepted. Thus was born "Wristonization," by all standards

---

* Not incidentally, even prior to the 1974 pay raise, the average federal salary had more than *doubled* since passage of the Salary Reform Act of 1962, according to the Tax Foundation, Inc. See "Federal Pay Doubled in Decade, Study Says," *Los Angeles Times*, February 25, 1974. Salaries range, as of November 1974, from $10,520 for Class VIII, Step 1, to $36,000 in Class II, Step 3, and above. FSOs in Classes I and II are impacted at a federal career ceiling of $36,000.

** Civil service personnel, i.e. general schedule (GS), serve under different legislation and operate under different salary scales, recruitment, promotion, and retirement policies.

the most sweeping foreign affairs personnel change to the present time, and variously depicted as progress or disaster, depending upon one's point of view. Among critics of the move, John Francis Campbell, a Foreign Service Officer, assailed it as contributing to the postwar decline of the Department of State.[15]

In 1962 the Herter Committee recommended that the personnel of other "foreign affairs agencies in the United States who are now in the Civil Service system should be redesignated as foreign affairs officers and employees, and should be brought within the structure of the foreign affairs services."[16] In effect, Herter wished to amalgamate the Civil Service and the foreign services of State, USIA and AID. With the failure in 1967 of the Hays bill, designed to accomplish this amalgamation for USIA, that agency persevered and secured its own career service legislation the following year. Unfortunately, the 1968 act created a system which locks USIA foreign service officers into a specialist category since they are designated by the law as Foreign Service Information Officers. Congress also created the category of Foreign Service Reserve Officer Unlimited (FSRU).* The parameters which Congress imposed reflect the persistent efforts within the department and in Congress to maintain a distinction between Foreign Service Officers of the Department of State and all other Foreign Service personnel categories. AID has continued to struggle for career legislation without success.

Diplomacy for the 70's noted that "16 years after the Wriston Committee recommendations, many officer level positions in the Department are still under the Civil Service system." It therefore recommended that "all officer level positions in the Department and abroad be brought into a unified personnel system under the Foreign Service Act."[17] *Diplomacy* said that the new category of Foreign Service Reserve Officer with unlimited tenure (FSRU), which was established by the 1968 legislation, would "permit establishment of a career system of Foreign Affairs Specialists (FAS) parallel to the Foreign Service Officer Corps" and should be drawn from the Civil Service employees of the department.[18]

The plan drew immediate criticism from Civil Service personnel, both in the Department of State and in USIA, where a similar recommendation was broached. Many civil servants regarded it as an effort to push them out of the security of the Civil Service into second-class status in the Foreign Service and subject to the selection out process.**

* The term is inherently contradictory because a "reserve" category normally refers to officers who serve on active-duty status for limited periods of time or in an emergency.

** Foreign service retirement eligibility is established at age fifty with twenty years of service; civil service retirement eligibility is established at age fifty-five with thirty years of service, at age sixty with twenty years of service, or at age sixty-two with five years of

Nevertheless, since it could do so administratively under provisions of P.L. 90-494, the department announced a program early in 1971—entitled "Toward a Unified Personnel System: the Foreign Affairs Specialist Corps"— to induce departmental Civil Service employees of officer level, Foreign Service Reserve Officers, and Foreign Service Staff Officers to convert to the newly established Foreign Affairs Specialist Corps (FAS) by designating almost all officer positions of the department as either Foreign Service Officer or Foreign Affairs Specialist positions.[19] Under the FAS category, individual officers would have FSRU status and be subject to selection out. FSR, FSSO, and GS employees of the department were also invited to apply for conversion to Foreign Service Officer status if they preferred, although entrance standards were higher and an examination was required. The objective was to include all career employees in either the FSO or FAS category. The conversion program to FSO ended December 31, 1973, while the FAS conversion program has continued.[20] In response to criticism, and as an inducement to conversion, the new appointees were provided exemption from selection out for performance ranking for two full performance and rating periods.[21] By 1974, more than ten percent of the Foreign Service Officer Corps consisted of employees appointed under the new program. Meanwhile, the continuing FAS conversions from other departmental employee categories will eventually produce a department and Foreign Service manned almost entirely by FSOs and FAS officers.

Job Responsibility and Promotion   In response to complaints from junior Foreign Service Officers that their talents were being underutilized, *Diplomacy for the 70's* recommended "systematic reclassification of job levels to move responsibility back down the ladder."[22] The study proposed greater functional specialization within the Foreign Service but not at the expense of the "inter-functional" or generalist posture characteristic of the higher-level FSO positions.

Another section of the study recommended a new system of semiautomatic promotion in the middle FSO grades to counteract unfavorable reaction to the department's expanded utilization during the 1960s of

---

service. Civil service retirement is mandatory at age seventy with fifteen years of service; foreign service employees must retire at age sixty. Foreign Service Reserve Unlimited Officers (FSRU) compete for promotion and retention and are eligible for foreign service retirement. Foreign Service Staff Officers (FSSO) in classes 7 to 1, Foreign Service Staff Employees (FSS) in classes 11 to 8, and Foreign Service Limited Reserve Officers (FSRL) are not eligible for foreign service retirement and do not compete for promotion and retention. They are governed by civil service retirement provisions, except that Foreign Service Staff Officers may convert to foreign service retirement after ten years of consecutive service.

Section 633 of the Foreign Service Act. Section 633 provides for involuntary separation (selection out) of Foreign Service Officers who are not promoted within an administratively determined time period. In 1956 selection out because of low rank-order within a Foreign Service class was added as a criterion under Section 633.

In response to the study, the Board of the Foreign Service adopted changes in 1971 which provided for "stringent appraisal" of junior Foreign Service Officers, who are considered in a "career-conditional status" until they reach "full career status" upon promotion to Class V. "Once safely past this 'first threshold,' officers would have virtual assurance of twenty additional years of service during mid-career.[23] By instilling an appropriate mix of competition for promotion and of career security among officers, the department said, an individual officer would feel encouraged to offer "forthright expression of views on policy matters which might be at variance with the views of his superviser."[24]

Recruitment   Recruitment for the career Foreign Service has scarcely been a problem in terms of the number of applicants for appointment. In December 1973 a total of 13,736 candidates took the written Foreign Service examination, the greatest number in the history of the Foreign Service. Less than 1600 received a passing grade entitling them to proceed to the oral examination, the second step in appointment. The applicants were competing in 1973-74 for approximately 165 appointments as FSOs and about twenty appointments as FSIOs.[25]

Diplomacy for the 70's was critical of the written examination which, as the study said, "was, until recently, more an academic hurdle than a device for identifying the best possible candidates."[26] Calling for greater reliance upon the oral examination, longer probation periods, and better in-service training programs, the reform study was acknowledging the demands for democratization of the Foreign Service.

Personnel Reform and Rising Demands   Most of the recruitment-training reform recommendations were put into effect, but the consequences for the foreign policy subsystem were unexpected. Just as the economic and social measures of the Johnson administration's "Great Society" prompted ever greater demands and expectations, so too have Foreign Service personnel reform measures. Unmet, and largely unanticipated, demands arose for collective bargaining, grievance appeals, and women's rights. A movement within the Foreign Service to achieve collective bargaining resulted, in 1972, in an election battle between the American Foreign Service Association (AFSA)—the traditional FSO club-like organization—and the American

Federation of Government Employees (AFGE)—a union associated with the AFL-CIO—for the exclusive right to represent Foreign Service employees. Although AFSA won the election, it emerged from the struggle as a far more politicized body. Acting in its new role as exclusive bargaining agent for the Foreign Service, the AFSA urged issuance of a presidential order which would empower it to negotiate employee grievance procedures rather than leaving them to management to develop in consultation with the employee groups as proposed by the department.

The grievance and selection out battles, meanwhile, were beginning to be reflected in Congress and the courts. As early as mid-1971 Senator Birch Bayh (D.-Ind.) and Representative John Ashbrook (R.-Ohio) proposed dismissal appeals systems. In mid-1972 the Senate voted 56 to 27 to establish a grievance and appeals system for Foreign Service employees. The climax came in December 1973 when U.S. District Court Judge Gerhard A. Gesell ordered full hearing rights for Foreign Service Officers involved in the selection out process, including legal representation, presentation of witnesses, and the right to confront and cross examine witnesses who had provided derogatory information against them. The court said that selection out, in consequence of a low ranking by the department's evaluating boards, as constituted when the suit was brought by the American Federation of Government Employees, was "constitutionally defective" in that it denied officers "adequate hearing comporting with the requirements of due process under the fifth amendment."[27]

Allegations, meanwhile, were mounting against the department's traditional position toward women. Under fire was the role-playing expected of wives of Foreign Service personnel serving abroad, as well as discriminatory practices in recruitment, promotion, and job opportunities for women employees in the Foreign Service.

One of the departmental task forces which contributed to *Diplomacy for the 70's* made concrete suggestions as to the expected role-playing of wives of officers serving abroad. These suggestions were based upon the views of twenty-seven women who participated in the task force. Recommendations of the task force were converted to policy with publication in June 1971 of Management Reform Bulletin No. 20, *Guidelines for Representational Responsibilities of Wives in Our Posts Abroad*, and provoked immediate criticism. The basic theme of the policy document was that "the official rank of an officer applies to his wife insofar as certain courtesies and many responsibilities come to her because of her husband's position." This concept was challenged on the ground that it perpetuated "the traditional view in our society that a woman finds her identity, position and meaning for her life through her husband. Her efforts therefore must be channelled through and for him."[28] Some Foreign Service wives alleged that they were required to serve as "ladies-in-waiting" to ambassadors' wives at field posts. Also criticized was the inclusion of an evaluation section pertaining to his wife and family in the Foreign Service Officer's annual efficiency report. Instead of resolving conflict and satisfying demands, the department found that its *Guidelines* of June 1971 had precipitated new demands for a "bill of rights" for Foreign Service wives.

Departmental discrimination against women Foreign Service Officers also came under scrutiny with establishment of the Women's Action Organization (WAO) in 1970. By 1972 WAO had 800 members (ten percent male) and was drawing attention to severe inequalities, especially to the minimal number of women in the FSO Corps. In 1957, women constituted 8.9 percent of the FSO Corps. By 1972, there were only 152 women among 3086 men—less than five percent.[29]

Responding to pressures for recognition of the rights of female employees, the department, for the first time in its history, held a meeting on the subject in January 1971. In consequence, no woman is required to resign when she marries. Additional policy changes include: (1) marriage or intention to marry is no bar to recruitment; (2) in the case of husband and wife officer "teams," the department will make every effort to assign them to posts where both may serve and if such arrangement is not possible, the nonworking spouse will be given leave without pay until opportunity for a suitable double assignment arises; (3) a married woman officer will be given leave without pay to stay home with young children and can return to active duty later.[30]

By 1972 some 55 "working couples" were on the Foreign Service payroll, including two ambassadors, Carol Laise in Nepal and her husband, Ellsworth Bunker, in Vietnam. However, according to some feminist observers, only the tip of the iceberg of discrimination has been exposed and destroyed. The upper ranks of the Foreign Service continue to be dominated by men.

Among other personnel practices in the Foreign Service which have been criticized is the recruitment of ambassadors from outside the career service. The appointment of major political campaign fund contributors has had a long political history. Since an ambassador is the personal representative of the president, chief executives have often looked outside the career service for diplomatic appointees. However, in the last two decades, approximately seventy-five percent of the ambassadors appointed have been from the ranks of the career Foreign Service. Among the twenty-five percent who are political appointees, by no means all of these have been campaign contributors (for example, Patrick C. Moynihan, ambassador to India; Philip K. Crowe, ambassador to Ceylon, South Africa, Norway, and Denmark; Robert G. Neumann, ambassador to Iran and Morocco).

In 1973 some observers concluded that the escalation of the Watergate scandals had further dampened tendencies toward such practices. A *Washington Star News* survey of all ambassadorial nominations by the White House from the date of President Nixon's reelection in November 1972 through June 1973 showed that "only 3 of the 28 new diplomatic plum assignments since election day went to major campaign contributors," less than eleven percent.[31] However, in February 1974 the first criminal charge ever made for *selling an ambassadorship* was preferred by Watergate Special Prosecutor Leon Jaworski against Herbert W. Kalmbach, President Nixon's personal lawyer. On February 26, Kalmbach pleaded guilty to the charge of trading an ambassadorship for a specific dollar level in political contributions to Republican senatorial candidates in 1970 and to President Nixon's reelection campaign in 1972. This admission prompted both Jaworski and the House Judiciary Committee to investigate other possible "sales."[32]

The American Foreign Service Association, editorially noting Kalmbach's guilty plea, said the incident "has once again brought to public light the urgent need to do something serious and constructive about a long-standing abuse." The AFSA's proposed solution is legislation which would make major political contributors ineligible for consideration as ambassadors.[33] In the meantime, the AFSA has requested the opportunity to testify before the Senate Foreign Relations Committee on nominations of *non-career* ambassadors. On April 10, 1974, Thomas D. Boyatt, president of the governing board of AFSA, questioned the suitability of Leonard K. Firestone, President Nixon's nominee for Ambassador to Belgium. Boyatt's appearance before the Foreign Relations Committee was the first input in history by an organization representing Foreign Service Officers into the confirmation process of American ambassadors.

Old and New Diplomacy

System maintenance in foreign affairs presumes an ability to play effectively the role of "super power," which the United States has assumed in the post-World War II era. This new role and the new problems arising from the "decolonization" of many areas of the world required, in the eyes of many, a new approach to the technique of diplomacy. For example, the "Young Turks" in the Department of State distinguished between an "old diplomacy," which emphasized individual experience and intuition, and a "new diplomacy," which called for a "new breed of diplomat-manager," utilizing contemporary analytical techniques and "backed by a Department organized on modern management principles."[34] Realization of the potentials such changes may offer is dependent, according to *Diplomacy for the 70's*, upon adoption of a special group of recommendations that cut across the two categories of management and personnel. These recommendations center upon "creativity" and "openness."[35]

Creativity is the ability to innovate, an activity which can flourish best, according to the study, in an atmosphere of democracy and participation and through use of "temporary groupings," the latter concept tying in directly with Alvin Toffler's ideas of "adhocracy."[36]

The reformers pointed out that the concept of creativity was lacking in earlier reform considerations. Innovation was indeed inhibited under the "old diplomacy." The cumbersome clearance procedure, both horizontal and vertical, besides being time-consuming, almost assured an unsatisfactory compromise. The inevitable result was a tendency toward collective responsibility, where no single officer may be faulted, at the expense of individual initiative which, if faulty, can result in penalty to the author. The reformers called for elimination of "clearing" in favor of coordination by means of ad hoc committees which would include all officers concerned with a particular issue. They also recommended the inclusion of alternative data and interpretations in submission of policy inputs.[37]

The demand of the reformers for "creativity" was an attack against the inhibitions which have traditionally characterized the Foreign Service. One reformer, an ex-Foreign Service Officer, writing in 1970, emphasized that the Foreign Service Officer "loses autonomy and merely resonates to the expectations of others" if he expects to get ahead. "Your chief will write your efficiency report," he warns, "so it is vitally important that he like you."[38] Other FSOs have argued that emphasis on conformity produces individuals more concerned with trying to be something rather than do something.

The second major recommendation, for openness, cuts across traditional categories of management and personnel. The State Department, as *Diplomacy for the 70's* recognized, "is not an autonomous organization," nor is it "the sole source of wisdom on foreign affairs." It must shed its "insularity," and create "shock points within the Department so that the foreign affairs process might be opened to the view. of outside persons," and it must develop "much closer relations with Congress."[39] The study called for the temporary exchange of personnel with other government agencies, business, professional, and academic communities; easier lateral entry; emphasis on training; and " 'democratizing' our missions abroad" by dismantling "the hierarchic structure which has grown up around the traditional somewhat authoritarian concept of the role of the ambassador."[40]

FROM REFORM TO REVERSION

The stage was set in mid-1971 for the Department of State to reassert its role as the primary actor in the foreign policy subsystem, with reforms designed to underscore and reinforce the legitimacy of the seventh-floor decision-making role. The formal responsibilities of seventh-floor principals were broadened and their foreign affairs management role emphasized. Resource allocation and policy were linked by the PARA concept in a version of the program-planning-budget-system so popular during the McNamara years at the Department of Defense, but the PARA concept was broadened to utilize *all political resources*—not merely budgets—to achieve foreign policy goals. A supportive subsystem for evaluation was added. Capstone of the reform was formal recognition by the department of rising demands of the "Young Turks" for assignments which would permit "creativity" to flourish. The need for an "atmosphere of democracy" and a sense of "participation," the encouragement of "innovation," and assurance that innovative and advocate views would survive their upward journey through the hierarchy were all clearly and even painstakingly enunciated. Finally, "openness" was assured by creation of "shock points within the Department so that the foreign affairs process might be opened to the views of outside persons."

Despite the vigorous recommendations contained in *Diplomacy for the 70's* and the "180 Day Progress Report" of July 1971, the Department of State almost immediately began to engage in behavior which suggested the exact opposite of "openness" and "participation." Actors and role-playing outside the department were the primary cause.

Leaks to the Press

The reversion to secrecy in place of "openness" was set in motion on June 13, 1971, when the *New York Times* began to publish a series of articles based on a massive and top-secret official study which had been "leaked" to the *New York Times* by Daniel Ellsberg, a former Department of Defense employee with access to classified documents. This study delineated the roles of the departments of Defense and State concerning U.S. intervention in Indochina during the years 1946 to 1968. The articles, which became known as the *Pentagon Papers*, were of such a secret and sensitive nature that the government tried through court action to prevent further publication. The decision of the Supreme Court on June 30, 1971, upheld the right of the *New York Times* to publish the material, although several justices pointed out that legal authority was available to the government to permit it to censor news; the Justice Department had simply not invoked that authority.*

---

* The Espionage Act of June, 1917, as amended to March 28, 1940, was not cited in the government's brief before the Supreme Court, nor was the State of National Emergency Proclamation of December 16, 1950. Justice Byron White, with whom Justice Potter Stewart joined in a dissenting decision, stated that the fact "that the government

On July 23, 1971, less than a month after the Supreme Court decision on the *Pentagon Papers*, the *New York Times* published the substance of U.S. proposals for the strategic arms limitations talks (SALT) with the Soviet Union before Washington had even communicated them to Moscow. In consequence, according to the press, Secretary of State Rogers requested certain departmental officers to undergo lie detector tests and used the incident as a rationale to impose restrictions on the flow of information within the department.[41] In August 1971 newspaper columnists Rowland Evans and Robert Novak alleged that "what is undermining morale at the State Department even more gravely than suffocation from the White House are the extraordinary new rules of secrecy recently laid down by Rogers." According to Evans and Novak, Rogers' instructions warned against "written memoranda raising questions about such dramatic policies as Mr. Nixon's new approach to Mainland China."[42]

Secrecy in the department became so pervasive by October 1971 that, according to the *New York Times*, "the vast majority of the Department's officials learned through the Federal Bureau of Investigation about President Nixon's plans to visit the Soviet Union next May." According to the *Times*, a routine FBI intelligence advisory concerning the trip reached the department just a few days prior to the formal announcement of October 12, 1971. Adding humiliation to the whole affair, the *Times* said, was the fact that the FBI "had learned from an informant that Gus Hall, general secretary of the American Communist Party, had been advised of the plans for the trip several days before by a Soviet diplomat." Reportedly only Secretary Rogers and a few senior officials knew of the plans before the general secretary of the American Communist party knew of them![43]

Secrecy, instead of openness, appeared to intensify. According to the *Washington Evening Star*, "the top floor of the Department has put strict limits on circulation of messages from US ambassadors among the country desk officers who are fundamentally concerned with sorting out policy toward those countries." The messages "now are read first by the regional

---

mistakenly chose to proceed by injunction does not mean that it could not successfully proceed in another way. . . .

"The criminal code contains numerous provisions potentially relevant to these cases. Section 797 makes it a crime to publish certain photographs or drawings of military installation.

"Section 798, also in precise language, proscribes knowing and willful publication of any classified information concerning the cryptographic systems or communication intelligence activities of the United States as well as any information obtained from communication intelligence operations." "Text of Ruling on Viet Papers," *Los Angeles Times*, July 1, 1971, p. 16. See also Benno C. Schmidt, Jr., "The American Espionage Statutes and Publication of Defense Information," in Thomas M. Franck and Edward Weisband, eds., *Secrecy and Foreign Policy* (New York: Oxford University Press, 1974).

Assistant Secretary of State concerned, and then forwarded to Rogers' secretariat for decision on wider distribution."[44] The *New York Times* reported a memo of November 17, 1971, to the secretary of state in which the president "directed that all official statements relating to the conference on disarmament henceforth will be cleared at the White House." Henry Kissinger signed the order.[45]

This instruction followed a "similar standing instruction" of the Bureau of East Asian and Pacific Affairs "prohibiting any discussion with newsmen of Nixon's forthcoming trip to China."[46] At exactly the same time, Benjamin Welles, writing in the *New York Times*, reported that the State Department on November 4, 1971, "cabled about 300 chiefs of missions and other principal officers overseas warning them that reports of dissent by younger officers must not be allowed to leak to Congress or the press."[47] Deputy Under Secretary Macomber, supporting these actions of the department, responded to press queries that "the right of dissent is very important—and no one's been pushing for it harder than I. But we want to keep it in the house. . . ."[48]

The department had moved quickly and comprehensively within its own structure, virtually destroying the openness concept in the process. However, a new and highly visible leak was discovered in the presidential element of the foreign policy system. Journalist Jack Anderson reported in December 1971 that President Nixon had ordered a "tilt" toward Pakistan, inclining the United States to favor that nation during the Indo-Pakistan War. Anderson claimed that Nixon's order was directed to the National Security Council through Henry Kissinger who, Anderson said, told the NSC that the president had given him "hell" about the NSC's reportedly equivocal attitude toward the war in South Asia.[49]

Anderson's detailed, nationally syndicated newspaper columns, and the alleged NSC reports upon which he said they were based, quickly became widely known as the *Anderson Papers*. The journalist, of course, refused to divulge his "sources." The *Anderson Papers* appeared literally on the heels of the alleged department leak about the SALT negotiations; the published reports about subjection of Department of State officials to lie detector tests; and the published reports of new rules of the department to enforce secrecy, to prohibit dissent, and to limit distribution of information. In the minds of many persons, the Anderson disclosures tended to be linked with the earlier Department of State leak, regardless of the fact that Anderson specifically ascribed his reports of alleged leakage to the National Security Council. Deputy Under Secretary Macomber subsequently may have reinforced the confused public reaction about the source of the "tilt toward Pakistan" leak. In March 1972 he responded to criticism about departmental restraints and secrecy by stating, "Denigration of the State Department by people either inside or outside the Department is contrary to the national interest. If it keeps up, it will eventually weaken this essential asset to the Government."[50]

Irony of Politics

The unfortunate reversal of the reform toward openness, which the department itself had recommended and initiated in 1971, was the direct consequence of the climate of concern for security engendered following publication of the *Pentagon Papers* in June 1971. In his statement of May 22, 1973, President Nixon stated that the publication of the *Pentagon Papers*

> created a situation in which the ability of the government to carry on foreign relations even in the best of circumstances could have been severely compromised. Other governments no longer knew whether they could deal with the United States in confidence. Against the background of the delicate negotiations the United States was then involved in on a number of fronts—with regard to Vietnam, China, the Middle East, nuclear arms limitations, U.S.-Soviet relations, and others—in which the utmost degree of confidentiality was vital, it posed a threat so grave as to require extraordinary actions.
> Therefore during the week following the Pentagon Papers publication, I approved the creation of a Special Investigations Unit within the White House—which later came to be known as the 'plumbers.' This was a small group at the White House whose principal purpose was to stop security leaks and to investigate other sensitive security matters.[51]

The change in attitude of the seventh floor of the Department of State —from an emphasis upon "openness" to demands for secrecy and conformity along its elements—began in July-August 1971 and coincided with the activation of the "plumbers' unit."

It is the irony of politics that the Department of State's carefully prepared internal reform which emphasized openness was foredoomed from its inception by a series of political interactions over which it had no control. Had it not been for a disillusioned Department of Defense employee, who by his own admission had not read the 1945-54 history of Vietnam until August-September 1969,[52] and who, according to Admiral Elmo R. Zumwalt, overruled him in 1963 when Zumwalt opposed involvement of U.S. ground troops in Vietnam,[53] it is unlikely that the *Pentagon Papers* would have been made public as and when they were. Had it not been for the clumsy prosecution by the Justice Department of its case against the *New York Times* and the *Washington Post* to stop publication of the *Pentagon Papers*, the government would probably not have lost its appeal to the Supreme Court. Had the Justice Department not failed in the Supreme Court case, leaks might not have continued to emerge from the State Department and the National Security Council. Had the Nixon administration not been so frustrated by the judicial process in its efforts to prevent security leaks, the "plumbers' unit" might not have been formed with the broad mandate from President Nixon which permitted it to be as active and determined throughout the executive subsystem as the Watergate invesgations* later proved it to be. Had the climate of fear over maintaining secrecy not become so pervasive in the executive branch, the Department surely would not have reversed itself about openness as it did.

Influence of Nixon and Kissinger

The roots of secrecy in the department had origins other than those arising from the public disclosure of the *Pentagon Papers*. They grew also out of the styles of Richard Nixon and Henry Kissinger.

During the period 1969 to 1971, at the very time openness was being formulated as a system maintenance technique within the department, officials of the department were being subjected to telephone wiretapping, which was coordinated, according to President Nixon, through "my assistant for National Security Affairs"—Henry Kissinger.[54] During that same period of time—according to disclosures in January 1974—a military "spy ring" was operating within the National Security Council for the purpose of passing on NSC documents to the Pentagon. The need for the "spy ring" arose, it was reported, because documents emanating from "Kissinger's secret Washington Special Actions Group," a committee of the NSC, were not being transmitted to the Pentagon as were formal NSC documents. The Department of Defense, it was reported, would otherwise have been unaware of Kissinger's secret diplomatic initiatives toward China, North Vietnam, and the Soviet Union.[55] The advent of Henry Kissinger as secretary of state in September 1973 hardly portends a period of greater openness in the department in the foreseeable future, given Kissinger's predilection for secrecy.

Perhaps the most important factor, however, was the attitude of President Nixon, who was especially sensitive about secrecy in foreign policy and admitted it. On May 14, 1974, in an interview he gave to columnist James J. Kilpatrick, Nixon expressed his conviction that secrecy is necessary for the conduct of foreign affairs. "You cannot in today's world," the president said, "have successful diplomacy without secrecy. It is impossible." Kilpatrick reported that, according to the president, the dialogue with China, begun in

---

* Investigation of the presidential subsystem and the personal affairs of President Richard Nixon as the result of the break-in of the Democratic party national headquarters in the Watergate apartment-hotel in Washington, D.C. on June 17, 1972.

1971-72, "never would have occurred without the highest secrecy. Nobody knew about the overtures save the President, Henry A. Kissinger and a few aides sworn to secrecy."[56]

The resignation of President Nixon and the assumption of that office by Gerald Ford has not had an appreciable effect upon Department of State procedures. President Ford, during his first six months in office, has vigorously endorsed Kissinger and supported his role of international peace-broker, a role which essentially depends upon personal interface and confidentiality.

MACRO-REFORM: THE MURPHY COMMISSION

In the midst of these leaks, charges, and countercharges, a new reform commission, much wider in scope, began its work in late 1973. Proposals for change in the foreign affairs subsystem have now come full cycle—from the general to the particular and back to the general and on an even broader scale. The Hoover Commission of 1949 had a broad mandate to make recommendations concerning the entire executive branch. The Wriston and Herter committees were concerned primarily with personnel problems of the three foreign affairs agencies. *Diplomacy for the 70's* recommended internal reform of the Department.

The new Commission on the Organization of the Government for the Conduct of Foreign Policy—the Murphy Commission (chaired by former ambassador Robert D. Murphy)—is authorized by the Foreign Relations Authorization Act of 1972 to "study and investigate the organization, methods of operation, and powers of all departments, agencies, independent establishments, and instrumentalities of the United States Government participating in the formulation and implementation of United States foreign policy."[57] The range of the Murphy Commission is government-wide. Its mandate extends far beyond the three foreign affairs agencies, beyond the military and intelligence subsystems within the executive branch, and beyond the executive branch itself to the role of Congress in foreign policy role-playing and to congressional-executive interactions. The body is authorized to hold hearings and subpoena witnesses, as well as to make proposals for constitutional amendments, legislation, and administrative action appropriate to its mandate.[58]

The report of the Murphy Commission is due for submission to the president and Congress on June 30, 1975, a time frame which suggests that a massive effort is indeed expected.

In August 1973 the Murphy Commission announced it would examine the impact of "the changing world environment and the manner in which foreign relations are conducted" as well as "the changing role of the United States."[59] In carrying out its investigation of *all* elements of the foreign policy system, the commission is sponsoring independent research under the following categories:

A. *Presidential Responsibility and Interagency Coordination:* How can the presidential powers in foreign affairs be properly delegated and agency responsibilities most effectively coordinated, especially with respect to better integration of policy planning and decision-making in diplomatic actions and activities?

B. *Public Opinion and Public Accountability:* How should public opinion make itself felt on and be dealt with by the Congress and the Executive? As a difficult but important aspect of this problem, how should the matter of confidentiality in foreign policy be handled?

C. *Substantive Problem Areas:* How can the Government be organized to deal effectively with some substantive problem areas which touch upon widely divergent governmental interests, such as:

  population and food resources
  energy crisis
  natural resources and the environment
  seabed and ocean floor

D. *Domestic Interests and Foreign Affairs:* How can the Government be organized to deal more effectively with the wide range of problems, including many of the foregoing, but especially economic matters— trade, monetary, agriculture, resources—which heavily involve important domestic interests and considerations as well as foreign policy?

E. *Cultural Affairs and Public Information Abroad:* How can the cultural affairs and information processes be organized to support more effectively the foreign policy of the United States?

F. *National Security, Military Policy and Arms Limitation:* How can the government organization and procedures be arranged most effectively to mesh national security and military affairs with general foreign policy matters? How can arms limitation policies be most effectively handled?

G. *Intelligence and Information Handling:* How can the organization be improved for collection of intelligence and information, for reporting, for evaluation and analysis and for dissemination?

H. *Personnel for Foreign Affairs:* How can the personnel systems in the foreign affairs effort be improved?

I. *Budget Process and Resource Allocation:* How can the budget process, including planning and programming, be improved?

J. *Overseas Establishments:* How can the control, coordination and communications systems in the overseas establishments be made more effective and efficient?[60]

During its first year of work, the commission devoted itself to discussions with foreign policy system-related elements throughout the government and it commissioned independent study groups to identify problems. During its second year the commission has focused on problems about which it will make recommendations.

For its part, the American Foreign Service Association has stated that its inputs to the commission will not emphasize "internal organizational changes in the three Foreign Affairs Agencies, as that has [sic] been overlystudied." Instead, the association will raise bureaucratic problems, "such as the excessively parochial and client-oriented approaches of some agencies, or the unnecessary proliferation of non-Foreign Service personnel overseas." The association agrees that "a wide-ranging study of this kind is long overdue," affording an "unprecedented opportunity for us to shape our own destiny and it deserves our utmost attention."[61]

It appears obvious that many aspects of the system by which foreign policy role players are recruited and utilized require change and modernization. A fragmented Foreign Service, vulnerable to politicization, subjected to the outrage of wiretapping, locked into conformity, limited in the inputs of its actors, and suffering morale problems, is hardly conducive to maintenance of a functional bureaucratic subsystem in the foreign policy process. And, regardless of the importance and roles of the host of other structural elements, such as the presidential subsystem, Congress, interest groups, and the external political environment, the Foreign Service occupies the central role in formulation of policy alternatives and in the conduct of relations with foreign states.

The American Foreign Service Association, in a meeting of its officers with Secretary of State Kissinger in February 1974, stressed the need to maintain an independent and increasingly unified Foreign Service, one which would advance professionalism and allow Foreign Service employees to make meaningful inputs.

Problems which face the Foreign Service are traceable in part to legislation under which it operates. The Foreign Service Act of 1946 is obsolete. It cannot provide a personnel organizational base which can cope with the complexity and diversity of contemporary foreign policy activity. Despite advances in specific personnel areas such as women's rights, the personnel system as presently constituted is in disarray. The visible conflict within the Foreign Service tends to discredit that bureaucracy and further to circumscribe its role. Conflict, of course, is a hallmark of any organization. Hopefully the new Murphy Commission, with its mandate to examine *all* governmental inputs to foreign policy organizational structures, can do much to reduce conflict about and within the foreign policy bureaucracy and thus restore its prestige.

SUMMARY

The basic problem common to all post-World War II reform efforts in foreign affairs management has been their limited scope. The Wriston and Herter studies focused largely upon personnel. The Hoover, Brookings, and Macomber-initiated (*Diplomacy for the 70's*) efforts stressed organization, work flow, and authority within the department. The studies and the changes they precipitated had little effect upon foreign policy-related bureaucracies outside the Department of State and its subsystems. The fundamental questions of parameters of authority throughout the foreign affairs bureaucracies and definitions of appropriate relationships among elements of the foreign affairs community were, essentially, not addressed, except for the administrative efforts of 1966 to reinforce departmental authority (see Chapters 3 and 4). These measures were principally intradepartmental and were unable to contain the pressures from defense, intelligence, and the White House (especially under Nixon) to play a major role in foreign policy decision-making.

The Murphy Commission, however, has a broader mandate than any of the earlier reform initiatives. For the first time, problems of foreign affairs management are being considered in their totality and from a government-wide standpoint. The Murphy Commission's authority to examine all facets of the foreign policy process provides an unparalleled opportunity to discover what kinds of relationships are necessary if the foreign policy system is to achieve maximum functionality and to recommend the necessary institutional changes to facilitate it.

Reform efforts, however, must be viewed realistically. Reforms may result in greater subsystem responsiveness and efficiency, but they can do little to change human nature. Foreign policy actors will continue to aspire to status and influence, as will actors in any political system, and they will seek it regardless of formal constraints imposed by reform. Bureaucracies, like societies, will continue to be divided into the few who exert influence and the many who do not.

Epilogue

David Easton's emphasis on decisions as outputs of political systems has prompted scholars to examine the structure and process of bureaucracies in an effort to identify their contributions to decision-making. In consequence, the bureaucratic role as a focus for study of the foreign policy process has become a major research area. Research conclusions are still tentative and differ from scholar to scholar. The authors of this volume, using the bureaucratic model as a guide and reflecting upon their combined forty years of participation in the foreign policy bureaucracy, suggest that the contribution of the bureaucracy is an essential prelude to foreign policy decision-making, and that the contribution of the bureaucracy to policy implementation is equally essential. Within such a context, the Department of State and its subsystems are the critical actors in the foreign policy process.

Notes

CHAPTER 1

1. John P. Lovell, *Foreign Policy in Perspective* (New York: Holt, Rinehart and Winston, Inc., 1970), p. 212.

2. For analysis of the systems approach, see Talcott Parsons and Edward A. Shils, eds., *Toward a General Theory of Action* (New York: Harper and Row [Torchbooks], 1962); David Easton, *A Framework for Political Analysis* (Englewood Cliffs, N.J.: Prentice-Hall, 1965); Marion J. Levy, Jr., "Functional Analysis," *International Encyclopedia of Social Sciences* (New York: Macmillan Company and the Free Press, 1968).

3. "The Secretary of State Interview," Bureau of Public Affairs, Office of Media Services, Department of State release of October 13, 1974. Also published October 13, 1974, in the *New York Times* as an interview with Secretary of State Kissinger by *Times* editor James Reston.

CHAPTER 2

1. Morton H. Halperin and Arnold Kanter, *Readings in American Foreign Policy: A Bureaucratic Perspective* (Boston: Little, Brown and Company, 1973), p. 3.

2. Margaret Truman, *Harry S. Truman* (New York: William Morrow and Company, 1973), pp. 418-19.

3. Dwight D. Eisenhower, *Waging Peace, 1956-61* (Garden City: Double & Company, 1965), p. fn. 246.

4. Arthur M. Schlesinger, Jr., *A Thousand Days: John F. Kennedy in the White House* (Boston: Houghton Mifflin Company, 1965); Roger Hilsman, *To Move A Nation* (Garden City: Doubleday & Company, 1967); Theodore C. Sorensen, *Decision-Making in the White House* (New York: Columbia Univ. Press, 1963); Robert F. Kennedy, *Thirteen Days* (New York: Norton, 1969).

5. Cf. Henry F. Graff, *The Tuesday Cabinet: Deliberation and Decision on Peace and War Under Lyndon B. Johnson* (Englewood Cliffs, N.J.: Prentice-Hall, Inc., 1970).

6. Walt W. Rostow, *The Diffusion of Power* (New York: The Macmillan Company, 1972), p. 360.

7. Lyndon Baines Johnson, *The Vantage Point: Perspectives of the Presidency 1963-1969* (New York: Holt, Rinehart and Winston, 1971). See also David Halberstam, *The Best and the Brightest* (New York: Random House, 1972) for exhaustive but undocumented impressions of the Tuesday Lunch Bunch and their influence on Johnson.

8. Rostow, p. 36.

9. The substance of the following analysis of the NSC subsystem in the Nixon administration is drawn from remarks by Philip O'Deen, director of program analysis, National Security Council, at a meeting of political scientists on the Contemporary American Presidency at the Western White House, San Clemente, California, October 13, 1972.

10. Frank Cormier, "Nixon Prefers Solitude in Deciding Issues," *Los Angeles Times*, November 16, 1972, Pt. 7, p. 1.

11. I. M. Destler, *Presidents, Bureaucrats and Foreign Policy: The Politics of Organizational Reform* (Princeton: Princeton Univ. Press, 1972), p. 122. See also I. M. Destler, "The Nixon System: A Further Look," *Foreign Service Journal*, February 1974, pp. 9-14, 28-29. Alexander L. George, "The Case for Multiple Advocacy in Making Foreign Policy"; I. M. Destler, "Comment"; George, "Rejoinder"; *American Political Science Review*, September 1972, pp. 751-95.

12. See Robert C. Toth, "Budget Office Develops New Muscle, Political Clout," *Los Angeles Times*, June 26, 1974, Pt. I-A, p. 7.

13. William Beecher, "Foreign Policy: Pentagon Suffering Rebuffs as White House Expands Role," *New York Times*, January 21, 1971.

14. For a perceptive account of how the Pentagon exploits fear about national security to gain congressional and public acceptance of its programs, see John H. Averill, "Defense Budget Each Year Sees New Red Threat," *Los Angeles Times*, September 29, 1973; and J. W. Fulbright, *The Pentagon Propaganda Machine* (New York: Liveright Publishing Corporation, 1970).

15. See Halperin and Kanter, *Readings in American Foreign Policy*.

16. See John C. Donovan, *The Cold Warriors: A Policy-Making Elite* (Lexington, Mass.: D. C. Heath and Company, 1974), p. 178, and James A. Donovan, *Militarism, USA* (New York: Charles Scribner's Sons, 1970), p. 119.

17. James A. Donovan, p. 132.

18. Beecher, "Foreign Policy: Pentagon Suffering Rebuffs as White House Expands Role."

19. Townsend Hoopes, *The Limits of Intervention* (New York: David McKay Company, Inc., 1969), p. 35.

20. Harry Howe Ransom, *Strategic Intelligence* (Morristown, N.J.: General Learning Press, 1973; Module 3030V00), p. 2.

21. "U.S. Intelligence Costs Put at $6 Billion a Year," *Los Angeles Times*, April 11. 1973.

22. George Sherman, "Soviet Mideast Tactics Puzzling," *Washington Star-News*, December 5, 1973.

23. Harry Rositzke, "President Must Balance Interests, Share Planning," *Los Angeles Times*, October 6, 1974, Part VIII, p. 1.

24. Quoted in *Washington Star-News*, October 20, 1974, Section G, p. 3.

25. Benjamin Welles, "Nixon Dissatisfied with Size and Cost of Intelligence Setup," *New York Times*, January 22, 1971.

26. Welles, "Nixon Dissatisfied with Size and Cost of Intelligence Setup."

27. Richard Helms' address to the Foreign Service Association, February 1970.

28. "Senate Favors Limitation on CIA," *Washington Star-News*, June 4, 1974.

29. Ransom, *Strategic Intelligence*, p. 2.

CHAPTER 3

1. James W. Davis, Jr., *The National Executive Branch* (New York: The Free Press, 1970), pp. 194-95.

2. John C. Ries, *Executives in the American Political System* (Belmont, Calif.: Dickenson Publishing Company, Inc., 1969), p. 58.

3. Ries, p. 39.

4. See Walt W. Rostow, *The View from the Seventh Floor* (New York: Harper and Row, 1964); Dean Acheson, *Present at the Creation* (New York: Norton, 1969); George Ball, *The Discipline of Power* (Boston: Little, Brown, 1968); John Franklin Campbell, *The Foreign Affairs Fudge Factory* (New York: Basic Books, 1971); George F. Kennan, *Memoirs 1925–1950*, (Boston: Little, Brown, 1967); Robert Murphy, *Diplomat Among Warriors* (Garden City, N.Y.: Doubleday, 1964).

5. Campbell, p. 135.

6. For a highly perceptive analysis of decision-making behavior by a Foreign Service officer, see John W. Bowling, "How We Do Our Thing: Crisis Management," *Foreign Service Journal*, May 1970, pp. 19-21, 48.

7. *The Pentagon Papers*, as published by the *New York Times*, edited by Neil Sheehan (New York: Bantam Books, Inc., 1971), pp. 354-55.

8. *The Pentagon Papers*, pp. 357-59.

9. *The Pentagon Papers*, pp. 294-95.

10. *The Pentagon Papers*, p. 299.

11. See *The Pentagon Papers*; David Halberstam, *The Best and the Brightest* (New York: Random House, 1972); Lyndon B. Johnson, *The Vantage Point* (New York: Holt, Rinehart and Winston, 1971).

12. Ries, p. 57.

13. Eugene V. Rostow, *Peace in the Balance* (New York: Simon and Schuster, 1972),

P. 71. Rostow seemingly overlooks the differences in views between McNaughton and Bundy shown in their memoranda reproduced in *The Pentagon Papers*.

14. See James E. Dougherty and Robert L. Pfaltzgraff, Jr., Chapter 11, "Decision-Making Theories," pp. 312-44, in their *Contending Theories of International Relations* (Philadelphia: J.B. Lippincott Company, 1971); and William D. Coplin, *Introduction to International Politics: A Theoretical Overview* (Chicago: Markham Publishing Company, 1971), pp. 48-54, who analyzes with perception influences and tendencies in bureaucratic decision-making.

15. Robert J. Art, "Bureaucratic Politics and American Foreign Policy: A Critique," *Policy Sciences,* December 1973, pp. 467-69.

CHAPTER 4

1. Jusserand's remark is recalled by Robert H. Ferrell, *American Diplomacy* (New York: W. W. Norton & Company, Inc., 1969), p. 3.

2. *Department of State Newsletter,* February 1973, p. 6.

3. Lyndon Baines Johnson, *The Vantage Point* (New York: Holt, Rinehart and Winston, 1971), pp. 192-202.

4. Harry Eckstein, "Authority Patterns: A Structural Basis for Political Inquiry," *American Political Science Review,* December 1973, p. 1153.

5. David Howard Davis, "State Department Structure and Foreign Policy Decision Rules," a paper presented at the American Political Science Association Annual Meeting, September 8, 1972, uses regression techniques in developing a rule for determining the size of an embassy by the Department of State.

6. Quoted by Sheldon Appleton, *United States Foreign Policy* (Boston: Little, Brown and Company, 1968), p. 161.

7. *Diplomacy for the 70's—Summary* (Washington: U.S. Government Printing Office, Department of State Publication 8560, 1970), p. 4.

8. *Diplomacy for the 70's—Summary,* p. 4.

9. *Diplomacy for the 70's—Summary,* p. 4.

10. Personal interview with Ambassador Edwin W. Martin, February 1, 1974, Claremont, California.

11. Arthur J. Dommen, "U.S. Life Gets Complicated in Cambodia," *Los Angeles Times,* August 17, 1971, p. 19.

12. U.S. Department of State, Bureau of Public Affairs, *Gist,* No. 48, February 1971.

13. *Gist,* February 1971.

14. Arnold Abrams, "Growing U.S. Military Role in Cambodia," *San Francisco Chronicle,* November 6, 1971, p. 9.

15. Dommen, p. 19.

16. Dommen, p. 19.

17. Abrams, p. 9.

18. Dommen, p. 19.

19. Abrams, p. 9.

20. *The Pentagon Papers,* p. 163 ff.

21. Arthur Dommen, "War Full-Time Job for Our Man in Laos," *Los Angeles Times*, April 1, 1971, p. 1.

22. Dommen, p. 1.

23. Henry S. Bradsher, "More Saigon Aid?. . .," *Washington Star-News*, October 8, 1974, p. A-5.

24. See Harry Howe Ransom, "Strategic Intelligence," *General Learning Press Module 3030V00* (Morristown, N.J.: General Learning Press, 1973), especially p. 10.

25. "CIA Chief on Secret Operations," *Los Angeles Times*, October 6, 1974, Part VIII, p. 4.

26. Editorial, *Foreign Service Journal*, September 1973, p. 6. The Magnuson bill would have established an International Commerce Service within the Department of Commerce.

27. "Secretary Asks for Increased Efforts to Aid American Business Abroad," *Department of State Newsletter*, February 1974, p. 10.

28. James W. Gould, "Evolution of An Idea Whose Time Has Come (and Gone)," *Res Publica* (Claremont, Calif.: Claremont Men's College, Vol. 2, No. 1, 1974), p. 8.

29. See *Volunteers in ACTION*, ACTION Pamphlet 4000-8 (7/73), p. 4.

30. Gould, p. 7.

31. Gould, p. 7.

32. *Volunteers in ACTION*, p. 5.

CHAPTER 5

1. Jack C. Plano, *et al*, *Political Science Dictionary* (Hinsdale, Ill.: The Dryden Press, 1973), p. 307.

2. United States Advisory Commission on Information, *The 26th Report* (Washington: Government Printing Office, 1973), Chart II.

3. See Herbert I. Schiller, *Mass Communications and American Empire* (Boston: Beacon Press, 1971).

4. *The 26th Report*, p. 21.

5. Charles Frankel, *The Neglected Aspect of Foreign Affairs* (Washington: Brookings Institution, 1966).

6. Principal studies on USIA include Wilson P. Dizard, *The Strategy of Truth* (Washington: Public Affairs Press, 1961); Ronald I. Rubin, *The Objectives of the U.S. Information Agency* (New York: Praeger, 1966); Robert E. Elder, *The Information Machine* (New York: Syracuse University Press, 1968); and John W. Henderson, *The United States Information Agency* (New York: Praeger, 1969).

7. See Stanley Karnow, "Tarnished USIA," *Washington Post*, January 2, 1972, pp. 1-2.

8. See Stanley Karnow, "Era of Glamor Passes for USIA," *Washington Post*, January 3, 1972, Pt. I, p. 16; and Marilyn Berger, "USIA Will Shift Posts to Meet Communism," *Washington Post*, April 2, 1971, p. A-16.

9. Editorial, *Foreign Service Journal*, September 1973, p. 6.

10. "The World," *Los Angeles Times*, March 27, 1974, p. 2.

11. "USIA Will Aid Tourism and Trade," *USIA World*, November 1973, p. 1.

12. For a recent analysis of the information and cultural role, see George N. Gordon and Irving A. Falk, *The War of Ideas: America's International Identity Crisis* (New York: Hastings House, 1974).

13. United States Information Agency, *40th Semiannual Report to the Congress, January 1 - June 30, 1973*, p. 28.

14. *The 26th Report*, pp. 26-27.

15. "Statement of Thomas D. Boyatt," *Foreign Service Journal*, May 1974, p. 40.

16. Leslie Albion Squires, "USIA Mechanism vs. Function," *Foreign Service Journal*, May 1974, pp. 17, 29.

CHAPTER 6

1. See United States Information Agency, *40th Semiannual Report to the Congress, January 1 - June 30, 1973* (Washington, 1973).

2. Quoted in United States Advisory Commission on Information, *The 26th Report* (Washington: Government Printing Office, 1973), p. 22.

3. United States Information Agency, *Facts About USIA* (Washington, February, 1974), p. 1.

4. *Facts About USIA*, February 1974.

5. Personal communication, Margita E. White, Assistant Director, USIA (Public Information), May 8, 1974.

6. As of February 1, 1974, according to a USIA office in Washington, VOA overseas stations were located in the following countries: Philippines, 21 transmitters (13 at Tinang and 8 at Poro); Greece, 14 (11 at Kavala and 3 at Rhodes); Morocco, 10; Liberia, 8; England, 6; Germany, 5 (at Munich); Okinawa, 4; Sri Lanka, 3; South Viet Nam, 1; and Thailand, 1.

7. "The Radio Broadcasting System of the U.S. Information Agency," issued by the USIA Office of Public Information, January, 1974, p. 5. All statistical statements in this discussion are drawn from this source.

8. *The 26th Report*, p. 39.

9. David Martin, "Color TV Thrives on Zanzibar," *Los Angeles Times*, May 22, 1974, p. 12.

10. See Marvin Miler, "US Will Launch TV Sateillite to Help Educate Isolated Groups," *Los Angeles Times*, May 23, 1974, Part II, p. A-1.

11. *The 26th Report*, p. 21.

12. *40th Semiannual Report to the Congress*, p. 23.

13. John W. Henderson, *The United States Information Agency* (New York: Praeger, 1969), p. 202.

14. *40th Semiannual Report to the Congress*, p. 23.

15. *40th Semiannual Report to the Congress*, p. 25.

16. *40th Semiannual Report to the Congress*, p. 26.

17. *The 26th Report*, p. 43.

18. See Stanley Karnow, "Tarnished USIA," *Washington Post*, January 2, 1972, pp. 1-2; and Stanley Karnow, "Era of Glamor Passes for USIA," *Los Angeles Times*, January 3, 1972, Part I, pp. 16-17.

19. Margita E. White, personal communication.

20. Morton H. Halperin and Arnold Kanter, eds., *Readings in American Foreign Policy: Bureaucratic Perspective* (Boston: Little, Brown and Company, 1973), p. 10.

21. See Aaron Wildavsky, *The Politics of the Budgeting Process* (Boston: Little, Brown and Company, 1964).

22. Stanley Karnow, "Tarnished USIA."

23. Stanley Karnow, "Tarnished USIA."

24. Marilyn Berger, "USIA Will Shift Posts to Meet Communism," *Washington Post*, April 2, 1971, p. A-16.

25. "Director spells out USIA's new directions for Senate Committee," *USIA World*, April 1974, p. 5.

26. "Summary of Recommendations," *The 26th Report*, p. i.

27. Robert K. Merton, *Social Theory and Structure*, enl. ed. (NY: The Free Press, 1968). p. 105.

28. Henderson, p. 194.

CHAPTER 7

1. Statement of Director James Keogh reported in the *USIA World*, April 1974, p. 6.

2. *Data for Decision*, January 14-20, 1974, Regional Reference Service of the Press Foundation of Asia, Manila, Republic of the Philippines, p. 1495.

3. "Public Diplomacy in a Changing World," editorial, *Foreign Service Journal*, June 1974, p. 4. AFSA defines the term "public diplomacy" as "the effort to ensure understanding of America and its policies."

CHAPTER 8

1. Contained in President Nixon's addresses to the nation November 3 and 15, 1969, and the president's Report to the Congress on the State of the World, January 1970.

2. See P. T. Bauer's slashing attack on assistance programs, particularly the self-perpetuating nature of British and American aid agencies. "Foreign Aid, Forever?", *Encounter*, March 1974, London.

3. President Kennedy's inaugural address, January 20, 1961.

4. For a harsher rationale of assistance, particularly to Europe, see Richard M. Freeland's *The Truman Doctrine and the Origins of McCarthyism* (New York: Alfred Knopf, 1972), an example of revisionist history.

5. For some of the early history see Jacob A. Rubin, *Your Hundred Billion Dollars* (New York: Chilton Books, 1964). Best on the European aspect is Harry B. Price, *The Marshall Plan and Its Meaning* (Ithaca, N.Y.: Cornell University Press, 1955).

6. There are many good studies of policy dynamics and mechanism of coordination. See David A. Baldwin, *Foreign Aid and American Foreign Policy* (New York: Praeger, 1966); Robert E. Asher, *Development Assistance in the Seventies* (Washington, D.C.: Brookings Institution, 1970); Willard L. Thorp, *Reality of Foreign Aid* (New York: Praeger, 1971); Paul S. Clark, *American Aid for Development*, (New York: Praeger, 1972); Robert A. Packenham, *Liberal America and the Third World: Political Development Ideas in Foreign Aid and Social Science* (Princeton: Princeton University Press, 1973).

7. Max F. Millikin and W. W. Rostow, *A Proposal: Key to an Effective Foreign Policy* (New York: Harper, 1957).

8. For an inventory of these institutions, see *Directories of Development Research and Training Institutes* for Africa, Asia, Latin America etc., prepared by the Development Center of the Organization for Economic Cooperation and Development, Paris, 1972–74.

9. Annual Reports of the International Rice Research Institute, Los Banos, Republic of the Philippines, 1970–73; Ministry of Agriculture Yearbooks, 1972–73, Government of Vietnam, Saigon.

10. A short evaluation of the accomplishments and "State of the Art" of the population program is found in *Population: A Progress Report*, OECD Development Center, Paris, 1974.

11. For examples of projects in South Korea, Taiwan, Thailand, Mexico, Israel, and Peru, see Kenneth M. Dolbeare and Murray J. Edelman, *American Politics* (Lexington, Mass.: D. C. Heath & Co., 1971), p. 191.

12. See *Current Technical Service Contracts*, June 30, 1974, AID, Washington, D.C.

13. See *Food for Peace—Annual Report, P.L. 480 Program*, U.S. Department of Agriculture, Washington, D.C.

14. See *Primer on Title IX*, AID, Washington, 1970; "Political Development," *Foreign Service Journal*, Vol. 47, No. 3, March, 1970; *Employment and Income Distribution, Status Report*, AID, Washington, October 7, 1973.

15. *First Steps, Report of the First Three Years*, Inter-American Foundation, Rosslyn, Va., 1974.

16. AID's Congressional Presentation for 1974 highlighted attention to growing problems of income distribution and unemployment. See *Introduction to the FY 1974 Development Assistance Program Presentation to the Congress*, AID, Washington, 1973.

CHAPTER 9

1. Letter dated May 29, 1961. See *Department of State Bulletin*, Vol. 45, pp. 993-94, December 11, 1961.

2. For a good analysis of, and model for, measuring the correlation of voting and foreign aid see Samuel J. Bernstein and Eugene J. Alpert, "Foreign Aid and Voting Behavior in the UN; the Admission of Communist China," *Orbis*, Fall 1971.

3. For a complete analysis of the civic action programs, see Hugh Manning, *The Peaceful Uses of Military Forces* (New York: Praeger, 1967).

4. For a summary of the machinery operating to coordinate the major programs of development loans and grants, see *Development Cooperation*, report by Edwin M. Martin, DAC chairman (Paris, 1973), pp. 60-61.

5. Report to the president from the Task Force on International Development, *U.S. Foreign Assistance in the 1970s: A New Approach* (Washington, D.C.: Government Printing Office, 1970).

6. President's message proposing a transformation of foreign assistance, September 15, 1970. 91st Congress, 2nd Session, House Document 91-385.

7. Report of the Commission on International Development, Lester G. Pearson, Chairman, *Partners in Development* (New York: Praeger, 1969).

8. Richard Nixon, State of the World Report: "U.S. Foreign Policy for the 1970s: The

Emerging Structure of Peace." Report to the United States Congress, February 9, 1972 (Washington, D.C.: Government Printing Office, 1972), p. 3.

9. See "Employment in the 1970s: A New Perspective," *International Development Review*, vol. XIII, no. 4, 1971.

CHAPTER 10

1. Committee on Foreign Affairs Personnel, *Personnel for the New Diplomacy* (Washington: Carnegie Endowment, 1962), p. 165.

2. William B. Macomber, Jr., "The First 180 Days: Progress Report on the Management Reform Program," *Department of State Newsletter*, July 1971, p. 9.

3. *Department of State Newsletter*, May 1972, p. 8.

4. *Personnel for the New Diplomacy*, p. 14.

5. *Diplomacy for the 70's: Summary* (Washington: Government Printing Office, 1970), p. 8.

6. *Diplomacy for the 70's: Summary*, p. 12.

7. *Diplomacy for the 70's: Summary*, p. 14.

8. "Secretary Rogers Announces Modernization Changes," *Department of State Newsletter*, July 1971, p. 2; and "The Seventh Floor," *Management Reform Bulletin, No. 24.* July 6, 1971.

9. "Secretary Rogers Announces Modernization Changes," p. 2.

10. "Secretary Rogers Announces Modernization Changes," p. 3.

11. "Secretary Rogers Announces Modernization Changes," p. 3.

12. "Tarr to Oversee all U.S. Military Aid Programs," *Washington Evening Star*, April 12, 1972.

13. *Hoover Commission Report* (New York: McGraw Hill Book Company, Inc., 1949), p. 175.

14. "Initiation of Recommendations in the Wriston Report," *Department of State Bulletin*, vol. XXX, no. 783, June 28, 1954, p. 1004.

15. John Campbell, *Foreign Affairs Fudge Factory* (New York: Basic Books, 1971), p. 114. Campbell accuses the Wriston Committee of taking "a meat axe to the personnel system of the Foreign Service," p. 119.

16. *Personnel for the New Diplomacy*, p. 30.

17. *Diplomacy for the 70's: Summary*, p. 16.

18. *Diplomacy for the 70's: Summary*, p. 17.

19. See Department of State, *Management Reform Bulletin, No. 8*, February 16, 1971.

20. "Special Lateral Entry Program Ends," *Department of State Newsletter*, March 1974, p. 18.

21. "Special Lateral Entry Program Ends," p. 18.

22. *Diplomacy for the 70's: Summary*, p. 18.

23. Macomber, "The First 180 Days," p. 5.

24. *Diplomacy for the 70's: Summary*, p. 22.

25. "Record Number Took Foreign Service Exam," *Department of State Newsletter,* March 1974, p. 18.

26. *Diplomacy for the 70's: Summary,* p. 23.

27. Joseph Young and David Pike, " 'Selection Out' Ploy Rejected by Court," *Washington Star News,* December 13, 1973.

28. Carol Pardon, "The Foreign Service Wife and 'Diplomacy in the 70's'," *Foreign Service Journal,* September 1971, p. 34.

29. Sandy Vogelgesang, "Feminism in Foggy Bottom: Man's World, Woman's Place?" *Foreign Service Journal,* August 1972, p. 4.

30. " 'A Fairer Shake for Women,' says Macomber," *Foreign Service Journal,* March 1971.

31. Jeremiah O'Leary, "Fewer Donor-Envoys," *Washington Star News,* July 6, 1973.

32. See John M. Crewdson, " 'Sale' of Envoy Posts Eyed," *Washington Star News,* March 17, 1974.

33. Editorial, "Selling Embassies," *Foreign Service Journal,* April 1974, p. 2.

34. *Diplomacy for the 70's: Summary,* p. 4.

35. *Diplomacy for the 70's: Summary,* p. 8.

36. See Alvin Toffler, *Future Shock* (New York: Random House, 1970).

37. See John D. Glassman, "The Foreign Service Officer: Observer or Advocate," *Foreign Service Journal,* May, 1970, pp. 29-30, 45.

38. Craig Eisendrath, "The Quiet Battles," *Foreign Service Journal,* April 1970, p. 18.

39. *Diplomacy for the 70's: Summary,* pp. 9-10.

40. *Diplomacy for the 70's: Summary,* pp. 9-10.

41. Kenneth J. Freed, "News Leak Probe Extended by FBI," *Washington Evening Star,* September 3, 1971, p. 2.

42. Rowland Evans and Robert Novak, "Foggy Bottom Faces a Trauma," *Los Angeles Times,* August 30, 1971.

43. Quoted in "Nixon Secrecy on Trip Nettles U.S. Officials," *Washington Evening Star,* November 23, 1971.

44. George Sherman, "Sickness at Foggy Bottom," *Washington Evening Star,* March 7, 1972, p. A-4.

45. "Nixon Secrecy on Trip Nettles U.S. Officials."

46. "Nixon Secrecy on Trip Nettles U.S. Officials."

47. Quoted in "State Department Tells Envoys to Mute Dissent," *Washington Evening Star,* November 22, 1971, p. A-5.

48. "State Department Tells Envoys to Mute Dissent," p. A-5.

49. Jack Anderson syndicated column, *Pomona Progress-Bulletin,* December 16, 1971.

50. "Sickness at Foggy Bottom," p. A-4.

51. "Text of Nixon's Review of Case," *Los Angeles Times,* May 23, 1973, p. 20.

52. Daniel Ellsberg, *Papers on the War* (New York: Simon and Schuster, 1972), p. 29.

53. "Ellsberg Overruled Him on Vietnam — Zumwalt," *Los Angeles Times,* April 19, 1974, p. 4.

54. "Text of Nixon's Review of Case," p. 20.

55. *Facts on File, Inc.,* New York, January 19, 1974.

56. James J. Kilpatrick, "Nixon Emphatically Rules Out Resignation," *Los Angeles Times,* May 17, 1974, p. 7.

57. Quoted in "On Organizing the Government for the Conduct of Foreign Policy," *Department of State Newsletter,* February 1974, p. 6.

58. "On Organizing the Government for the Conduct of Foreign Policy," p. 7.

59. "On Organizing the Government for the Conduct of Foreign Policy," p. 6.

60. "On Organizing the Government for the Conduct of Foreign Policy," pp. 6-7.

61. Editorial, "And Now a Meaningful Commission," *Foreign Service Journal* (September 1973), p. 6.

Recommended Reading

In addition to the sources utilized in the preparation of this volume as given in the notes for each chapter, supplementary documents, books, and periodicals are suggested below, by chapter, for the interested student. Periodical literature is not included unless especially relevant. The materials cited are selective rather than comprehensive and are mainly contemporary.

CHAPTER 1

A comprehensive presentation of the extent of nation-state foreign relations is found in Annette B. Fox, Alfred O. Hero, Jr., and Joseph S. Nye, eds., "Transnational Relations: The U.S. and Canada," *International Organization*, Fall 1974.

Most contemporary concepts of the nature of politics are derived from the milestone work of Harold D. Lasswell, *Politics: Who Gets What, When, How* (Cleveland: World Publishing, 1958). See also Robert A. Dahl, *Modern Political Analysis*, 2nd ed. (Englewood Cliffs, N.J.: Prentice-Hall, 1970).

Official and unofficial contacts among states are differentiated in system approaches. See Charles A. McClelland, *Theory and the International System*

(New York: Macmillan Company, 1966). Major contributors to the system concept in political science include Gabriel A. Almond and G. Bingham Powell, Jr., *Comparative Politics: A Developmental Approach* (Boston: Little, Brown and Company, 1966); Karl W. Deutsch, *The Nerves of Government* (New York: Free Press, 1969); and James N. Rosenau, ed., *Linkage Politics* (New York: Free Press, 1969).

For a recent and informed study of presidential interaction with other foreign policy subsystems, see Francis O. Wilcox, *Congress, The Executive and Foreign Policy* (New York: Harper & Row, 1971).

James A. Robinson, *Congress and Foreign Policy-Making*, rev. ed. (Homewood, Ill.: The Dorsey Press, 1967) is an excellent study of the congressional role in legitimizing foreign policy initiatives. See especially the exhaustive bibliography. Bernard Schwartz, *A Commentary on the Constitution of the United States* (New York: Macmillan, 1963) is a standard reference which delineates impact of the judiciary on foreign policy.

CHAPTER 2

Almost all contemporary research and literature on the foreign policy politics of the presidential subsystem through mid-1972 are cited in Alexander L. George, "The Case for Multiple Advocacy in Making Foreign Policy"; I. M. Destler, "Comment"; George, "Rejoinder," *American Political Science Review*, September 1972, pp. 751-95, and in I. M. Destler, *Presidents, Bureaucrats and Foreign Policy: The Politics of Organizational Reform* (Princeton: Princeton University Press, 1972), both cited in the text. An especially insightful account is Aaron Wildavsky, "The Two Presidencies," Douglas M. Fox, ed., *The Politics of U.S. Foreign Policy Making* (Pacific Palisades, Calif.: Goodyear, 1971). See also Henry Jackson, ed., *The National Security Council* (New York: Praeger, 1965) and Keith C. Clark and Laurence J. Legere, eds., *The President and the Management of National Security* (New York: Praeger, 1969).

Samuel P. Huntington is possibly the leading scholar on military input to foreign policy formulation. See his *The Common Defense* (New York: Columbia University Press, 1961) and *The Soldier and the State* (New York: Vintage, 1964). Other important studies include Burton M. Sapin and Richard C. Snyder, *The Role of the Military in American Foreign Policy* (Garden City, N.Y.: Doubleday, 1954); Warner Schilling, Paul Hammond, and Glenn Snyder, *Strategy, Politics and Defense Budgets* (New York: Columbia University Press, 1962); Adam Yarmolinsky, *The Military Establishment* (New York: Harper & Row, 1971); Stephen E. Ambrose and James A.

Barber, Jr., eds., *The Military and American Society*, (New York: Free Press, 1972); C. W. Borklund, *The Department of Defense* (New York: Praeger, 1969); Laurence I. Radway, *Foreign Policy and National Defense*, (Glenview, Ill.: Scott, Foresman, 1969); and Charles Walton Ackley, *The Modern Military in American Society* (Philadelphia: Westminster Press, 1972).

For several decades Harry Howe Ransom has dominated scholarly investigation of the role of intelligence in the American political system. See, for example, his *The Intelligence Establishment* (Cambridge, Mass.: Harvard University Press, 1970) and *Central Intelligence and National Security* (Cambridge, Mass.: Harvard University Press, 1958). For an account by a former director of the CIA, see Allen Dulles, *The Craft of Intelligence* (New York: Harper & Row, 1963).

The much publicized work by Victor L. Marchetti and John D. Marks, *CIA: The Cult of Intelligence* (New York: Alfred A. Knopf, 1974), whose disclosures have been contested in the courts by the CIA, is unfortunately a hastily written polemic. Other works include: Lyman B. Kirkpatrick, Jr., *The Real CIA* (New York: Macmillan, 1968) and *The U.S. Intelligence Community* (New York: Hill & Wang, 1973); Young H. Kim, ed., *The Central Intelligence Agency: Problems of Secrecy in a Democracy* (Lexington, Mass.: D. C. Heath, 1968); Thomas M. Franck and Edward Weisband, eds., *Secrecy and Foreign Policy* (New York: Oxford University Press, 1974); David Wise and Thomas B. Ross, *The Invisible Government* (New York: Random House, 1964); Alfred Vagts, *The Military Attaché* (Princeton, N.J.: Princeton University Press, 1967); and Sherman Kent, *Strategic Intelligence for American World Policy* (Princeton, N.J.: Princeton University Press, 1949).

CHAPTER 3

Documentary materials concerning the organization and operations of the Department of State, the United States Information Agency, and the Agency for International Development are regularly found in the monthly *Department of State Newsletter*. New departmental directives are summarized in the *Newsletter*. The *Foreign Service Journal*, the monthly journal of professionals in foreign affairs, is published by the American Foreign Service Association. The *FSJ* contains advocate articles, humor, news of the Foreign Service and editorials. The weekly *Department of State Bulletin*, devoted principally to official United States government foreign policy statements, also includes information about the Department of State and its subsystems.

Contemporary works by students and observers of the Department of State include:

George W. Ball, *The Discipline of Power* (Boston: Atlantic-Little, Brown, 1968).

W. Wendall Blancke, *The Foreign Service of the United States* (New York: Praeger, 1969).

Ellis Briggs, *Farewell to Foggy Bottom* (New York: McKay 1964).

"How the Secretary of State Apportions His Time," *The Department of State Bulletin*, April 25, 1966, pp. 651-54.

Charles Frankel, *High on Foggy Bottom: An Outsider's Inside View of the Government* (New York: Harper & Row, 1969).

Morton A. Halperin, *Bureaucratic Politics and Foreign Policy* (Washington, D.C.: Brookings, 1974).

John E. Harr, *The Professional Diplomat* (Princeton, N.J.: Princeton University Press, 1969).

H. Field Haviland, Jr., *The Formulation and Administration of U. S. Foreign Policy* (Washington, D.C.: Brookings, 1960).

Roger Hilsman, *The Politics of Policy-Making in Defense and Foreign Affairs* (New York: Harper & Row, 1971).

Henry M. Jackson, ed., *The Secretary of State and the Ambassador* (New York: Praeger, 1966).

Richard A. Johnson, *The Administration of American Foreign Policy* (Austin: University of Texas Press, 1971).

John P. Leacocos, *Fires in the In-Basket* (New York: World, 1968).

Dean E. Mann and W. Doig Jameson, *The Assistant Secretaries: Problems and Processes of Appointment* (Washington, D.C.: Brookings, 1965).

Frederick C. Mosher, *Programming Systems and Foreign Affairs: An Attempted Innovation* (New York: Oxford University Press, 1970).

Charlton Ogburn, Jr., *The Formulation and Administration of United States Foreign Policy* (Washington, D.C.: Brookings, 1960).

Elmer Plischke, *Conduct of American Diplomacy,* 3rd ed., (New York: Van Nostrand Reinhold, 1967).

Don K. Price, ed., *The Secretary of State* (Englewood Cliffs, N.J.: American Assembly, 1961).

W. W. Rostow, *View from the Seventh Floor* (New York: Harper & Row, 1964).

Francis E. Rourke, *Bureaucracy and Foreign Policy* (Baltimore: Johns Hopkins University Press, 1973).

Ernest Satow, *Guide to Diplomatic Practice,* edited by Nevile Bland (New York: Longmans, Green, 1958).

Warner Schilling, "The American Foreign Policy Making Process," in Douglas M. Fox, ed., *The Politics of U.S. Foreign Policy Making* (Pacific Palisades, Calif.: Goodyear, 1971).

Smith Simpson, *The Anatomy of the State Department* (Boston: Houghton Mifflin, 1963).

Richard C. Snyder, H. W. Bruck, and Burton Sapin, eds., *Foreign Policy Decision Making: An Approach to the Study of International Politics* (New York: Free Press, 1962).

Henry S. Villard, *Affairs at State* (New York: Crowell, 1965).

Bradford H. Westerfield, *The Instruments of American Foreign Policy* (New York: Crowell, 1963).

Davis K. Willis, *The State Department* (Boston: Christian Science Publishing Society, 1968).

CHAPTER 4

The Internal politics of U.S. diplomatic missions has been virtually unexplored. Hopefully future research will focus upon the foreign policy significance of intramission conflict, as well as the matter of impact of mission elements upon host country political actors and groups. At present the student must depend principally on accounts of ambassadors and a very few interested observers. Each of the following provides useful information: William Attwood, *The Reds and the Blacks* (New York: Harper & Row, 1967); Ellis Briggs, *Anatomy of Diplomacy* (New York: McKay, 1968); Harlan Cleveland, *NATO: The Transatlantic Bargain* (New York: Harper & Row, 1970); Charles Frankel, *The Neglected Aspect of Foreign Affairs* (Washington, D.C.: Brookings, 1965); and John Kenneth Galbraith, *Ambassador's Journal* (Boston: Houghton Mifflin, 1969).

CHAPTERS 5, 6, AND 7

Materials pertaining to the United States Information Agency as a political subsystem can be divided into several categories:

History and Organization of the Agency

Robert E. Elder, *The Information Machine* (Syracuse, N.Y.: Syracuse University Press, 1968).

John W. Henderson, *The United States Information Agency* (New York: Praeger, 1969).

Ronald I. Rubin, *The Objectives of the USIA* (New York: Praeger, 1966).

Oren Stephens, *Facts to a Candid World* (Stanford, Calif.: Stanford University Press, 1955).

The Role of Cultural Affairs

American Assembly, Columbia University, *Cultural Affairs and Foreign Relations,* Paul J. Braisted, ed. (Washington, D.C.: Columbia Book Company, 1968).

Philip H. Coombs, *The Fourth Dimension of Foreign Politics* (New York: Harper & Row, 1964).

Charles Frankel, *The Neglected Aspect of Foreign Affairs* (Washington, D.C.: Brookings, 1965).

Walter H. C. Laves, *Cultural Relations and U.S. Foreign Policy* (Bloomington: Indiana University Press, 1963).

Thomas C. Sorensen, *The Word War* (New York: Harper & Row, 1968).

The Informational Role

E. W. Barrett, *Truth Is Our Weapon* (New York: Funk & Wagnalls, 1953).

Wilson P. Dizard, *The Strategy of Truth* (Washington, D.C.: Public Affairs Press, 1961).

Arthur Goodfriend, *The Twisted Image* (New York: St. Martin's Press, 1965).

Propaganda and Foreign Policy

George N. Gordon and Irving A. Falk, *The War of Ideas: America's Identity Crisis* (New York: Hastings House, 1973).

John Hohenberg, *Between Two Worlds: Policy, Press and Public Opinion in Asian-American Relations* (New York: Praeger, 1967).

John L. Martin, *International Propaganda: Its Legal and Diplomatic Control* (Minneapolis: University of Minnesota Press, 1958).

Arthur E. Meyerhoff, *The Strategy of Persuasion* (New York: Coward-McCann, 1965).

Terence H. Qualter, *Propaganda and Psychological Warfare* (New York: Random House, 1962).

Wilbur Schramm, *The Process and Effects of Mass Communication* (Urbana: University of Illinois Press, 1954).

Joyce Walter, *The Propaganda Gap* (New York: Harper & Row, 1963).

Bradford H. Westerfield, *The Instruments of American Foreign Policy* (New York: Crowell, 1963).

John B. Whitton, ed., Princeton University Symposium, *Propaganda and Cold War* (Washington, D.C.: Public Affairs Press, 1963).

CHAPTERS 8 AND 9

Studies of the role of economic assistance in the foreign policy process can be broadly categorized. Some of the more useful analyses by category follow:

Theoretical Bases

Gabriel A. Almond and G. Bingham Powell, *Comparative Politics: A Developmental Approach* (Boston: Little, Brown, 1966).

David A. Baldwin, *Economic Development and American Foreign Policy, 1943-1962* (Chicago: University of Chicago Press, 1962).

Lloyd D. Black, *The Strategy of Foreign Aid* (New York: Van Nostrand, Reinhold, 1968).

Robert A. Goldwin, ed., *Why Foreign Aid?* (Chicago: Rand McNally, 1963).

Jacob J. Kaplan, *The Challenge of Foreign Aid* (New York: Praeger, 1967).

John Montgomery, *Foreign Aid in International Politics* (Englewood Cliffs, N.J.: Prentice-Hall, 1967).

Economic Assistance as an Instrument of Foreign Policy

George Liska, *The New Statecraft: Foreign Aid in American Foreign Policy* (Chicago: University of Chicago Press, 1960).

Edward S. Mason, *Foreign Aid and Foreign Policy* (New York: Harper & Row, 1964).

John Montgomery, *The Politics of Foreign Aid* (New York: Praeger, 1962).

Joan M. Nelson, *Aid, Influence and Foreign Policy* (New York: Macmillan, 1968).

Michael K. O'Leary, *The Politics of American Foreign Aid* (New York: Atherton Press, 1967).

Andrew F. Westwood, *Foreign Aid in a Foreign Policy Framework* (Washington, D.C.: Brookings, 1966).

Particularized Applications of Foreign Assistance

Robert E. Asher, *Developing Assistance in the Seventies: Alternatives for the United States* (Washington, D.C.: Brookings, 1970).

Francis C. Byrnes, *Americans in Technical Assistance* (New York: Praeger, 1965).

Maurice Domergue, *Technical Assistance: Theory, Practice, and Politics* (New York: Praeger, 1968).

John F. McCamant, *Development Assistance in Latin America* (New York: Praeger, 1968).

Willard L. Thorp, *The Reality of Foreign Aid* (New York: Praeger, 1971).

Eugene R. Wittkopf, *Western Bilateral Aid Allocations: A Comparative Study of Recipient State Attributes and Aid Received* (Beverly Hills, Calif.: Sage Professional Papers in International Studies, 1972).

For further investigation the researcher must rely mainly on documentation prepared by AID for Congress and the extensive reports issued by the four congressional committees which review aid legislation: House Foreign Affairs, Senate Foreign Relations, and the subcommittees of the Appropriation Committees of each body. In those bodies, country programs and projects are examined in great detail. The president's annual aid message and the *Congressional Record*'s coverage of floor debate provide extensive public documentation of the entire aid program for each year.

For a broader spectrum of worldwide economic development, consult the annual reports of the United Nations, the International Bank for Reconstruction and Development, and similar lending institutions. The annual review of aid provided by members of the Development Assistance Committee (DAC) of the Organization for Economic Cooperation and Development (OECD) summarizes data and discusses practical operational problems from the donors' viewpoint. AID publishes an annual compendium of program information, *U.S. Overseas Loans and Grants*, which is available from the AID Statistics and Reports Division, Department of State, Washington, D.C. The U.S. food program (Public Law 480) is treated in an annual United States Department of Agriculture report, *Food For Peace*.

CHAPTER 10

For a complete bibliography of research, literature, and documents pertaining to reform and reorganization of the Department of State and its subsystems, see William I. Bacchus, "Diplomacy for the 70's: An Afterview and Appraisal," *American Political Science Review*, June 1974, pp. 736-48. Bacchus, a staff member of the Commission on the Organization of the Government for the Conduct of Foreign Policy, has included all relevant materials since World War II on reform and reorganization (some of them unpublished but nevertheless significant by reason of their authorship).

Index

Cones, career, 81, 93

Congo, 184-85

Congress (U.S.), 5-7, 8, 25, 30, 37-38, 57, 217, 223, 226, 235; foreign assistance programs, 168-72, 186-87, 188, 193, 195-96, 197, 210, 212, 215; interaction with USIA, 111, 117-20, 135-36, 138, 144-45

Congress of Vienna, 66

Constitution of the United States, 6-7, 9, 66

Consul, 66, 98-99; general, 99

Consular: agencies, 67; officers, 66, 99; section, 70, 98-99

Consulates, 66, 67; general, 66, 67

Coordinator for Security Assistance, 220

Coordinator of Inter-American Affairs, 108

Costa Rica, 176

Country Analyses and Strategy Papers (CASP), 200, 218

Country director, 47, 54, 55-64, 219-20. See also State, Department of

Country plan, 153-59. See also USIS

Country team, 79-80, 162, 200-1; in Philippines, 86-87. See also Diplomatic mission

Courts. See Judiciary

Creel, George, 108

Crowe, Philip K., 227

Cuba, missile crisis, 19, 28, 35

Cultural affairs: officer, 74-75, 150, 163-64; role, 108, 110, 146; section, 95, 163-64. See also USIA: USIS

Customs, Bureau of, 13, 104

Davis, James W., Jr., 39

Decision-making, 47, 59, 63-64; categories of, 63; criteria, 48n; personalization of issues, 49

Defense, Department of, 12, 13, 16, 23, 26-33, 48, 59, 60, 220, 234; foreign assistance, 182-84, 196-98; interaction with USIA, 111-12, 139; military elements at diplomatic missions, 67, 71, 88-89

Defense Intelligence Agency, 33

Defense Programs Review Committee, NSC, 24

Deputy chief of mission, 92, 161-62. See also Diplomatic mission

Despatch, foreign service. See Communications, mission

Destler, I. M., 23

Development, as foreign aid goal, 175-76

Development Assistance Committee (DAC), 189n, 207, 212

Development Loan Fund, 190, 203

Diplomacy, 65, 69, 217; old and new, 228-29

Diplomacy for the 70's, 217-21, 235; resource allocations, 218

Diplomatic mission, 50, 61, 65-105; AID interaction with, 199-205; internal competition, 71-104, 162, 200-1; micro political systems, 68-71; military interaction with, 73, 74-75, 78, 79-81, 85-91, 204-5; Public Law 480, use of, 193; USIS interaction with, 149-64

"Dirty tricks," 36, 93-94

Dominican Republic, 68, 75n

Donovan, William J., 108

Draper, William, 188

Drug Enforcement Administration, 13, 101, 104, 205

Dulles, John Foster, 110, 112

East Asian and Pacific Affairs, Bureau of, 47, 49-59. See also State, Department of

Easton, David, 239

Eckstein, Harry, 71

Economic section, 70. See also Diplomatic mission

Economic/commercial section, 96-97, 98, 203. See also Diplomatic mission

Economic Cooperation Administration, 182-84, 191

Educational and Cultural Agency, U.S., 120

Educational exchange, See Exchange of persons program; USIS

Egypt. See Arab Republic of Egypt

"Selling of the Pentagon," 29

Senate, 5, 7; Foreign Relations Committee, 120, 170, 171, 228

Senior Interdepartmental Group (SIG), 23

Senior Review Group, National Security Council, 21, 23, 24, 83-84, 201

Seventh Fleet, U.S., 62, 85-87

Seventh floor. See State, Department of

Seventh Floor Management Team, 218, 220

Shakespeare, Frank, 114, 118, 133, 142, 143, 164, 166

Sharp, U. S. Grant, 51

Shortwave broadcasting. See Voice of America

Sihanouk, Norodom, 56, 58, 88

Six-day War, 35

Snyder, Richard C., 62

Somalia, 76

South East Asia Treaty Organization (SEATO), 86-87, 150

Southeast Asian War. See Vietnam, war

Soviet Union, 21, 25, 28, 29, 36, 75-76, 116, 118, 128, 129, 132, 143, 173; Committee of State Security (KGB), 94n; trade, 8

Spain, 172, 175, 198

Sputnik, 111, 115

Squires, Leslie A., 120

Stassen, Harold, 184

State, Department of:
— authority, 7, 9, 12, 23, 41, 96-97
— bureaus, functional, 42-43; Educational and Cultural Affairs, 134, 141
— bureaus, regional (geographic), 42-43, 47-50, 54-59; East Asian and Pacific Affairs, 47, 55-59; Inter-American Affairs, 218
— cultural role, 108-10
— floor hierarchical organization, 40-44; first, 43; second, 43; third, 43; fourth, 43; fifth, 43, 59-63; sixth, 42-43, 47-59; seventh, 40-42, 44-46, 54-59, 82, 220
— foreign assistance programs, 182-84, 197. See also Foreign assistance; Agency for International Development
— informational role, 108-10
— personnel, 40, 141; counselor, 42, 45;

country director, 47, 54, 55-64, 219-20; deputy secretary, 42, 45, 220; deputy under secretary for management, 220; executive secretary, 219; regional assistant secretaries, 47-59; secretary of state, 42, 45-46, 48, 218-20; under secretaries, 42, 45-46, 48, 220
— policy planning staff, 82
— pressures on, in Cambodia, 88-89 reversion to secrecy, 229-35; in Pentagon Papers, 230-31
— staff meetings: ad hoc, 55, 229; "larger," including functional specialists, 54, 55-59; "smaller," country directors, 54
— subsystems, 13; USIA, 106-50; USIA interaction with, 109-12, 125, 138, 139, 140, 144, 146-47

State Department reform, 216-38
— and Murphy Commission, 120, 235-38; scope of investigation, 235-36
— in system maintenance, 216-29; chain of command, 217, 218-21; definition of objectives, 217-18; Diplomacy for the 70's, 217-19, 223-26, 228-29, 235, 238; new and old skills in diplomacy, 217, 228-29, 230, 233, 234; personnel policy, 217, 221-28

Station chief. See Central Intelligence Agency

Stevenson, Adlai, 148

Strategic arms limitation talks (SALT), 21, 24, 29, 35, 104, 231, 232

Streibert, Theodore, 114

Subic Bay Naval Base, 50, 62, 85-88

Sukarno, 58

Surveillance. See Electronic

Swank, Emory C., 88-89

Swaziland, 150

Symington, Stuart, 90

Syria, 2, 25

Systems approach, 3-4; maintenance, 216-38; structure as interaction, 44

Taiwan, 15, 115, 118, 154, 172, 173, 186, 195, 210

Taylor, Maxwell, 20, 23, 30, 31, 51, 78

Technical Cooperation Administration, 182, 183